LOYAI
THE CORE?
Orangeism and Britishness in Northern Ireland

JAMES W. McAULEY
JONATHAN TONGE
ANDREW MYCOCK

IRISH ACADEMIC PRESS
DUBLIN • PORTLAND, OR

First published in 2011 by Irish Academic Press

2 Brookside
Dundrum Road
Dublin 14, Ireland

920 NE 58th Avenue, Suite 300
Portland, Oregon,
97213-3786, USA

www.iap.ie

British Library Cataloguing in Publication Data
An entry can be found on request

978 0 7165 3087 9 (cloth)
978 0 7165 3088 6 (paper)

Library of Congress Cataloging-in-Publication Data
An entry can be found on request

Printed by Good News Digital Books, Ongar, Essex

Contents

List of Tables

List of Abbreviations

AOH	Ancient Order of Hibernians
DUP	Democratic Unionist Party
IRA	Irish Republican Army
LOL	Loyal Orange Lodge
NOP	National Opinion Poll
PSNI	Police Service of Northern Ireland
PSA	Political Studies Association
RC	Roman Catholic
RUC	Royal Ulster Constabulary
SDLP	Social Democratic and Labour Party
SF	Sinn Féin
SOD	Spirit of Drumcree
TUV	Traditional Unionist Voice
UDA	Ulster Defence Association
UUC	Ulster Unionist Council
UUP	Ulster Unionist Party
UVF	Ulster Volunteer Force

Acknowledgements

The authors acknowledge with grateful thanks the assistance of the Economic and Social Research Council, whose grant award RES-000-23-1614 facilitated the membership survey of the Orange Order, interviews and focus groups. We are extremely grateful to the Orange Order who offered unstinting cooperation and thank all those who assisted in the project from Grand Lodge to private Lodge. In particular, we thank David Hume MBE, Director of Services, David Scott, Education Officer at Grand Lodge, Jonathan Mattison, Grand Lodge archivist and the Reverend Mervyn Storey. We are also grateful to Dr Catherine McGlynn, Professor Jocelyn Evans, Robert Jeffrey and Dr Tina McAdie for assistance with data collection and analysis. We are also indebted to our respective families for their considerable forbearance regarding the time out we have each taken to produce this book.

Notes on Contributors

James W. McAuley is Associate Dean for Research and Enterprise and Professor of Political Sociology and Irish Studies in the School of Human and Health Sciences at the University of Huddersfield. He has researched and written extensively on Northern Irish politics and society for many years. His latest books include *Ulster's Last Stand? Reconstructing Unionism After the Peace Process* (2010) and *Ulster Loyalism After the Good Friday Agreement* (edited with Graham Spencer, 2011).

Jonathan Tonge is Professor of Politics at the University of Liverpool. Recent books include *Abandoning the Past? Former Political Prisoners and Political Reconciliation in Northern Ireland* (2010) with Peter Shirlow, James W. McAuley and Catherine McGlynn; *Politics in Ireland: Convergence and Divergence in a Two-Polity Island* (2009) with Maura Adshead; *Irish Protestant Identities* (2008) (co-edited); *Northern Ireland* (2006); *Sinn Féin and the SDLP* (2005) with Gerard Murray; and *The New Northern Irish Politics?* (2005). Recent articles include contributions to *The British Journal of Politics and International Relations*; *Political Psychology*; *Electoral Studies*; *Party Politics*; *Political Studies*; *Terrorism and Political Violence*; *Space and Polity*; *Irish Political Studies* and *West European Politics*.

Dr Andrew Mycock is a Senior Lecturer in Politics at the University of Huddersfield. His key research and teaching interests focus on post-empire citizenship and national identity, particularly in the UK and the Russian Federation, and the impact of citizenship and history education programmes. He has published widely on the 'Politics of Britishness', education policy, citizenship, and democratic youth engagement. He was a Youth Citizenship Commissioner as part of the Governance of Britain reviews in 2008–9 and is co-convenor of the Academy for the Study of Britishness.

Introduction

The Orange Order remains an important part of Protestant–Unionist–British life in Northern Ireland. It offers distinctive social, religious and cultural traditions which continue to impact upon many Protestants in the region. With approximately 40,000 members, its size, although reduced in recent decades, still more than quadruples the combined memberships of all Northern Ireland's political parties. Amid the Troubles and direct rule from Westminster, the Orange Order found itself removed from political power. Since the 1998 Belfast Agreement, the Order has undergone radical change in its search for political and social influence. These changes include severance of its century-old formal link with the Ulster Unionist Party (UUP), the political 'defection' of many of its supporters to the Democratic Unionist Party (DUP) and the attempted rebranding of the climax of its religious and cultural Battle of the Boyne commemorations as a more benign 'Orangefest'. The Order has struggled for relevance amid societal secularisation, political isolation and alternative cultural influences. It has offered a particular view of Britishness, one inextricably linked to the Protestant religion and monarchy, one based on unyielding loyalty yet sometimes criticised by opponents as dated, even anachronistic.

This book examines recent developments, exploring distinct aspects of the Orange Order's raison d'être and its attempted adaptation to reduced circumstances. It draws upon entirely new data, taken from the first ever membership survey of the Orange Order. That survey was undertaken by the authors as part of a project funded by the Economic and Social Research Council from 2006 to 2008. This data is revelatory in terms of why Orange Order members join the organisation and how members perceive themselves, their organisation and 'outsiders'. The survey sheds light on the views of Orange Order members of republicans, Catholics, unionists and loyalist political parties. It offers a guide to the attitudes of Orangemen to future constructions of Orangeism, as the Order attempts to maintain cultural, religious and

political relevance. The quantitative survey of members is comple-
mented by extensive qualitative interviews with Orangemen, ranging
from senior officials in Grand Lodge to ordinary members of private
Lodges.

Through the interplay of historical, sociological and political analysis,
allied to the survey data, this book locates Orangeism within the wider
debate over what constitutes the essential features of Britishness.
It assesses the extent to which Orange loyalties to faith, crown and
country make Orangeism a very distinctive outworking (and outpost)
of Britishness. The book then explores sociological aspects of
Orangeism as family inheritance, communal belonging and solidarity,
before explaining the political switch of support of Orange Order
members to the Democratic Unionist Party and exploring the permanence of re-alignment. Additionally, the book considers the Orange
Order's religious role as a harbinger of an uncompromising Reformed
Protestant tradition.

A recent surge in literature on the Orange Order reflects the
importance of the topic. Kevin Haddick-Flynn has already provided a
detailed history of the Orange Order and the focus of this book is very
much upon the contemporary.[1] Ruth Dudley Edwards' work, *The
Faithful Tribe: An Intimate Portrait of the Loyal Institutions*,[2] offered
useful insights into the Orange Order as a social entity, but contains
little that is political. It offers a sympathetic account of the important
social and cultural functions of the Order, particularly in rural areas.
The book by Mervyn Jess on the Order is a basic, lucid descriptive
account of some of the controversies, such as the long-running saga
surrounding the Drumcree parade, that have engulfed the organisation.[3]

The most detailed studies of the contemporary Orange Order have
been provided by Eric Kaufmann. His detailed examination, *The
Orange Order: A Contemporary Northern Irish History*, is a vital book,
grounded in serious political science.[4] It uses data regarding Orange
Order and Protestant density to assess the strength of Orangeism in
different localities and does offer some explanation of the UUP versus
DUP debate within Orangeism. Kaufmann highlights the tensions
between 'rebel' Orange unionists and those more deferential to the
leadership of the organisation provided by Grand Lodge. If Kaufmann's
monograph does much to dispel common impressions of the Orange
Order as a united, homogeneous monolith, his joint work with Henry
Patterson, *Unionism and Orangeism in Northern Ireland: The Decline
of the Loyal Family*, does likewise in respect of the old UUP–Orange

Order relationship.[5] This excellent work highlights the episodic tensions between the two and charts the decline of the alliance. Graham Walker's outstanding detailed consideration of the Ulster Unionist Party also offers much analysis of the nature of the UUP–Orange relationship and its impact upon both parties,[6] and the position of the Order within the UUP (a state of affairs no longer pertaining) is also assessed in David Hume's book.[7]

Brian Kennaway's book, *The Orange Order: A Tradition Betrayed*, is of a very different type.[8] This is a closely argued, insider lament over the perceived changing nature of the Orange Order from a religious organisation to one which became unnecessarily involved in controversies over parades. It criticises the indiscipline of the Orange Order leadership and members and seeks a return to the Order's supposed original role of the articulation of the worthiness of a Christian life.

While all of the above accounts possess considerable value, this book expands our knowledge of the Orange Order by assessing what its members think of their organisation and how they perceive the present and future of Orangeism. The study also locates Orangeism within broader debates over Britishness, provides the most complete data yet seen on the switch within the Order to political support for the DUP and offers sociological analysis of the Orange Order as a family/ social/cultural tradition. The aim is to provide an objective analysis of the perceived and actual roles of the Orange Order, allowing the individual and aggregate views of its members to be heard.

THE PLAN OF THE BOOK

Chapter 1 analyses the Orange Order's promotion of British identity and assesses how far its conceptualisation of Britishness is distinctive. A number of statistical studies have highlighted the relative decline in ascription to a British national identity across the UK, particularly during the past decade. Amid a plethora of suggestions as to how a sense of cohesive Britishness could be promoted, including the creation of a 'British' Day, teaching Britishness in schools, citizenship ceremonies for young people, or flying the Union flag more often on government buildings, government 'solutions' to issues of identity have often omitted reference to Northern Ireland amid the promotion of 'Britishness', not 'UK-ness'. This has drawn criticism from Ulster unionists and members of the Orange Order, who see the monarchy and Protestantism as central to their understanding of Britishness and who draw on a range of institutions and cultural practices which have been largely omitted from government articulations of British citizenship and identity.

This chapter explores whether members of the Orange Order might become 'last-gasp Britons', defined by their ascription to an imperial Britishness which others have rejected. Drawing on interviews with Orange Order members, it will consider what are the key cultural dynamics and institutions that form a sense of Britishness. The chapter draws upon public statements and media reportage to explore the extent to which public expressions of Britishness differ from constructions of British identity elsewhere in the UK. It assesses the extent to which the Orange Order draws on articulations of a 'defensive Britishness' as an expression of political and cultural loyalty, or whether a new 'Ulster-Britishness' has emerged. The chapter will explore the extent to which distinct Ulster-Scots or Northern Irish identities complement or subvert ascription to an enduring sense of Britishness. The chapter argues that since the signing of the Belfast Agreement, a re-imagining of political and cultural identity has encouraged a fragmentation in constructions of Britishness within the Orange Order, reflected through the views of its membership.

Chapter 2 assesses the 'imperial Britons', looking at the influence of the Orange Order beyond the UK. The current focus on 'new' Britishness articulates a common UK citizenship and identity founded on a range of nationally-located institutions, and sustained by a common language, history and set of distinct British values. The notion of enduring transnational affiliations to a common British identity is contested, but, as Bridge and Fedorowich note, 'Britishness outside Britain persists well beyond the demise of the British Empire.'[9] For a significant though dwindling number of people, particularly those who lived through the Second World War or who were educated under an imperial school system, the notion of an 'ethnic Britishness' persists which is founded on common shared ethno-cultural rituals, symbols and other ties. Even if, as Stuart Ward suggests, a common Britishness has been strongly diluted by the mother country's actions in nationalising citizenship and pursuing a European integrationist agenda, the political and cultural legacy of former colonial ties continues to flag enduring notions of a shared (predominantly white) British past.[10]

Enduring transnationalism within the Orange Order is seen by some to promote and reinforce a common sense of Britishness beyond the UK. The Orange diasporas extend, in a non-exhaustive list, to the

Republic of Ireland, Scotland, England, North America, New Zealand and Australia. This chapter considers the extent to which transnational constructions of Orangeism are founded on common cultural and political articulations of identity which are British in origin. It explores the centrality of Britishness in expressions of transnational Orangeism by the Imperial Grand Orange Council, and the extent to which the autonomous Commonwealth and United States Orange Lodges project a common identity which draws on British institutions and ethno-cultural identity. Central to this analysis are two key questions: do Orangemen in Northern Ireland view other national Orders as culturally British or part of a distinct ethno-religious movement? To what extent, if any, do Orangemen outside Northern Ireland, England and Scotland view themselves as British? The chapter explores whether ethno-cultural dimensions of Orangeism draw on a common understanding of Britishness. It considers what impact political deliberations in the 'Dominions' and elsewhere has had on loyalty to the monarchy, and the extent to which competing nationalisms compromise or complement a common-held Orangeism. The chapter assesses the legacy of Britishness within the modern Orange Order and whether this continues to project a common transnational identity.

The third chapter examines the Orange Order as a cultural entity. Although its current membership has reduced dramatically from previous decades and overt patronage is a thing of the past, the Orange Order still plays a crucial role in the organisation of religious, political and social life for many Protestants. This is particularly true in rural areas where most villages with a significant Protestant population have an Orange Lodge or a designated Orange Hall and the Orange Order remains important within many Protestant communities. The continuing strength of these links should not be under-estimated. One crucial role of the Orange Order, therefore, is the passing on through generations of a distinct history and the promotion of a particular worldview through an identifiable Orange mythology (most importantly perhaps the folklore surrounding the siege of Derry in 1689 and the Battle of the Boyne in 1690). Such symbolism of these Protestant victories remains deeply rooted.

In most developed societies, political identities and political structures are reinforced by the transmission of a set of values from generation to generation. In Northern Ireland, however, such political socialisation is restricted almost exclusively to a reproduction of the values of one's respective political community. Central here is an understanding of how 'politics' is transmitted from generation to generation of Orange Order membership. Both political socialisation and subjective orientations shape people's responses to their situations. Thus, political orientations and actions are due not only to external circumstances but also to enduring differences in processes and patterns of cultural learning. Within Orangeism this has both formal and informal dimensions. The processes of political socialisation often involve the more or less unconscious inculcation of particular values. More overtly it takes place through the ritualisation of particular forms of political behaviour and expressions of identity.

The fourth chapter explores patterns of socialisation in the maintenance of the Orange tradition. Processes outlined in the previous chapter reinforce, and in turn are reinforced by, strong self-perpetuating political frames, and this chapter highlights the construction of contemporary political ideologies and discourses within Orangeism. It considers how these have been used to position the organisation, through political and cultural reactions to recent events in Ireland. In so doing it draws directly upon public declarations and texts produced by the Orange Order and those carried in its monthly publication, the *Orange Standard*, and utilises material drawn from interviews with members.

Within this, two important bands of discourse need to be recognised. First, those that contain 'internal' messages; second, those that project 'external' messages seeking to frame and position the Order within distinct moral, social and political arenas of life. Beyond this, we identify several, sometimes overlapping, discourses of 'Britishness', 'faith' and 'loyalty' that give it political expression. Membership of the Orange Order is a marker of ethnic identity and belonging and within the organisation an ideology is continually reproduced that suggests the defence of the union and the defence of Protestantism has become indistinguishable.

The Orange Order continues to play a significant role in the socialisation of its members. As commonly displayed in the *Orange Standard*, Orange families often comprise several generations and longevity of membership can be considerable. Induction into this identifiable worldview, a fixed social milieu, promotes ideas that integrate Protestantism with unionism and finds expression through Britishness. Core to this is resistance to anything that is seen to diminish the standing of Protestant unionism. Central therefore to this chapter is a detailed discussion of the strength and form of social and political reproduction within Orangeism.

Chapter 5 draws upon extensive quantitative data, taken from the Orange Order membership and from the authors' earlier survey of the Ulster Unionist Council, to assess the dramatic re-alignment of Orange politics since the 1998 Belfast Agreement. That Agreement marked the beginning of the end of the alliance between the UUP and the Orange Order. Seven years after the deal, the Orange Order, which had opposed the Agreement, severed its formal links to the UUP, ending a century-old association. This chapter examines the reasons for that severance, exploring whether moral concerns of the Orange Order were more important than political and constitutional worries. The chapter measures the extent to which the Orange Order's members have shifted allegiance from the UUP to the DUP – and assesses the reasons why the DUP is now the main party of choice.

This section of the book reveals striking attitudinal and party choice differences according to age and social class among Orange Order members, with older sections continuing to be more sympathetic to the UUP. It assesses the extent to which power-sharing and cross-border bodies are supported by the Orange membership. The chapter also analyses the prospects for two alternative scenarios for Northern Ireland Protestants. The first is a thawing of inter-bloc rivalries; in this re-spect the significance of our survey data revealing that one-third of Orange Order members might even consider lower preference voting across the sectarian divide is explored. The second scenario is that of a hardening of Orange opinion, indicated by feelings of betrayal over power-sharing with Sinn Féin and sympathy or support for the Tradi-tional Unionist Voice party, opposed to mandatory coalition government.

The final chapter explores the political and religious challenges to the Orange Order. In an era in which the DUP shares power with the historic 'enemy' and with Northern Ireland not immune to broader secular forces, how has the Orange Order updated and modernised its message in an attempt to remain relevant? This chapter takes a close look at the relationship between Orangeism and the main Protestant churches. It examines the denominations from where the Orange Order draws its members.

The chapter assesses to what extent the fusion of political realism with traditional moral values apparent within the DUP has been matched within the Order. To what extent do Orange Order politics go beyond defence of the constitution and the upholding of 'moral/religious' positions on, for example, worship, Sunday trading or abortion, towards social concerns? To what extent can Orange Order members be described as Right or Left? This section of the book then explores how the Order has attempted to re-brand itself as a forward-looking religious and political organisation, amid charges of sectarianism and outdated attitudes. Its members remain hostile to the Catholic Church, to ecumenical projects and to inter-marriage between Protestants and Catholics, yet are insistent that their hostility is to the doctrines of Rome, with no ill-will held towards Catholics. The chapter examines the desire among some within the Orange leadership to promote a more benign and inclusive Orangeism, manifest in the rebranding of Orange 12th of July celebrations as an 'Orangefest' cultural celebration, which the Order wishes to be promoted as a tourist attraction. To what extent do members want change – and why?

The book is an attempt to understand the rationale behind each facet of the Orange Order. From the outside it may appear an anachronistic manifestation of a sectarian Protestant Britishness based upon loyalty to the crown that has long departed other parts of the United Kingdom, if such an outlook ever existed. Yet the Order is much more than this, offering a cultural dimension to Protestant life in Northern Ireland which continues to attract interest and sympathy extending beyond its paid-up members to large swathes of the broader unionist population. Moreover, the Orange Order is not impervious to change, as it wrestles with often difficult issues of modernisation, secularisation and political upheaval. This book chronicles and assesses that wrestling.

NOTES

1. K. Haddick-Flynn, *Orangeism: The Making of a Tradition* (Dublin: Merlin, 1999).
2. R. Dudley Edwards, *The Faithful Tribe: An Intimate Portrait of the Loyal Institutions* (London: HarperCollins, 2000).
3. M. Jess, *The Orange Order* (Dublin: The O'Brien Press, 2007).
4. E. Kaufmann, *The Orange Order: A Contemporary Northern Irish History* (Oxford: Oxford University Press, 2007).
5. H. Patterson and E. Kaufmann, *Unionism and Orangeism in Northern Ireland since 1945* (Manchester: Manchester University Press, 2007).
6. G. Walker, *A History of the Ulster Unionist Party: Protest, Pragmatism and Pessimism* (Manchester: Manchester University Press, 2004).
7. D. Hume, *The Ulster Unionist Party, 1972–1992* (Belfast: Ulster Society, 1996).
8. B. Kennaway, *The Orange Order: A Tradition Betrayed* (London: Methuen, 2006).
9. C. Bridge and K. Fedorowich, 'Mapping the British World', *Journal of Imperial and Commonwealth History*, 31, 2 (2003), pp.1–15.
10. S. Ward (ed.), *British Culture and the End of Empire* (Manchester: Manchester University Press, 2001).

CHAPTER ONE

'Last-Gasp' Britishness? The Orange Order and British Identity

The Orange Order continually stresses the contribution of Northern Ireland within the union. Amid post-empire constructions of UK citizenship and British national identity, the Order emphasises more traditional forms of Britishness. The institution has been critical of what is construed as a politically-motivated de-emphasising of the centrality of the monarchy and Protestantism in promoting a common Britishness.[1] This stress on forms and symbols of Britishness which have diminished elsewhere in the United Kingdom has placed the Orange membership as what Nairn describes as 'last-gasp Britons', defined by their ascription to an imperial identity which others have rejected.[2]

This chapter will explore the extent to which the Orange Order continues to project a coherent collective political identity founded on a common ethno-religious 'Protestant-Britishness'.[3] It will consider conceptual complexities inherent in relationships between citizenship and nationality that inform competing constructions of Britishness, of which the Orange variant is but one. It will explore how recent developments concerning the politics of identity in the UK have impacted on constructions of Orange Britishness. By drawing on interviews with Orange Order members, it will consider what are the key cultural dynamics and institutions that inform its sense of Britishness.

NATION, STATE, EMPIRE AND IRELAND

The Orange Order has played a crucial role in defining popular constructions of Britishness for many Northern Irish Protestant unionists.[4] It has provided a teleological connection that allows current generations to link with their ancestors in the defence of the union. The Order's institutional role has proved crucial for many in the shaping of a historical narrative that celebrates a particular view of the British national past to legitimate the present. Moreover, it is an institution that seeks an active role in articulating and propagating a view of history whereby ties with the rest of the United Kingdom are seen as organic, founded on a common ascription to the British crown and the Protestant faith. For Orange Order members, pivotal moments both in British constitutional history such as the siege of Derry in 1689 and the victory of crown forces led by King William III at the Battle of the Boyne, together with the sacrifices of Ulstermen at the Battle of the Somme in 1916, underline the legitimacy of Northern Ireland as part of the union.

Recent political developments in Northern Ireland and across the remainder of the UK have however drawn attention to the potential for such political and cultural ties to be radically reformed or even severed. The Devolution Acts of 1998 diffused political power from the UK government to national political institutions in Scotland, Wales and Northern Ireland. The accession to power of secessionist national-ists through minority government in the Scottish parliament, coalition in the Welsh Assembly and through consociational power-sharing in the Northern Irish Assembly has raised the potential for the eventual breakup of the UK state. Moreover, the signing of the Belfast Agree-ment confirmed the right of citizens to hold both British and Irish citizenships and the recognition of the birthright of all the people of Northern Ireland to identify as either Irish or British – or both.

Such moves have raised a number of important questions as to the existence and relevance of a British nationality and its relationship to the citizenship conferred by the UK state, thus highlighting the blurred and often ambiguous conceptual relationships between nation, multi-national state and former empire. It is now widely accepted that nations and their nationalism are defined by a confluence of ethnic and civic dynamics that reflect the historical distinctiveness or unique-ness of each nation. The ethnic nation and its associated nationalism is founded on the belief of shared primordial ties that stress common ancestry, culture, religion, history and ethnicity that are tied to a common 'homeland'. Its civic counterpart is seen as modern and constructed, conceived within largely political and legal contexts, drawing on shared institutions and political practices within a defined sovereign territory.

Ernest Gellner notes how nations intuitively seek to establish their own state but that congruence between the two has rarely – if ever – been achieved.[5] Most western nation-states have therefore evolved from ethnic-based statehood to adopt an incorporative civic nationalist model that draws on and embeds many of the political and cultural institutions, rituals and practices of a dominant ethno-national group or groups.[6] The acquisition of statehood therefore has typically involved nation-building through state-led cultural homogenisation and the repression (or nation-destroying) of claims by rival ethno-national groups through the relegation or even attempted eradication of competing minority nationalisms.[7]

However, from the late eighteenth century onwards the construction – or invention – of imagined political communities highlighted the importance of ethno-symbolism and the stressing of the antiquity of the nation in legitimising and authenticating the state. The importance of pre-modern ethnic nations and their national myths, historical memories and culture, the primary role of an ethno-national group, was and continues to be reflected in the language, symbols and rituals of modern sovereign nation-states. Therefore civic and ethnic nationalisms are often conflated in the construction of national past and how modern citizenship and nationality are understood in most nation-states.

Citizenship and nationality are thus often understood as being synonymous and interchangeable, indicating that nationality confers rights and responsibilities on citizens, and that every citizen is a national of a particular state. Such a view is erroneous. Nationality is a cultural concept founded on the basis of a shared national identity whereas citizenship is a political concept that defines the relationship between citizen and state.[8] Attachment to a particular territory can be framed within historical narratives that identify certain institutions, symbols and rituals to sustain claims for contemporary citizenship and statehood. But such factors can also tie an ethno-national people to a national homeland – both those who reside within the modern borders of the nation-state but also diasporas elsewhere which continue to associate with the 'mother country'. Citizenship and nationality can therefore be founded on common cultural dynamics such as religion, language and representative institutions such as the Orange Order, which draw on a common historical past to legitimate political and cultural constructions of a national community and a state that do not necessarily co-terminate.

In avowedly multi-national states such as the UK such conceptual complexities are realised in the conflated and multi-layered nature of state and sub-state frameworks of citizenship and national identity. The domination of the English ethno-nation in the establishment of the British state was reflected in the adoption of many of its political, economic and cultural values, institutions and practices, thus raising pertinent questions about 'internal colonialism'.[9] Concerns over the potential threat of rival nationalisms to the unity of the multi-national state meant overt expressions of English national chauvinism or triumphalism were tempered in favour of a more inclusive Anglo-Britishness. The gradual 'blending' of the political and cultural dynamics of each constituent nation encouraged an overarching British civic and cultural national consciousness and identity.[10]

Recognition of the plurality of Scottish, Welsh and Irish nationalisms was also encouraged as long as they did not pose a threat to the Anglo-British state and nationalism. As the British Empire expanded, a British national-imperial consciousness slowly emerged that more readily reflected multi-nationality within the UK. The centrality of war, Protestantism and the monarchy in defining a uniform, if not universal, transnational British identity which drew strongly on common Anglo-British institutions, symbols, cultural practice and 'invented traditions' is well documented.[11] The British imperial experience was one where political, social or cultural interchange was not bounded within a discrete national or indeed multi-national state framework. This meant that ethnic and civic identities were contingent, both overlapping with and merging within national, multi-national and transnational imperial contexts to ensure that British nationality and citizenship were simultaneously plural while also being necessarily under-defined to negate accusations of Anglo-British messianism.

The borders between metropole and imperial periphery were as such ambiguous. Empire saw extensive British plantation in some imperial territories that emphasised the core attributes of an ethnicised and racialised national-imperial Anglo-Britishness but also extended the borders of the Scottish, Welsh and Irish ethno-national groups. Distinctions in imperial relationship reflected delineations between settled dominions such as Australia, New Zealand and Canada and colonies like India, the West Indies and African possessions. Ireland's status within the empire is a subject of intense debate, founded on a key binary that locates it as either a British colony or one of the colonising nations that established and ran the British Empire.

David Fitzpatrick argues that Ireland's status oscillated between periphery and metropole – formally integrated into the United Kingdom but often considered 'akin to a colony'.[12]

This, according to Stephen Howe, indicates that 'degrees of coloniality' ensured Britishness was a plural identity that could therefore be understood in both national and imperial terms, though many of the central tenets were common.[13] Religion and ethnicity proved central to constructions of Britishness within both contexts and were also crucial determinants in how citizenship was and continues to be understood. Protestant settlers in the north of Ireland often construed political and cultural relations with the British state in markedly different ways to their Catholic counterparts. This, in part, was due to the framework of ethno-religious values and institutions that lay at the core of the British imperial state and its Anglo-British multinational identity. Though both Protestants and Catholics contributed to the expansion and maintenance of empire, the position of Ireland vis-à-vis the rest of the imperial metropole differed considerably.

ORANGE ALLEGIANCE

The Orange Order's allegiance to the UK has its origins in the fear of the perceived Catholic threat to the political order established in the wake of the Glorious Revolution of 1688, the Protestant Ascendancy and the continued exclusion of Catholics from politics and the monarchy. The Order's founding constitution, *Qualifications of an Orangeman*, emphasised the ethical and religious commitments of membership. Its origins were both national and multi-national, being in part a reaction to the rise of Irish nationalism in the late eighteenth century, but also located in broader concerns about the threat of Catholicism in Europe. Although the Order's founding principles were primarily religious, its Protestantism was defined by loyalty to the British monarch and ascription to a common national-imperial Britishness.

Kaufmann argues that, in Northern Ireland, the *raison d'être* of the Orange Order is 'that of an *ethnic* association representing the Ulster-Protestant people' (original emphasis).[14] Although the Protestant religion was the key delineator in defining group commonality and identity, other cultural markers were also important. These drew on a range of rituals, practices and institutions which sought to emphasise a shared British past but also reflected the distinctiveness of Ireland's position in the union. The Protestant faith of Orange adherents provided the boundary marker between the Catholic-Irishness of the 'disloyal' nationalist community and that of the Protestant-British who remained loyal to crown and empire.

As we shall discuss in Chapter 2, the ethno-cultural associations of the Orange Order extended beyond Ireland. By the end of the nineteenth century, the Orange Order had firmly established itself within British society both at home and across many parts of the empire. Many of those who settled across the empire were infused with a sense purpose, what Kumar describes as a 'missionary nationalism' which infused ideologies of empire during the eighteenth and nineteenth centuries.[15] Orange Order members saw their role in empire as a civilising one whereby the Protestant faith was a crucial component in shaping the political and cultural values of settler communities and colonised subjects alike. However, the imprecise boundaries between metropole and colony ensured that missionary religiosity and hierarchy were prevalent in Ireland too.

It was widely accepted that the union provided the best defence against perceived and actual threats of Catholic expansionism. Threats to the union in the form of secessionist Irish nationalism increasingly highlighted the political underpinnings of Orangeism. Union in 1801 did not stimulate a comparable process of incorporation as with Scotland or Wales, and the growth of Irish counter-state nationalism during the nineteenth century, together with the failure to devolve political power through home rule, led to insurrection. The role of the Orange Order was one increasingly linked to the defence of the union, thus politicising its position explicitly and highlighting the extent to which its members were prepared to maintain their constitutional position. Between 1912 and 1918 Orange Order members indicated a preparedness both to go to war against and in defence of the British state.

The partition of Ireland secured the dominant position of the Protestant majority within the emergent Northern Irish statelet and in the short term also secured its place in the union. Many of the elites who took the reins of power in the extensively devolved 'Orange state' were drawn from an elite social background whereby Orange Order membership was widespread. Partition also highlighted the potential for further redefinition of constitutional arrangements. Although Orangeism continued to be defined by loyalty to the British crown, Protestant identity in Northern Ireland no longer instinctively prioritised Britishness over allegiance to Ulster.[16] The decline of the

British Empire during the twentieth century slowly undermined many of the transnational political and cultural commonalities of the Orange Order, thus encouraging the nationalisation of Northern Irish Orangeism in most contexts. The rapid social and political change of post-war Britain further diluted a sense of common UK-wide Britishness. Secularisation, immigration, multiculturalism and other social phenomena increasingly signposted divergence between the values and practices of communities on the 'mainland' and those of Protestants (especially Orange ones) in Northern Ireland. Moreover, the growth of Scottish and Welsh civic and ethno-cultural nationalism allied with demands for political devolution or even secession from the UK state highlighted the pluralised network of identities across the UK of which the British variant was but one.

This sense of 'otherness' was also reflected in the governance of the self-proclaimed 'Orange state' whereby religion demarked sectarian divisions in Northern Ireland's politics, economy, and society. From partition until the late 1960s, the Orange Order played a significant role in the redefinition of citizenship and national identity in the province and the development of a discrete Northern Irish historical narrative to legitimate the dominant position of Protestants in government. A common UK citizenship and Britishness was de-emphasised in favour of a distinctive Ulster unionist identity that continued to prioritise the Protestant faith but also acknowledged the emergence of devolved Northern Irish political and social citizenship.

The erosion of Protestant political and economic power from the 1960s, combined with shifts in the composition of Northern Irish society and its attitudes provided significant challenges to the Orange Order. The commencement of the Troubles saw a significant growth in British government running of Northern Ireland. This increasingly placed the interests of the Protestant community at odds with those of Westminster, particularly in respect of efforts to encourage equality for Catholics and the sharing of political power. It elicited contradictory responses from the Protestant community whereby membership of the Orange Order fell but the intensity of its activities grew in response to political processes viewed as part of an ongoing dilution of Britishness.[17] The signing of the Anglo-Irish Agreement in 1985 stimulated an increase in the number of marches, the routes of some proving controversial and stimulating intense debate about equality of civil rights and the freedoms to express 'cultural traditions' founded on allegiance, history and identity. Central to such displays was the importance of Protestant and British identity which have seen Orange marches defended by supporters as not sectarian or political but as expressions of cultural and religious identity, a defence of a particular form of Britishness.

The Orange Order was therefore a significant political and cultural force in both encouraging a common hybrid Ulster-British identity among Protestants while also underscoring the divergence of constructions of Britishness and the conditionality of loyalty to the British state. This was reflected in the partial replacement of British identity with one allied to Ulster unionism. As loyalty to the crown and Protestant faith is not necessarily founded on a common UK citizenship, the Orange Order's allegiance to Britishness highlights the tensions between citizenship and nationality. Although the Order remains steadfastly committed to the maintenance of the union, the coherence and cohesion of Orangeism in relation to Britishness has begun to fragment, thus revealing the inherent complexities of an identity founded on a merged and layered civic and ethno-cultural nationalism.

THE POLITICS OF BRITISHNESS IN NORTHERN IRELAND

Public survey data suggests that there has been a relative decline in ascription to a British national identity across the UK, particularly during the past decade or so, and growth in sub-state national identities.[18] In a response to concerns about this dilution of Britishness, the Labour government invested considerable political capital in articulating a shared and inclusive post-empire UK citizenship and British national identity. This was applied within a range of policies to educate young people and new migrant citizens, build community cohesion, and suppress 'home-grown' terrorism. A plethora of suggestions were forwarded as to how a sense of cohesive Britishness could be promoted, including the creation of a 'British' Day, teaching Britishness in schools, citizenship ceremonies for young people, flying the union flag more often on government buildings, and a museum and/or an Institute of Britishness.[19]

Key to such deliberations was a number of pervasive themes linked to the modernisation of the UK state and its constitution allied to the 'rediscovery' of a discrete framework of British national values such as tolerance, liberty, responsibility and internationalism that were shaped by a 'golden thread' of British constitutional progression. This unique combination of British values was shaped by a range of national institutions such as the National Health Service (NHS), the armed forces, museums and the BBC which furnished a shared patriotic purpose underpinning a common Britishness.[20] There were, however, significant omissions from this narrative. Few Labour politicians were prepared to publicly acknowledge the role of the monarchy or established Church of England in constructions of modern British national identity.

The emergence of the 'politics of Britishness' as a key theme of Labour's period in government was in part a response to what former prime minister Gordon Brown described as 'the dangerous drift in anti-union sentiment' in parts of the UK.[21] Secessionist nationalists such as the Scottish National Party (SNP) were highly critical of this state-sanctioned Britishness and sought instead to convince Scots of the terminal decline of a UK state whose multi-nationality is too complex to govern in a sustainable manner. This was in part due to the 'redundant' parliamentary structures that were 'rotten to the core' and unable to arrest economic and social decline in its constituent nations.[22]

There was, however, uncertainty as to the multi-national remit of Labour's 'politics of Britishness' and whether it was predominantly located in 'Britain' rather than the 'United Kingdom'. Government policy tended to focus on the three nations of Britain – England, Scotland and Wales – while often overlooking the place of Northern Ireland within the union as it sought to counter secessionist nationalism in Scotland and, to a lesser extent, Wales. Such an oversight was not entirely accidental and drew attention to the uncertain and contested nature of the borders of UK citizenship and British national identity and highlighted ambiguity as to whether the government was promoting Britishness or UK-ness.[23]

Debates about British identity have been somewhat characterised by a general absence of Northern Irish voices or acknowledgement of the contribution of Northern Ireland when understanding Britishness. Although Labour was keen to make political capital out of their role in the Northern Irish peace process, they often avoided reference to Ireland when talking about citizenship and Britishness. For example, in an article defending the union, Gordon Brown noted, 'I am Scottish and proud of it, but I am no less proud to be British – just as there are millions who are proud to be Welsh and British and English and British too.'[24] This oversight was not unique and politicians from across the political spectrum have found it easier to discuss Britishness or other national identities without reference to Northern Ireland. However, Brown's oversight provoked a swift response, with Democratic Unionist Party (DUP) MP Nigel Dodds describing the omission as a 'major error'. He noted that if Brown was 'serious about promoting Britishness, he has to encompass all its component parts'.[25]

In opposition Conservative party leader David Cameron was highly critical of Labour's promotion of Britishness, suggesting Brown approached the 'the question of national identity like a brand manager trying to launch a new product on the market'.[26] However, the Conservatives have drawn on a similar framework as Labour, promoting British values and institutions in an effort to counter 'the ugly stain of separatism seeping through the Union flag'.[27] There are subtle distinctions though that reflect a belief in an orthodox, understated and organic Britishness. Cameron has argued that his view of Britishness is defined by 'forgotten institutions' such as the monarchy, while other leading Conservatives have argued that Anglican Christianity 'has been important to developing Britishness'.[28]

Cameron has suggested the union is 'built around shared belonging, shared past and a shared destiny'.[29] This suggests that multi-national commonalities define contemporary Britishness, shaped by an inclusive national past that is teleologically projected into the future. But such a view raises questions about the extent that such perspectives can draw on ethno-religious constructions of Britishness that emphasise the role of the Protestant faith. Moreover, Cameron's evoking of a shared past, present and future overlooks the sectarian binary which continues to define Northern Ireland. It also conflicts with the multicultural civic Britishness expounded by Conservatives elsewhere.[30]

The Conservatives' preparedness to 'defend' the union and promote a British national identity that emphasises the role of the crown and church draws them closer to Northern Ireland's Protestants and the Orange Order than the previous Labour administration. Addressing the Ulster Unionist Party (UUP) conference in 2008, Cameron noted, 'I passionately believe in the union and the future of the whole United Kingdom. We're better off together – England, Northern Ireland, Wales and Scotland – because we all bring our strengths to the mix.'[31] Conservatives briefly sought to tie this defence of the union with efforts to 'normalise' politics through union with the UUP, thus offering a 'new opportunity to participate in the mainstream of British politics'.[32] The creation of a 'dynamic new political and electoral force' meant that the Conservatives, according to

Cameron, were the only 'party of the union'. The depth of this union was dealt a blow in the 2010 general election when the UUP failed to win any seats. Relations between the parties have subsequently become more distant, leading some to suggest that this relationship was now best described as that not of 'brothers' but 'cousins'.[33]

Cameron's assertion that 'I will never be neutral on our union' highlights a clear tension between how they understand Britishness and the union and the demands of the peace process .[34] The Conservatives appear unsure about how their explicit support for the union balances with claims that in government they 'will never side with one part of the community over another',[35] a claim surely compromised by their (admittedly temporary) alliance with the UUP. 'Secret talks' organised by then shadow Northern Ireland secretary Owen Patterson with the UUP and DUP in January 2010 to discuss the potential for an electoral pact in the event of a hung parliament led leading Northern Irish Conservatives to raise concerns about the potential 'triumph of tribalism over inclusive, secular politics'.[36] Social Democratic and Labour Party (SDLP) deputy leader Alasdair McDonnell responded to the talks by suggesting, 'this is playing the orange card, it's being sectarian, it's being divisive.'[37]

The Conservatives drew attention to the supposedly regressive nature of the former links between the UUP and the Orange Order in portraying their own link as progressive,[38] even though the UUP leader at the time of the resurrection of the Conservative–UUP link, Sir Reg Empey, was also a member of the Orange Order. The Conservatives explicitly stated that the Orange Order had 'no influence' on the pact with the UUP and urged their partner party to not 'look backwards' and to seek voters 'irrespective of which church they go to or how they worship God or which part of the community they come from'.[39]

For all its strength, there remains a lack of clarity in defining and expressing a unionist British identity. Although Nairn suggests that Ulster's unionists seek the 'customary ethos of Britishness to stay in place … to maintain the Kingdom's last resort, sovereignty over Northern Ireland', he overlooks divisions within the unionist community in Northern Ireland or the conditionality of Ulster unionism.[40] As Todd has shown, unionist identity is multiple, differentiated between 'Ulster loyalist' and 'Ulster British' traditions, which Porter suggests is reflective of diverse ethnic and civic constructions of Britishness.[41]

THE ORANGE ORDER AND BRITISHNESS

The Orange Order has emerged as a key institution to defend and promote Britishness in Northern Ireland. Indeed for some unionists the Orange Order is an institution aiming 'to promote true cultural equality'.[42] It has engaged in an extensive revision and rebranding of its image, activities and place within Northern Irish civil society since 1998, thus tapping into the ongoing 'culture wars' across the UK as a whole. Sustained efforts have been made to develop the educative role of the Orange Order with outreach programmes into schools offering citizenship and other classes to explain how its heritage continues to shape understanding of Protestant and unionist identities and to address 'the myths and misconceptions people have'.[43]

The Order views itself as a key institution in explaining the history of the Protestant community, thus emphasising its cultural and religious roles. As we note in chapters 4 and 6, the rebranding of 'the Twelfth' as 'Orangefest' was a deliberate attempt to answer accusations of sectarianism by offering the opportunity for all communities to come together and celebrate the cultural richness of the Orange tradition. But the development of Orangefest is not seen by leading members of the Orange Order as promoting 'cultural neutrality' in Northern Ireland. Ex-Orange Order deputy grand master Reverend Stephen Dickinson argued, 'this is about Protestantism, this is about Britishness – it's not about cultural tourism.'[44] According to Dr David Hume, the director of services of the Grand Lodge of Ireland, 'the Twelfth' provided for Northern Ireland's unionist community to 'take a stand for their Britishness and to help strengthen the union'.[45]

The Orange Order claim they have 'a role to play in standing up for being British' and to be 'the common thread in the fabric of the Protestant community'.[46] Such statements support claims that religious and national identification continue to be frequently conflated, with such overlaps often informing less than favourable views of other communities.[47] The role of religion and nationality is crucial in understanding how Protestants construe and articulate political and cultural constructions of community with Northern Irish and overarching British contexts. Coakley rightly notes that the Belfast Agreement means that citizenship is no longer a matter of involuntary affiliation as Northern Irish citizens can choose to hold both British and Irish citizenship.[48] He notes however that recent survey evidence indicates a strong tendency for Protestants to define themselves as British citizens without any recognition of the potential for joint citizenship.

But whereas citizenship is often seen within instinctively reductive contexts, the Protestant community does not express its identity affiliations within similarly monolithic terms. Concerns about the dilution of ascription to a British national identity across the rest of the UK are somewhat mitigated in Northern Ireland by the political and cultural drivers that ensure identity politics reflects established community divisions. Protestants overwhelmingly identify themselves as British, thus indicating some realignment from the pre-Troubles period when almost as many opted for 'Ulster' in such surveys.[49] Recent studies suggest about two-thirds of Protestants see themselves as British, a significantly higher response than any other part of the UK, including England.[50] However, nearly a quarter self-identify as 'Northern Irish' and nearly one in ten ascribe to an 'Ulster' identity. A 2007 survey found that although three-quarters of Protestants prioritise British identity over its Irish counterpart, one in five see their Irishness as equal to or more important to a sense of British-ness.[51] This would suggest that Britishness is seen by many as part of a layered identity framework that acknowledges the importance of the Northern Irish nation or Ulster region in expressing a sense of community identity.

When asked to describe their national identity, Orange Order members were similarly divided. Preference for a 'British' identity was favoured by 63.1 per cent, underlining the continued importance of the overarching union for nearly two-thirds of respondents. Only 11.2 per cent of members defined their identity as 'Northern Irish', about half the number within annual Northern Ireland Life and Times surveys of the Protestant community, and 11 per cent of members saw their identity as primarily 'Ulster'. Claims for a revival in Ulster-Scots heritage were not significantly realised in the survey, with only 1.7 per cent of members prioritising this identity. However, 11.7 per cent of respondents to the survey we undertook expressed a range of hybrid British identities such as British/Ulster (4.1 per cent), British/Northern Irish (2 per cent), British/Northern Irish/Ulster (2.5 per cent) or British-Irish (3.1 per cent). It is clear from the survey that the self-identification patterns of Orange Order members replicated many of the complexities of citizenship and national identity within a multi-national, post-empire state.

Leading figures within the Orange Order have also acknowledged this layering and hybridisation of national identity, also evident in interviews with Order members. Moreover, it reflects the complicated relationship between Britishness and Irishness, particularly in light of the changing nature of cross-border relations with the Republic and increased political, economic and cultural cooperation.[52] The extent to which the Orange Order recognises Irish dimensions of its identity is variable, often defined by the context in which links are articulated. For David Hume, the Orange Order offers the potential to extend British nationality to Protestants in the South, noting because 'it is a British Institution, themes of loyalty and British identity are inherent within its composition, including among those within it who live in the Irish Republic'.[53]

Some Order members were prepared to express a recognition of Irishness, with interviewees aware of the potential for cultural expressions of Irish identity to be misconstrued as a challenge to the British political union. One noted, 'I would like to be able to call myself Irish, but the connotation of calling yourself Irish could be misinterpreted entirely ... we're all Irish, you know.'[54] However, expressions of Irishness were often qualified. Thus one member noted that 'most times I would say Irish' but ... 'whenever I go on holiday generally ... you say you are British, and they say oh right you are English and I say no I'm not English'.[55] Another noted, 'I am an Irish-man, I was born in Ireland, I am an Irishman,' before continuing, 'but first of all I am a Christian. I owe allegiance to my god, my king and the throne and Ireland. Second to them I would be British, then I would be Irish.'[56]

More typically, a sense of Irishness was rejected outright: 'I'm born a British citizen and that's what I am ... I have no desire to be part of the Irish Republic and no desire to be Irish.'[57] Irish identity was instead understood as Northern Irish, often being distinguished from an overarching British nationality. For example, one commented, 'I would say I come from Northern Ireland ... if they asked me the nationality – its British.'[58] Another noted, 'I would describe myself as being a UK citizen in Northern Ireland.'[59] Northern Irishness was seen to be distinctive but did not contribute to the development of a competing sense of nationhood or nationalism. 'Ulsterness' was also a pervading theme, though as this quote from Hume highlights, this was often conflated with a Northern Irish identity: 'I see myself as an Ulsterman; my symbols are the Red Hand and the Northern Ireland flag. That is my regional identity and it is part of British identity.'[60]

Drawing distinctions between place of origin and nationality is instructive and raises interesting questions as to how and in what ways Orangemen understand and ascribe to a political or cultural sense of Britishness. When asked, many of those interviewed were certain in their Britishness; this was exemplified by a forthright member who noted, 'I would always say I'm British.'[61] Hume suggests the Orange Order itself 'is very clearly a British Institution. It does not have a monopoly on Britishness, of course, but it is part of the rich tapestry of our culture and identity and its membership strength makes it well placed to promote British values.'[62] Many were aware of attempts by Westminster politicians like Gordon Brown to take on this difficult task and some were generally supportive of the emphasis on Britishness. However, one Orangeman noted, 'I think when Gordon Brown talks about Britishness he is talking about England, Wales and Scotland – he is not talking about us in Northern Ireland.'[63]

Studies of popular attitudes to identity often focus on Britain rather than the UK as a whole and seek to explore shifts in ascription to national and other frameworks of communal identity.[64] Some surveys go further though and assess how popular constructions of Britishness are understood. When asked in a 2005 YouGov/*Daily Telegraph* poll what it means to be British, nearly three-quarters suggested 'accepting Britain's way of life', thus implicitly highlighting concerns that it might be under threat. Pride in the national past is a strong influence.[65] A 2008 YouGov/*Times* survey identified 'Britain's defiance of Nazi Germany in 1940' while the 2005 poll saw 38 per cent propose 'a willingness to fight to defend Britain' and 44 per cent found 'pride in Britain's historic achievements, including the Empire'.[66] Such responses draw attention to the importance of a celebratory view of the past that is sometimes founded in a defensive Britishness. However, a poll for the Political Studies Association (PSA) taken in 2005 suggested that nearly a third of Britons were 'often ashamed to be British'.[67]

Institutions were less prevalent in how British identity was understood. A poll by NOP/Nationwide in 2002 suggested that nearly 90 per cent of people were proud of the armed forces but only 64 per cent expressed similar sentiment towards the royal family.[68] The monarchy was identified by just over one-third of respondents in the YouGov/*Telegraph* poll while only 23 per cent in the YouGov/*Times* survey identified 'allegiance to the Queen' as important in defining Britishness. Civic institutions would appear to be similarly less influential. Just over one-third prioritised Westminster or the House of

Commons as a key British institution, though about half saw 'our parliamentary democracy' helped to define Britishness. Other institutions identified by politicians such as the BBC and the NHS were also peripheral in how British identity was understood. In both YouGov polls British values such as tolerance, fairness, and consideration to others were seen as important, while the PSA poll suggested three-quarters believed Britishness stood for justice and responsibility. This would suggest that the stress on values by politicians has had some success.

Such surveys also suggest that Britishness is predominantly understood in abstract terms and is strongly defined by a sense of emotional attachment that is supplemented by a diverse range of civic and civil institutions, values and constructions of the British national past. The focus of these surveys was, however, typically on Britain rather than the UK. Indeed the YouGov 2005 poll suggested nearly a third of those polled believed 'the fact that Britain consists of three countries: England, Scotland and Wales' was important in defining what it is to be British. This would suggest for a significant number of Britons, Northern Ireland is not seen as key to understanding citizenship and identity.

Our membership survey and interviews with Orange Order members provides some indication of commonalities and distinctions in how Britishness is understood by Northern Irish Protestants. The most important aspect of British identity for three-quarters of members was the crown. Members spoke of an 'attachment to the ideology of the British crown'.[69] Some felt 'the chain of the monarchy' provided a historical link that not only legitimated the place of Northern Ireland in the union but also the loyalty of the Orange Order.[70] According to one member, 'we are Her Majesty's most loyal subjects.'[71] Such responses alluded to subtle but important distinctions in the role the crown played in shaping citizenship and identity. The acknowledgement of 'subjecthood' is one largely absent from debates in the rest of the UK except for republicans of all hues. However, the importance of the crown meant some Order members were explicit that they were 'a British subject in the United Kingdom'. This awareness of the distinctions was outlined in an interview in which one member noted, 'we respect the idea of the British Monarch ... yes, there's a difference between being a British citizen and a British subject.'[72]

The role of the monarch as 'defender of the faith' was crucial in defining such near universal support. In our membership survey only

15 per cent indicated that faith was the most important aspect of British identity, a low figure given the importance of faith to Orangeism. The comparative lack of prominence of faith in shaping British identity indicates that for many Orange members the crown provides a dual role, underlining both the constitutional links with the rest of the UK that bind the union but also institutionally representing Protestantism. This was clearly outlined in an interview where it was stated, 'I do support the Queen, and again she's a figurehead for, for most British and Protestant people.'[73] Another member drew again on the importance of a shared history but also raised the idea of divinity, noting, 'you must not lose sight that the monarch of England is crowned on the basis of the line of David and even going back before that.'[74] It is evident that constitutional and religious elements of Britishness are strongly correlated and merged.

For some, though, there was an awareness of the potential for changes in this relationship. The intention of Prince Charles to undertake a symbolic change on accession to the throne to become 'Defender of Faith' highlights the potential for constitutional reform of the monarchy that would dilute the institution's link with the Protestant faith.[75] Although David Cameron has shelved plans to reform the Act of Settlement to allow a Catholic or anyone married to a Catholic to become monarch, it has cross-party political support across much of the UK.[76] Orange Order members are sensitive to potential change: 'the act of settlement is crucial … if there was an RC monarch then this institution would have to sit down and talk about the future.'[77]For some, a Catholic monarch would mean 'a whole new debate would open about the union'.[78]

Protestantism clearly remains integral to how Britishness is understood. Hume argues that the UK remains 'a majority Protestant nation and [retains] the ethos of the Protestant faith'.[79] Orange Order defence of the Protestant faith and support for the union is however seen as part of a broader 'cultural Christianity' that binds the UK together. In the 2001 census 71 per cent of UK citizens indicated they saw themselves as 'Christian'. This noted, the Orange Order construes Britishness in a similar fashion to many leading British politicians, recognising that people have multiple and layered identities. Hume suggests that 'being British is not about race, or creed or culture. Being British is about pluralism not uniformity, it is about respect for difference and about difference itself.'[80] He believes Britishness to be organic and that 'being British is not about being white. It is not about being Protestant. It is not even about where you are born. It is, I would assert, about how you feel.'[81]

Therefore the Orange Order operates as a pluralist institution in that its members hold a diverse range of views, but these are connected by an ascription to a common faith and set of values. Hume asserts, 'we are an organisation which is unashamedly Protestant but which also espouses civil and religious liberty for all.'[82] Such a view ties in with a shift in perspective whereby the Orange Order purports to be an institution that protects Protestant culture and Northern Irish Britishness within a broader British multiculture. It is however 'very clearly a British institution' whose principal role, according to some members, is 'to preserve the unionist British Protestant culture'.[83] For some, the reason for becoming an Orangeman was because 'the Orange institution was strong on keeping Northern Ireland inside the British family and the maintenance of the Union and loyalty to the Monarch'.[84]

The loyalty of Orange Order members to crown and union was a point of pride; one interviewee claimed, 'we protect all that's British.'[85] This ascription to the British state and its identity was felt to be often questioned and derided by others within Northern Ireland and other parts of the UK. It was, according to Hume, 'curiously ironic that people so desirous of being British are seen by some commentators as almost embarrassing'.[86] One member argued, 'our Britishness has been challenged since the day Northern Ireland was formed.'[87] Another felt that Orangemen 'should not be pushed into a position of embarrassment as to who we are'. In particular, it was felt that 'republicans are trying to chip away at our identity.'[88]

The Orange Order sees its role as a counterweight to an ideologically driven Irish republican and nationalist agenda to undermine Britishness and 'colonise' Northern Ireland.[89] Sinn Féin requests for the union flag not to be flown on 'neutral' public buildings are seen by unionists as evidence of a broader campaign of 'anti-British bigotry'[90] by republicans 'intent on gutting civic buildings of any reference to Britishness'.[91] Sectarian attacks on Orange Halls and limits placed on Orange marches are often flagged to support this narrative. Such attacks and restrictions, as well as other moves by Sinn Féin and others, are seen not only to be an attack on such cultural pluralism, but contributing to a politically correct form of ethnic cleansing. In response, the Orange Order has engaged in a sustained campaign against the Equality Commission for Northern Ireland, which they accuse of having 'a long-term strategy to wipe the face of Britishness from Northern Ireland'. Leading figures within the Orange Order have described the role of the Equality Commission as a 'continuous partial attack on the symbols of Britishness in Northern Ireland'.[92]

Some members interviewed suggested the Orange Order was engaged in a 'cultural war'. One argued:

> Whenever the republicans mentioned the British removal from Northern Ireland or from Ulster, they weren't talking to the British forces, they weren't talking to the British soldier in the street, they were talking to those who identified themselves as British citizens – they included me in that. And I think we were quite resilient and we resisted that attempt to be ethnically cleansed.[93]

Another member argued that Gordon Brown's promotion of Britishness was flawed, as 'he wants to fly the union flag but we are not allowed to.'[94] The union flag was seen as symbolic of the British union:

> It encompasses the union of the empires, of England, Scotland and Northern Ireland. It brings together the St George and St Patrick and St Andrew flag very nicely together and it's symbolic of the union that was created between us and Scotland, how best we can be together, you know, the monarch would be the Queen, the crown, the head of state.[95]

The idea of sacrifice is another persistent theme in defining Orange Britishness. As Southern notes, this draws attention to the extent that the Troubles have encouraged the persistence of forms of Britishness shaped by war.[96] Hume suggests, 'I come from the one part of the United Kingdom and the British Isles where, in our present generations, people have died because of their desire to remain British.'[97] County grand secretary of Fermanagh, Robert Dane, argues, 'Protestant culture is … often based around service to the crown in the uniform of the country.'[98] The Orange Order has been active in the memorialisation of the 'sacrifice' of its hundreds of members killed during the Northern Ireland conflict. The remembrance of servicemen who died in conflicts such as the First and Second World Wars, the Falklands and more recently in Iraq highlight that history and sacrifice are central to the reproduction of community memories. Such sacrifices mean that, to many Orangemen, the union 'is more than a mere concept', suggesting war continues to play a part in defining and celebrating British identity.[99]

Kaufmann notes that the ethno-cultural associations of the Orange Order remain crucial in presenting a politicised Protestant identity that is central to their understanding of Britishness.[100] However, the Orange Order has increasingly focused on civic constructions of identity, be they framed within British and Northern Irish frameworks. Some members saw Britishness as defined by a civic relationship between citizen and state based on sovereignty and law. One suggested, 'I'm first and foremost a British citizen. I hold a British passport',[101] while another argued, 'I'm a British citizen as it says on my passport, and I would intend to remain that way.'[102] This contractual framing of citizenship was exemplified by one member who noted, 'we obey the laws of the land, and that's basically the laws of the land being made and set by Westminster.'[103] Another noted, 'Britishness is the institutions set up in Westminster. That's why we elect our, our MPs and send them over there to, to look after our interests.'[104] Britishness was therefore a legal concept that was often framed as loyalty both to the (unwritten) constitution and parliament. Some were however mindful of the potential for Westminster to challenge the crown in defining Britishness. One member noted, 'Well I don't know what Gordon [Brown] means by Britishness ... I mean, to me, the Labour Party has always looked towards setting the head of state to the side and taking over the job themselves.'[105] Implicit here is not only the challenge to traditional constructions of British national identity but also the potential for a British republic. Resistance to this idea was strong. One suggested, 'they're always trying to do away with the Royal Family',[106] while another member simply stated, 'I don't like the idea of a republic.'[107]

However, the key dynamic that shapes loyalty to the union remains the Protestant crown rather than Westminster. The Order has argued that the UK government should not 'tinker' with the unwritten constitution and the principle of the 'head of state being of the majority religion'.[108] Moreover, concerns have also drawn attention to the lack of resonance of Northern Ireland in debates about the constitutional future of the UK. The Orange Order has encouraged members 'remind our fellow countrymen and women across the narrow strip of water that we are at least as British as they are'.[109] Hume argues that 'it is important that a sense of Britishness is not left carelessly lying on the political fringes of the nation'.[110]

CONCLUSIONS

The Orange Order continues to see itself as a vanguard institution to defend a particular variant of Britishness that has largely dissipated outside Northern Ireland. The leadership of the Grand Lodge of Ireland have developed a narrative that emphasises threats to British identity by republicans and highlights the continued loyalty of Ulster Protestants to the crown (but not the British government). Its role in promoting a cultural Britishness founded on the centrality of the Protestant faith is an important factor in why members join and continue to participate in the Order. However, many members are aware of the potential for constitutional arrangements to be reformed further, thus potentially forcing the Orange Order to reconsider the central tenets of Orange Britishness. There is an air of resignation that further reform could render the Britishness they hold dearly almost, if not entirely, obsolete.

The Orange Order has had to reposition itself following the political changes of the Belfast Agreement and the severing of formal political links with the UUP. The Order has sought to shift emphasis from the 'politics of the union' to adopt a more culturally tolerant view of Orangeism which stresses its legitimacy within a multicultural society. This suggests an acceptance that the Order's construction of Britishness is a minority view. In promoting a distinctive Britishness, leading figures within the Orange Order continue to make forays into the political arena in an attempt to unify the unionist parties in the defence of this threatened Britishness.[111] This is reciprocated in the manner by which many leading figures within the various unionist parties continue to link the 'politics of Britishness' to their membership of the Orange Order.

Attempts by Westminster politicians to identify the key dynamics of a civic Britishness have involved the promotion of British multiculturalism that recognised a complex patchwork of ethnic, religious and other communities. The representative institutions of many of these groups are lauded as promoting tolerance and a shared sense of British identity. But although the Conservative government has attempted to develop a UK-wide representative framework, the Orange Order remains marginalised, even seen by critics as a regressive institution that promotes division. This isolation is indicative of broader concerns about acknowledging the legitimacy of those groups who seek to promote a form of Britishness that continues to emphasise the historical role of the Protestant faith. It would appear that UK governments, irrespective of their political origins, remain suspicious of those who are prepared to vocally promote forms of Britishness that compromise narratives founded on the progressive nature of British values.

Our survey and interviews with members of the Orange Order revealed that most were sure of the role of the crown and Protestant faith in shaping their Britishness. When pushed further to define what the key elements of their British identity were, it was evident that many differing views were held. While some were prepared to acknowledge Irish dimensions of their identity, most located their reflections within a British context. However, it was interesting that the value-laden approach of British politicians was not replicated, and many identified institutions and banal national indicators such as the union flag. Some were more circumspect. One member successfully encapsulated the complexities and potential pitfalls, suggesting that defining Britishness was 'like nailing jelly to the wall. It is an idea that's out there ... it's not defined and that is part of its strength and it is not defined because if you define it then people will find something that they will react against.'[112]

Despite this, most members of the Order were keen to identify a range of institutions, attitudes and practices that they saw as fundamental to informing a sense of Britishness. These reflected the complex relationship between civic and cultural determinants that continue to underline the multi-nationality and multicultural constructions of UK citizenship and British identity.

NOTES

1. A. Dawar, 'Brown attacked for ignoring Ulster in article', *Guardian*, 27 March 2008.
2. T. Nairn, *Pariah: Misfortunes of the British Kingdom* (London: Verso Books, 2002).
3. J.W. McAuley and J. Tonge, '"For God and for the Crown": Contemporary Political and Social Attitudes Among Orange Order Members in Northern Ireland', *Political Psychology*, 28, 1 (2007), pp.33–52, at p.35.
4. See, for example, C. Kinealy, 'The Orange Order and Representations of Britishness', in S. Caunce, E. Mazierska, S. Sydney-Smith and J.K. Walton (eds), *Relocating Britishness* (Manchester: Manchester University Press, 2004), pp.217–36; E. Kaufmann, *The Orange Order: A Contemporary Northern Irish History* (Oxford: Oxford University Press, 2007).
5. E. Gellner, *Nations and Nationalism* (Ithaca, NY: Cornell University Press, 1983).
6. T. Kuzio, 'The Myth of the Civic State: A Critical Survey of Hans Kohn's Framework for Understanding Nationalism', *Ethnic and Racial Studies*, 25, 1 (2002), pp.20–39.

7. W. Connor, 'Nation-Building or Nation-Destroying?', *World Politics*, 24, 3 (1972), pp.319–55; W. Kymlicka, 'Nation-Building and Minority Rights: Comparing West and East', *Journal of Ethnic and Migration Studies*, 26, 2 (2000), pp.183–212.
8. D. McCrone and R. Kiely, 'Nationalism and Citizenship', *Sociology*, 34, 1 (2000), pp.19–34.
9. M. Hechter, *Internal Colonialism: The Celtic Fringe in British National Development* (Berkeley, CA: University of California Press, 1975).
10. K. Robbins, *Nineteenth-Century Britain: Integration and Diversity* (Oxford: Clarendon Press, 1988).
11. L. Colley, *Britons: Forging the Nation, 1707–1737* (New Haven, CT: Yale University Press, 1992).
12. D. Fitzpatrick, 'Ireland and Empire', in W.R. Louis (ed.), *The Oxford History of the British Empire, Volume III: The Nineteenth Century* (Oxford: Oxford University Press, 1999); C. Kinealy, 'At Home with the Empire: The Example of Ireland', in C. Hall and S.O. Rose (eds), *At Home with the Empire* (Cambridge: Cambridge University Press, 2006); T. Eagleton, 'Afterword', in T. McDonough (ed.), *Was Ireland a Colony? Economics, Politics and Culture in Nineteenth-Century Ireland* (Dublin: Irish Academic Press, 2005); L. Kennedy, *Colonialism, Religion and Nationalism in Ireland* (Belfast: Institute of Irish Studies, Queen's University, 1996); S. Howe, 'Questioning the (Bad) Question: "Was Ireland a Colony?"', *Irish History Studies*, 37, 142 (2008), pp.1–15.
13. Howe, 'Questioning the (Bad) Question: "Was Ireland a Colony?"'
14. Kaufmann, *The Orange Order: A Contemporary Northern Irish History*, p.2.
15. K. Kumar, *The Making of English National Identity* (Cambridge: Cambridge University Press, 2003).
16. Kinealy, 'The Orange Order and Representations of Britishness', p.226.
17. McAuley and Tonge, '"For God and for the Crown"', p.41.
18. L. Stone and R. Muir, *Who Are We? Identities in Britain* (London: Institute of Public Policy Research, 2007).
19. Department for Education and Skills, *Curriculum Review: Diversity and Citizenship* (London: The Stationery Office, 2007); G. Brown, 'The Future of Britishness', speech to the Fabian Society New Year Conference, 14 January 2006; R. Kelly and L. Byrne, *A Common Place* (London: Fabian Society, 2007); Ministry of Justice, *Citizenship: Our Common Bond* (London: The Stationery Office, 2008).
20. G. Brown, 'The golden thread that runs through our history', *Guardian*, 8 July 2004.
21. G. Brown, 'We need a United Kingdom', *Daily Telegraph*, 13 January 2007, p.12.
22. G. Kerevan, 'Independence vote offers only chance for Scotland to plan route to national prosperity', *The Scotsman*, 26 November 2009, p.15.
23. A. Mycock and J. Tonge, 'The Future of Citizenship', in Political Studies Association, *Failing Politics? A Response to 'The Governance of Britain' Green Paper* (Newcastle: Political Studies Association, 2008); C. McGlynn and A. Mycock, 'Introduction: A Special Edition on Britishness', *Parliamentary Affairs*, 63, 2 (2010), pp.223–8.
24. G. Brown, 'We must defend the union', *Daily Telegraph*, 25 March 2008, p.14.
25. Dawar, 'Brown attacked for ignoring Ulster in article'.
26. D. Cameron, 'Stronger Together, Weaker Apart', speech to Scottish Conservative party conference, 23 May 2008.
27. D. Cameron, 'Stronger Together', speech to Dynamic Earth Conference, Edinburgh, 10 December 2007, available at: www.timesonline.co.uk/tol/news/politics/article3030953.ece; accessed 4 April 2011.
28. D. Grieve, 'Britishness: Useful or Redundant?', 10th Annual Wilberforce Address, London, 6 May 2008.
29. D. Cameron, 'A New Political Force in Northern Ireland', available at: http://www. conservatives.com/News/Speeches/2008/12/David_Cameron_A_new_political_force_in_ Northern_Ireland.aspx, 6 December 2008; accessed 4 April 2011.
30. See, for example, D. Cameron, 'Islam and Muslims in the World Today', speech at Cambridge University, 5 June 2007; S. Warsi, 'Speech to *Guardian* race equality conference', London, 11 December 2007.
31. Cameron, 'A New Political Force in Northern Ireland'.

32. D. Cameron, 'Our Contract for Northern Ireland', available at: http://m.conservatives.com/News/News_stories/2010/05/~/link.aspx?_id=775B33AD61064823A502D8ACD1C11CA6&_z=z, 4 May 2010.
33. BBC, 'UUP and the Tories: How Brothers became Cousins', 6 October 2010, available at: http://www.bbc.co.uk/news/uk-northern-ireland-11485193; accessed 4 April 2011.
34. Cameron, 'Our Contract for Northern Ireland'.
35. 'Interview with David Cameron', *News Letter*, 5 December 2008.
36. H. McDonald, 'Northern Ireland Tories Condemn Secret Talks with Unionists', *Guardian*, 24 January 2010.
37. BBC, 'Tories Play the "Orange Card" – SDLP', 25 January 2010, available at: http://news.bbc.co.uk/1/hi/northern_ireland/8478174.stm.
38. Former vice-chairman of the Conservative party in Northern Ireland, Jeffrey Peel, controversially described the Orange Order as a 'backward-facing, history-obsessed parish pump society'. In response, UUP chief whip David McNarry, MLA suggested, 'the honourable thing for the Conservative Party to do would be to apologise to Orangemen.' N. McAdam, 'Anti-Orange remark stirs up dissent within the UUP', *Belfast Telegraph*, 21 August 2008.
39. 'No Unionist Pact – Cameron', *News Letter*, 29 January 2010; BBC, 'Conservatives – No Orange Order Influence on UUP Pact', 29 January 2010.
40. Nairn, *Pariah: Misfortunes of the British Kingdom*, p.116.
41. J. Todd, 'Two Traditions in Unionist Political Culture', *Irish Political Studies*, vol. 2 (1987), pp.1–26; N. Porter, *Rethinking Unionism: An Alternative Vision for Northern Ireland* (Belfast: Blackstaff Press, 1996).
42. N. Dodds, speech to Democratic Unionist Party annual conference, 1 November 2008, available at: http://www.dup2win.com/articles.asp?ArticleNewsID=315; accessed 4 April 2011.
43. Grand Lodge of Ireland, 'Education', undated, available at: http://www.grandorangelodge.co.uk/education/index.html; accessed 4 April 2011.
44. *News Letter*, 'Why the Orange Order Need to Change', 15 July 2008.
45. 'Unionists urged to take a stand for Britishness', *Londonderry Sentinel*, 12 July, 2008.
46. 'Orange Order condemns racist incidents', *Orange Chronicle*, June 2009.
47. O. Muldoon, K. Trew, J. Todd, N. Rougier and K. McLaughlin, 'Religious and National Identity after the Belfast Good Friday Agreement', *Political Psychology*, 28, 1 (2007), pp.89–103.
48. J. Coakley, 'National Identity in Northern Ireland: Stability or Change?' *Nations and Nationalism*, 13, 4 (2007), pp.573–97.
49. See E. Moxon-Browne, 'National Identity in Northern Ireland', in P. Stringer and G. Robinson (eds), *Social Attitudes in Northern Ireland: The First Report* (Belfast: Blackstaff Press, 1991), pp.22–30.
50. Northern Ireland Life and Times Survey, 2003, available at: http://www.ark.ac.uk/nilt/2003/Political_Attitudes/IDENTITY.html; accessed 4 April 2011.
51. Northern Ireland Life and Times Survey, 2007, available at: http://www.ark.ac.uk/nilt/2007/Identity/IRBRIT.html#religion; accessed 4 April 2011.
52. J. Coakley and L. O'Dowd, 'The Transformation of the Irish Border', *Political Geography*, 26, 1 (2007), pp.877–85.
53. D. Hume, 'The Orange Order and Britishness', speech as part of the 'New Perspectives on Britishness' seminar series, University of Huddersfield, 4 March 2010.
54. Interview with the authors, 3 November 2007.
55. Ibid.
56. Ibid., 2 November 2007.
57. Ibid., 3 May 2008.
58. Ibid., 2 November 2007.
59. Ibid., 3 November 2007.
60. Hume, 'The Orange Order and Britishness'.
61. Interview with the authors, 3 November 2007.
62. Hume, 'The Orange Order and Britishness'.

63. Interview with the authors, 25 January 2008.
64. See, for example, Stone and Muir, *Who Are We? Identities in Britain.*
65. YouGov/*Daily Telegraph*, 'Britishness', July 2005, available at: http://www.yougov.co.uk/extranets/ygarchives/content/pdf/TEL050101032_1.pdf; accessed 4 April 2011.
66. YouGov/*Sunday Times*, Survey results, http://my.yougov.com.
67. Opinion Leaders, 'Integration Agenda Needed to Strengthen Britishness', January 2006, http://www.fabians.org.uk/publications/extracts/integration-agenda-needed-to-strengthen-britishness; accessed 4 April 2011.
68. NOP/Nationwide, 'Brits Still Proud of Family Values and Great British Institutions', March 2002, available at: http://www.prnewswire.co.uk/cgi/news/release?id=83272; accessed 4 April 2011.
69. Interview with the authors, 3 November 2007.
70. Ibid., 2 November 2007.
71. Ibid., 3 November 2007.
72. Ibid., 2 November 2007.
73. Ibid., 3 November 2007.
74. Ibid., 3 May 2008.
75. A. Pierce, 'Prince Charles to be known as Defender of Faith', *Daily Telegraph*, 13 November 2008.
76. M. Greaves, 'Cameron drops plans to reform Act of Settlement', *Catholic Herald*, 5 July 2010, available at: http://www.catholicherald.co.uk/news/2010/07/05/cameron-drops-plans-to-reform-act-of-settlement; accessed 4 April 2011.
77. Interview with the authors, 25 January 2008.
78. Ibid.
79. D. Hume, speech at Grangemouth, *Orange Chronicle*, 28 June 2008, available at: http://www.orange-order.co.uk/chronicle/?item=david-hume-s-speech-at-grangemouth-scotland; accessed 4 April 2011.
80. 'Protestants must preserve heritage', *News Letter*, 26 April 2009.
81. Hume, 'The Orange Order and Britishness'.
82. Hume, speech at Grangemouth.
83. Interview with the authors, 3 May 2008.
84. Ibid., 26 January 2008.
85. Ibid., 3 November 2007.
86. Hume, 'The Orange Order and Britishness'.
87. Interview with the authors, 26 January 2008.
88. Ibid., 25 January 2008.
89. N. Southern, 'Post-Agreement Societies and Inter-Ethnic Competition: A Comparative Study of the Protestant Community of Londonderry and the White Population of Pretoria', *National Identities*, 11, 4 (2009), pp.397–415.
90. N. Dodds, speech to Democratic Unionist Party annual conference, 1 November 2008.
91. Ulster Unionist Party, 'Positive Progress for Unionist Identity', 29 May 2008, available at: www.uup.org.uk; accessed 4 April 2011.
92. Letter to *Belfast Telegraph*, 22 January 2008.
93. Interview with the authors, 2 November 2007.
94. Ibid., 25 January 2008.
95. Ibid., 3 November 2007.
96. N. Southern, 'Britishness, "Ulsterness" and Unionist Identity in Northern Ireland', *Nationalism and Ethnic Politics*, 13, 1 (2007), pp.71–102, at pp.84–5.
97. Hume, 'The Orange Order and Britishness'.
98. Grand Lodge of Ireland, 'Orange Culture Must be Respected', 1 July 2009, available at: http://www.grandorangelodge.co.uk/press/PressReleases-2009/090701orange_culture_must_be_respected.htm; accessed 4 April 2011.
99. Hume, speech at Grangemouth.
100. Kaufmann, *The Orange Order: A Contemporary Northern Irish History*, p.2.
101. Interview with the authors, 3 November 2007.
102. Ibid., 2 November 2007.

103. Ibid.
104. Ibid., 3 November 2007.
105. Ibid., 2 November 2007.
106. Ibid., 3 November 2007.
107. Ibid.
108. 'Tampering with the Constitution', *Orange Standard*, November 2008.
109. 'False Information Being Spread', *Orange Standard*, June 2008.
110. Hume, 'The Orange Order and Britishness'.
111. S. McBride, 'Unionism must unite – Saulters', *News Letter*, 21 May 2010.
112. Interview with the authors, 25 January 2008.

CHAPTER TWO

Imperial Britons: Orangeism and Transnational Britishness

INTRODUCTION

The Orange Order in Northern Ireland is strongly associated with the promotion of a particularistic Protestant Britishness. Orangeism is therefore traditionally understood to be founded in narratives that assert the political dominance of Protestants in Northern Ireland and a collective ethno-cultural Ulster identity. The organisation has attempted to challenge and overwrite established perceptions of the Orange Order as a sectarian entity, but with limited success. For many, both within and outside the Order, it continues to be representative of a particular view of the union founded on a merged religious and political Britishness.

Orangeism has sought to preserve the social and political unity of an increasingly divided Protestant community in Northern Ireland.[1] The Orange Order has also sought to maintain a sense of cohesion and common purpose among the network of Orange associations that extends beyond Northern Ireland. As such, the Orange Order plays an important role in promoting the Protestant reformed faith while also, in some countries, reinforcing a transnational cultural Britishness beyond its Ulster heartland. A number of studies have reflected on this transnationality of Orangeism, which covers the Republic of Ireland, the rest of the UK, North America and parts of the Commonwealth.[2] Yet, as we noted in Chapter 1, divisions exist within the Order in Northern Ireland as to how Orangeism and Britishness are understood which reflect the complexities of living in a post-empire multi-national state such as the UK.

This chapter will consider the extent to which transnational Orangeism is founded on common cultural and/or political articulations of identity which are British in origin. It will explore the centrality of Britishness in expressions of transnational Orangeism in other parts of the UK and how members in Northern Ireland view the union. It will also consider links outside the UK through the Imperial Orange Council, and the extent to which the autonomous Commonwealth and United States Orange Lodges project a common Orange ethno-cultural identity. It will explore whether Orangemen in Northern Ireland view other Order associations as culturally British or part of a distinct ethno-religious movement.

THE ORANGE ORDER AND THE UNION

The growth of the Orange Order during the nineteenth and twentieth centuries is strongly linked to the threat of counter-nationalist movements in the UK. Primarily the Order was an institutional response to the emergence of a resurgent Irish nationalism and perceived threat to the Protestant ascendancy. The movement gained further momentum through its resistance to home rule with the Order playing a pivotal role in uniting religious, cultural and political dynamics of unionism. The partition of Ireland underlined the determination of Northern Irish Protestants to remain within the union and to continue to prioritise their British identity.

Partition also formalised the peripheral nature of Northern Ireland with regards to the remainder of the UK. Devolution allowed for the design of an 'Orange state' dominated by Protestants with the tacit approval of Westminster. The political, cultural, social and economic development of Northern Ireland after 1921 reflected the distinctive nature of many aspects of its government. Britain and Northern Ireland continued to be part of the UK but became very different places to live. The Troubles further underlined such differences and many in Britain were reluctant to empathise with their Northern Irish unionist counterparts and may have gladly accepted Irish reunification.

The Orange Order's role in underpinning the ideological and institutional foundations of unionism has therefore proven pivotal in defending Protestantism from its traditional enemies of Irish nationalism and republicanism.[3] Increasingly this role was extended to oppose efforts by the UK government to weaken Northern Ireland's position in the UK. From the late 1960s onwards Westminster not only intervened in the governance of Northern Ireland, it engaged in a military conflict to defend its place in the union while also engaging in political agreements which afforded some influence to the Irish Republic in the affairs of Northern Ireland. Many Northern Irish Protestants are therefore unsure as to their surety of place within the union, fearing the upward trajectory of Dublin influence.

Since the signing of the Belfast Agreement in 1998, the political and social framework of Northern Ireland has undergone radical change. The formation of a coalition government headed by the Democratic Unionist Party and Sinn Féin was an unexpected outcome to the political process. Moreover, politicians and political parties in Northern Ireland would appear more sensitive, in the public realm at least, to the complex and inter-related factors that define the politics of citizenship and identity in the United Kingdom and the Republic of Ireland. This would appear, in part, to be in response to the stated intent of the Belfast Agreement for Northern Irish citizens to recognise 'the birthright of all the people of Northern Ireland to identify themselves and be accepted as Irish or British', promoting 'full respect for, and equality of, civil, political, social and cultural rights ... and of parity of esteem and of just and equal treatment for the identity, ethos and aspirations of both communities'.[4]

Although identity politics remain divisive, there has also been a greater preparedness of Irish nationalists and republicans to acknowledge the legitimacy of bi-nationalism, while also continuing to actively agitate for a united Ireland. Thus, Sinn Féin party leader Gerry Adams (2009) has argued that republicans should re-evaluate their perceptions of unionists, as 'in a United Ireland the agencies, management, symbols and emblems need to reflect the diversity of our society'.[5] Adams therefore formally acknowledges the potential for the Orange Order to enhance Irish multiculture, suggesting that 'Orange marches, albeit on the basis of respect and cooperation, will continue in a United Ireland' if its members so wished. This shift in the tone of rhetoric of the leadership of Sinn Féin has not however curtailed criticism of some Orange Order marches. Some republicans have also persisted in more direct action such as attacking Orange Halls and street protests against the small number of contested Orange parades. Clearly tensions remain as to the perceived cultural, religious and, indirectly, political legitimacy of Orangeism. This would suggest, for some, that the culture and identity of the Orange Order and its members continue to be associated with a fixed and belligerent oppositional Britishness, a colonial identity adopted by Ireland's misguided Protestant minority.

The signing of the Belfast Agreement has seen the border between Northern Ireland and the Republic become more politically and economically porous. The advent of new cross-border institutions has encouraged the development of a range of bodies that have transformed the Irish border.[6] But, as Cohen notes, the Belfast Agreement has failed to resolve many of the ethnic tensions allied to the partition of Ireland and in some cases it may well have exacerbated divisions.[7] Orange rituals such as parades have taken on greater political as well as cultural value for Northern Irish Protestants keen to express their defiance not only to republicans and the Irish government but also to a British state that has been prepared to modify Northern Ireland's constitutional politics in favour of institutionalised bi-governmentalism.

For Orange members their British identity is one continually under threat and must therefore be defended from Irish republicans and nationalists who are perceived to be aggressively attempting to undermine key facets of Britishness in Northern Ireland. As we noted in Chapter 1, such seismic constitutional change has not yet seen Orange Order members embrace their Irishness significantly in political or cultural terms. In interviews, members occasionally acknowledged that facets of their cultural identity had Irish origins but this never extended to a sense of common or dual citizenship. Although the Grand Lodge of Ireland has jurisdiction over Orange Lodges and parades on both sides of the border, many Northern Irish members continue to overlook Irish dynamics of their identity. Therefore, the transnationality of the Orange Order in Ireland is often sidestepped in favour of a UK-centric view of Orangeism. The primacy of UK citizenship and British national identity were encapsulated through loyalty to faith and crown, and to embrace Irish bi-nationality would be an act of disloyalty.

The peripheral nature of Protestantism and Orangeism in debates about citizenship and national identity in the Republic of Ireland is reciprocated in the North in so much that the Orange Order's role as political and cultural unionist organisation denies any potential for formal recognition of the dual citizenship open to its members. Orangeism is construed as an expression of a British, unionist and Protestant identity. This has meant that attempts to promote the Orange Order as cultural institution in the South have been strongly refuted by Irish nationalists and republicans. For the most part, loyalism and Orangeism are largely ignored by indifferent citizens in the Irish Republic. The last overt display of hostility came when a loyalist 'Love Ulster' march (not organised by Grand Lodge but containing some Orange Order members) was attacked in Dublin in 2006.

Even if the Orange Order sought to recognise its Irishness within political or cultural terms, it is unlikely that others would allow it to develop a more visible all-Ireland presence. Bryan suggests that distinctions in how southern Irish Orange members understand their identity mean 'key focus of identification is the Protestant faith and being a Protestant in Ireland, not being a unionist or being British'.[8] He argues that the focus of the Orange Order in Northern Ireland on the maintenance of the union often overlooks the fact that many Orange members in Ireland are citizens of another country and ascribe to its non-British national identity.

This noted, the British state's preparedness to negotiate with the Irish government and Irish republicans and nationalists in Northern Ireland draws attention to the conditionality of the union and also raises questions as to the extent that loyalty to the union is reciprocal. National identities are founded on a belief in a common past and shared cultural heritage that is often framed within a particular state. Therefore citizenship is underpinned by a state nationalism that is a hybrid of ethno-cultural and civic attributes. In the case of Protestants in Northern Ireland, the correlation between religion and British national identity is crucial and the Orange Order sustains a British nationalism which prioritises Protestantism in a manner distinctive from other parts of the UK.

The near-universal embrace of Britishness by Order members in Northern Ireland reflected a belief in the legitimacy of a political union founded on a shared past. One member went as far as to claim that he was 'sitting in the oldest part of the United Kingdom'.[9] The Orange Order has stated that 'Orangemen must take a lead in speaking out for the Union'[10] and has stressed that 'we support the Union. We want the Union. We are, and we remain, United by the Kingdom.'[11] But members were also much more aware of the distinctions between Britain and the UK than many of their fellow citizens on the 'mainland'. Many shared this member's view of the role of the Orange Order: 'We are in many ways the organisation that can maintain the link with Britain.'[12] A widely-shared sentiment was: 'we are a natural part of the British family', meaning 'the main thing is the union with Great Britain'.[13] Alluding to the Belfast Agreement, one noted that 'God ordained that we be in the United Kingdom. No matter what Tony Blair says or anybody else says, it will still be here.'[14] However, there is a palpable pessimism about the future of the UK which reflects what Aughey has identified in debates about the union as a shift from 'declinism' to 'endism'.[15] He notes that, for some, devolution in the wake of the Belfast Agreement was representative of an acceptance that the decline of ascription to a British national identity would be followed by the break-up of the union.

Such pessimism as to the future of the union was evident in interviews with members. One bluntly stated that 'Britain is about to collapse – there is no doubt whatsoever',[16] while another suggested that 'the union is going to evaporate like Scotland is going to go, Wales is going to go, there will be no United kingdom, there is going to be no realm to defend.'[17] The sense of resignation was palpable but tempered with typical defiance, with an older member suggesting that 'Britain is going to have its own problems without worrying about us. We will survive no matter what happens, it is whether Britain will or not.'[18]

ORANGEISM AND THE NATIONS OF BRITAIN

Boyd draws attention to the distinctiveness of the modern Northern Irish Orange Order across the UK, highlighting how unique political, cultural and geographical circumstances have shaped its distinctive understanding of British society and the union.[19] MacRaild argues that the Orange Order's view of the union is founded on a pan-Protestant Britishness that saw the appeal of Orangeism spread to other parts of the UK during the nineteenth century, particularly in areas of high Irish migration such as the north-west of England and the west of Scotland.[20] As the British Empire expanded, ties between the Orange Order in Northern Ireland and the rest of the UK were strengthened by the formation of numerous Orange Lodges in industrial cities such as Liverpool and Glasgow, where Protestants with no Irish connections also joined.[21] As Kinealy notes, by the end of the nineteenth century, 'the Orange Order had firmly established itself within British society.'[22]

Although ethno-national mobilisation of English and Scottish Protestant settlers in Northern Ireland from the nineteenth century onwards was founded on religious schisms that were evident across the UK, Coakley notes that citizenship and nationality have proven more complex in Ireland.[23] In interviews, Orange members appeared more sensitive to the layered nature of British and Northern Irish or Ulster identity, with one noting, 'It's a bit like being a Virginian or an American or a Texan or American, being British is the umbrella I think but there is a further breakdown meaning you are Scottish, Welsh or Northern Irish.'[24]

Pan-British Orangeism was defined by the strident expression of a belief in the Protestant ascendancy. Its development across Britain differed somewhat to that in Northern Ireland. This, in part, was due to the more pronounced secularisation of society in England, Scotland and Wales but also to the relative lack of development of the movement outside Ireland. Orange Lodges continued to prosper in Liverpool and in the west of Scotland where sectarian tensions endured, proving an important political and cultural institution for Protestants.[25]

For the first half of the twentieth century, Liverpool politics were dominated by informal alliances between Conservative and Protestant candidates, the latter often involved with the Orange Order. However, this waned to the point where Protestant candidates disappeared from the council in 1974. The Orange–Blue alliance was no longer of relevance, while Orange versus Green tensions diminished, although they remain a folk memory for older Liverpudlians. As late as 1990, Liverpool was described as 'England's last sectarian city' in a programme on the city's 'Billy Boys'[26] and a three-part television series on the city in 2008 featured the role of the Orange Order.[27] However, although the city was still claimed by the Order as 'still an Orange Citadel',[28] a combination of slum clearance and secularisation meant that the Orange Order had dwindled, and its modern Twelfth of July parades in Liverpool and Southport attract only 3,000 marchers.[29] While this is a far from negligible figure (most organisations would struggle to put on a demonstration anywhere near that size), it represents a mere one-third of the numbers marching in the 1960s. The Order still has over forty Lodges in Liverpool, although often small in membership size.

However, the dispersal of Orange communities via slum clearance does not automatically lead to a decline in Orangeism. In Glasgow and its surrounds, Orangeism has not endured a diminution to the extent seen in Liverpool, partly because sectarianism has a sporting outlet via regular Rangers versus Celtic soccer fixtures; as such, 'Orange versus Green' remains culturally and socially important, unlike on Merseyside. In 2009, there were 217 Orange parades in Glasgow, more than in Belfast and Londonderry combined.[30] The largest demonstration, held on the Saturday before the Twelfth, attracts around 10,000 marchers drawn from across approximately 180 Lodges. The Grand Orange Lodge of Scotland claimed a 'dramatic increase in membership' in 2010.[31]

Links with the Orange Order in Northern Ireland and the rest of the UK have remained strong, with Orange Lodges regularly sending marching bands to visit each other on the Twelfth. David Hume suggests that it is crucial in supporting the union across the UK: 'The Orange Order, whatever else may be said of it, is deeply loyal to the United Kingdom, whether its members are in Belfast, Glasgow, London or Manchester.'[32] Ties remain particularly strong with Orange Lodges in the west of Scotland and north-west England. Such links highlight that unionism is not a solely Northern Irish ideology and comparisons of Scotland and Northern Ireland highlight shared ethno-cultural and political dynamics. Shared commitments to the union are particularly strong among members of the Orange Order in Scotland and Northern Ireland. However, there are differences in focus of such expression due to distinctive pathways to union and divergence in institutional frameworks. This, according to Farrington and Walker, was reflected in the different devolution settlements which sought to address claims for national self-determination in Scotland but were an institutional method to resolve conflict in Northern Ireland.[33]

Although some claim that sectarianism and religious discrimination are declining features of Scottish society allied to a gradual secularisation of Scottish politics,[34] they continue to divide communities in some parts of Scotland.[35] The Orange Order continues to influence Scottish politics and society but, since the Scottish National Party (SNP) made concerted efforts to reject their traditional stereotype as a Protestant or 'Orange' party,[36] it lacks power and often makes the newspaper headlines because of the contentious nature of parades. Indeed, relations with the SNP have soured considerably, with threats from some Orangemen to take up arms if Scotland severed ties with the rest of the UK.[37]

The threat of Scottish nationalism and independence is seen as a shared threat for the Orange Order in Scotland and Northern Ireland. Drew Nelson, grand secretary of the Grand Orange Lodge of Ireland, noted, 'We believe that the people in Scotland who are calling for independence are misguided.'[38] Such analysis has chimed with a preparedness of the Grand Lodge of Scotland to 'mobilise to defend the Union'. Grand master Ian Wilson argued that the Orange Order needs to 'get real' about the threat of Scottish nationalism and has even gone as far as to encourage members in Scotland to vote Labour in an attempt to nullify the threat of the Scottish National Party.[39] In response, SNP politicians have raised concerns that Orange parades undermine 'togetherness and inclusion',[40] and there have been tighter regulations introduced on parades in Scotland in recent years.

The Orange Order has not simply focused on identity issues within Northern Ireland and has invested considerable effort in promoting a common Ulster-Scots community. As David Hume has noted, 'Ulster and Scotland have a shared heritage which includes the Orange tradition and the Institution.'[41] This has involved the promotion of the parades as an integral part of Ulster-Scots heritage but has also seen greater emphasis placed on common cultural and linguistic attributes.[42] However, attempts to re-imagine Ulster Protestantism as part of a broader Ulster-Scots community should be seen in part as a response to the growing threat of Irish nationalism.[43] It is therefore not devoid of political content and has involved calls for a united stand of 'the Grand Orange Lodges of England and Scotland in calling for the positive promotion of the benefits of the Union for our peoples'.[44] This would suggest that political exigencies motivating Ulster-Scots Orangeism are not founded in the necessity of any significant reciprocal affiliations or recognition of the political realities of contemporary Scotland.[45]

Some members were keen to express their ascription to a shared Ulster-Scots identity. One noted, 'I am part of the United Kingdom of Great Britain and Northern Ireland, as constitution states, but culturally I class myself as an Ulster-Scot.'[46] Another described himself as 'right along the bottom line British' before acknowledging the multinationality of the UK by noting 'there are Welsh British so we are Ulster-Scots British.'[47] Some were less sure, though. When asked about his layered identities, one noted, 'I would be British, then I would be Irish or Ulster Scots or whatever you want to call me.'[48] However, the Grand Lodge's promotion of Ulster-Scots appeared to lack resonance with many of its membership, as did the importance of affiliations with Scottish Orangeism. Most of those interviewed did not mention their Ulster-Scots identity and in our membership survey less than 2 per cent identified it as their primary identity.

Craith asserts that there is no doubt that Northern Ireland is currently witnessing a reinterpretation of Ulster-Scots culture and identity which draws on perceptions of a shared past and the reinvention of ancient tradition.[49] But, he continues, the re-awakening of Ulster-Scots is driven by political as much as cultural factors. Questions persist as to the extent to which Ulster-Scots is a distinctive and recognised linguistic nationalism either in Scotland or Northern Ireland. Moreover, the extent to which Orangeism in Scotland shares a common framework with its Northern Irish counterpart is open to question.[50] Kaufmann notes that Orangeism in Scotland is weaker and is as much influenced by local competition with Catholics as by broader issues relating to Ireland.[51] It would appear that devolution has had a divisive impact on how Orange identity and UK citizenship are understood and how distinctive national issues often drive debates in Northern Ireland and Scotland.

Some members did however express particular warmth towards the Scottish. One noted that 'people here [in Northern Ireland] would identify more with the Scottish people than they would with the English'.[52] A shared Scottish heritage was important for some: 'my connection route, where I come from ... as with a lot of people from here, you know they're of Scottish descent'.[53] But the ethno-nationalist dynamics of Ulster unionism meant that, if there was a sense of Ulster-Scotsness, members primarily located it within Northern Irish contexts with scant reference to Scotland itself. Indeed, when Scotland was discussed it was often framed within oppositional contexts. Sensitivity to the desire of Scottish nationalists to break up the union was prevalent in interviews as was an awareness of the instrumentalist nature of unionism in Scotland. One attempted to address such complexities:

> I am very proud to be Northern Irish. But I'm part of the union. In the same way as people in Scotland, those who are not of the nationalist agenda who want Scotland to go independent, would be quite within their rights to say I'm very much Scottish, and that's my background and my history but I'm part of the union which makes up the UK.[54]

A sense of powerlessness was evident, particularly in relation to the potential for Scottish independence. As one member commented, 'If Scotland wants to go their own way, well, it's going to ultimately raise the question in Northern Ireland.'[55]

But if debates about identity were not strongly influenced by a transnational sense of Ulster-Scots unionism or by historical links with Scotland itself, England and Englishness were frequently mentioned. This in part reflects the role of England in shaping the central tenets of an Anglo-Britishness that overlaps with Protestant Britishness but which also provides an oppositional dynamic for Northern Irish Orangemen.[56] Hume suggests that this confrontational dynamic is somewhat attributable to Anglo-British myopia:

> Sometimes we get the feeling that for English people the term

Britishness is taken to mean *them*. Because our sterling banknotes were not accepted as legal tender in England we could be forgiven for having a chip on our shoulder about what we see as ignorance at best.[57]

Peating notes that many unionist Protestants associate such attitudes in England with their loss of privilege in Northern Ireland and a lack of support for the union.[58] Awareness of the potential for negativity in English public attitudes towards Northern Ireland was evident in some responses: 'I think quite a high percentage of English folk would quite happily like to see the back end of us.'[59]

Some recognised that Orangeism differed in England, particularly the distinctive political environment that meant English Orangemen were less unified by their religion and loyalty to the union. When asked about how this difference was realised, one member noted, 'You wouldn't have all the Orangemen in England Conservatives and the political background wouldn't affect them the same.'[60] But some members sought to empathise with established narratives focused on the decline of British national identity in England. One argued that 'since the 1950s the Britishness has gone out of England'.[61] Another suggested that 'what English people need to do is to be proud about being English'.[62] There was some awareness of a growth in English political nationalism and the risk that this could finally break the union. One suggested that 'England will have its own parliament, there will be no United Kingdom any more in another twenty years. Tony Blair has wrecked the whole thing.'[63]

This idea that England had been (irreparably) changed was a strong theme in discussion with Orange members. Key was the impact of immigration and the influence of multiculturalism on English society. The conflation of England and the rest of the UK strongly shaped responses, somewhat mirroring the Anglo-centric focus of politicians and many academics when discussing issues relating to immigration and multiculturalism.[64] Patterns of population flow to Northern Ireland and the development of multiculture have been recognised as strongly divergent to the experience of England, with the Troubles limiting numbers of new citizens to the province.[65] Craith notes that politicians and communities in Northern Ireland have experienced difficulties in giving greater recognition to minorities beyond the two traditions.[66]

The shift from biculture to multiculture in the post-Belfast Agreement period continues to be strongly influenced by rival mono-cultural claims to Irishness and Britishness but has been aided by the significant increase in the number of migrants coming to Northern Ireland.[67] This has led some to suggest that a lack of experience of the challenges of living in a multicultural society has resulted in tensions developing in relation to some newer communities.[68] There was widespread acknowledgement that, as one noted, the UK has 'been multi-cultural certainly since, I suppose, just after the Second World War'.[69] Multiculturalism was seen to be 'affecting the Britishness quite a bit'.[70]

The Order insists that it is 'an Institution which stands for civil and religious liberty for all; there should be no doubt for us that we say no to racist mindsets and intimidation'.[71] This view was echoed by a member who spoke for many when suggesting immigration was 'not actually a bad thing ... I've no objection to anyone coming into the country to make a better living for themselves.'[72] Some members acknowledged the legitimacy of established migrant groups, particularly the Chinese community in Northern Ireland, who 'are as much British as we are'. One member suggested that some communities, 'after the third and fourth generation, they'll become, you know, Northern Irish' with the potential for 'perhaps even bringing them into the organisation'.[73] Some members were however suspicious of the origins of some new migrants, particularly those from what were seen as 'Catholic' countries such as Poland. One noted, 'We need to be ultra aware of nationalities and communities and what traditions they bring with them.'[74]

There was some awareness that the focus of government promotion of British identity was focused not at recalcitrant Irish republicans and nationalists but the failure of some newer citizens to integrate into British society. As one noted, 'This whole thing of the new Britishness is being delivered into this multi-cultural sort of cauldron now.'[75] Some members drew parallels with the threat of republicans to 'chip away at our identity' and the challenges of multiculturalism to an English identity. Such threats were often seen in religious terms, particularly in respect of the Muslim community. As one noted, 'I would say the English are being challenged in the same way by the Muslims.'[76] Mapping of the experiences of Northern Ireland was evident, with the presence of other religions understood as a potential threat to the Christian underpinnings of English society. Some expressed concern at the response in England to immigration: 'Is it apathy? Do they not see the danger?'[77]

Perceptions of difference were often founded on cultural difference. One commented, 'We are amazed here that there are certain boroughs, districts in Britain, in England, where the Queen's English is not spoken.'[78] One member voiced such concerns, arguing that 'we have absolutely no problem with another religion coming in and setting up in England, but they've come to England because they like England – don't try to change England to the place you've come from.'[79] The dilemmas of integration and assimilation were clearly evident as he continued, 'There's absolutely no problem people coming in and setting up and enjoying their own culture, expressing their own culture, but don't make everybody else conform to it.'[80] Such themes were reiterated in another interview:

> It has to be a tolerance to accept people in to the community but not to change the community. I mean if you want to come into the country then you are certainly welcome but the rules here are the boundaries. You are welcome to practise your religion and your own culture but don't try to change us.

For some members, immigrants were 'coming here for a free ride'. One suggested that 'when you get loads of people coming in and no chance to go home and they're starting to get people who are criminals or you know, lower levels of their own society getting out and coming into Britain, and you can see all the problems that that's sort of causing'.[81] Another member drew attention to shifting patterns of immigration, noting that 'it was people from the different Dominions of Britain coming in to take up jobs that was fine, but now … it's the type of people we're getting in, it's the people I think are coming in who are not coming in to contribute to society.'[82]

It was not clear whether such views were founded on first-hand experience or what the role of media and other sources were in shaping attitudes. One of the few members to relate their understanding of English society was a member invited to take part in an Orange parade in Corby in Northamptonshire. He noted that he had been warmly welcomed by many people he had met but while playing his Lambeg drum, 'we were stoned and there was not a white face among them – all black.'[83]

THE ORANGE ORDER AROUND THE WORLD

Unionism and Orangeism have a history of internationalism which reflects the importance of transnational constructions of Protestant and British identity.[84] The growth of the British Empire, particularly from the early nineteenth century onward, provided opportunities to develop Orange networks in new settled lands and undertake missionary work to civilise indigenous peoples across the empire. The development of Orangeism across the 'White Dominions', parts of Africa and the United States drew on a shared Protestantism, though overseas Orange associations proved less accommodating of formal expressions of sectarianism.[85] This reflected the multi-faith composition of the settler societies they were founded in and also the comparative lack of political sensitivity about the constitutional status of Ireland.

Although Orange associations were founded on some very broad cultural aspects, their development was markedly different in each country. For example, in Canada, Orangeism was evident from at least 1812 and initially had considerable influence over the country's political and cultural development.[86] Members enjoyed preferential access to networks that held considerable sway over the Canadian government and economy, particularly in some of the major cities such as Toronto. Such networks were replicated in other settler societies and some missionaries also sought to establish Orange Lodges in other colonies of the empire. The Order promoted a British way of life and opposed separatist nationalism, such as that found in French Quebec.

The attraction of Orangeism for many members outside of the UK was its pro-empire, pro-Protestant focus that allowed settlers and others to maintain some connections and express loyalty to the 'mother country'. The Orange Order was as such transnational from its earliest days, establishing itself across four continents. Kaufmann notes that in Australia and Canada, Orangeism was rooted in British-Protestant ethnicity that reproduced hierarchies of power evident in Ulster and the rest of the imperial metropole.[87] The British crown and Protestant faith were therefore central to transnational constructions of Orange Britishness. Orange associations across the empire and elsewhere were not however simply an organisation for displaced 'Ulstermen', attracting members from across settler societies.

The Orange Order declined in popularity and influence and the salience of Orangeism dissipated during the twentieth century as members of Lodges outside the UK shifted political loyalties towards their host states. The profile of Orangeism in most countries quickly declined and the Orange Order does not play a significant political role any longer. In many countries, Orange associations adapted to the particular conditions in which they were located, encouraging national identification in each country rather than a broader transnational

British identity. This reflected the divergent pathways of Orangeism in each country and the preparedness of member associations to adapt to changing political contexts.

Orangeism increasingly found expression as a cultural identity but not one focused on the defence of the union or a particular understanding of Britishness. The primary role of Orangeism across parts of the empire became increasingly built around the promotion of the Protestant reformed faith. In Australia, New Zealand and Canada it remains an institution that promotes loyalty to the crown and a shared Protestantism. However, Orange Lodges are founded on and promote a duality of loyalties, encouraging patriotism to their host country with equal, and often more, enthusiasm. In some Orange associations, practices have been adopted that are not evident in Ireland, such as mixed membership of men and women. The global movement of Orangeism is therefore a small group of member states whose practices and rituals can differ markedly, as can their role in civil society and political life in each country.

The Grand Lodge of Ireland places considerable emphasis on maintaining transnational links, noting that 'it is this great movement of Orangeism across the world encapsulating faith, determination and commitment that is the Institution's hope for the future.'[88] Such aspirations are founded on a number of connecting issues. The Grand Lodge is keen to promote common religious links to maximise claims of their status as a part of a broader cultural Orange movement. One member noted in an interview that the Orange Order was 'the biggest world organisation of Protestants'.[89] But the unique nature of Protestantism in Northern Ireland, particularly its strong political underpinnings and links with political parties, distinguishes it from its counterparts elsewhere. Issues concerning the preservation of the union are not central to the Orangeism of the other members of the Imperial Orange Council and some members are not always entirely sympathetic towards, or interested in, the more politicised form of Orangeism evident in Northern Ireland.[90]

For some members though, the presence of Orange Lodges encouraged transnational friendship. When asked what these links meant, one noted, 'in so much that if any of us were travelling the world we would make contact and feel safe'. Asked if he had personally made such contacts, he said, 'oh yes, particularly in Canada'.[91] Such sentiment was not however universal and one suggested, 'I do not feel it [Orange internationalism] is a major factor.'[92] A sense of history was important for some. One suggested:

There's a great strength in the United Kingdom of Great Britain and Northern Ireland as being a title to the British Empire, which probably isn't as good as it was, but, you know, to the same extent, you know, it's a powerful state, it's a powerful joined up force, and you know, how best can you bat the ball?

For some, a sense of mournful resignation fused with a reluctance to accept the end of empire. One noted that 'Britain has been a great blessing to the world' before somewhat mournfully adding, 'we may not have an empire now.'[93] Another agreed, believing that the 'British Empire may fade away too'.[94]

Links have been maintained since 1867 through the overarching Imperial Orange Council which comprises all Orange associations across the world and meets every three years. It has few significant powers over member associations and instead offers opportunities to build networks between Orange Lodges in different countries. At the 43rd Imperial Orange Council gathering in Belfast in 2009, delegates agreed that 'there is little or no distinction between the Christian message at the core of Orangeism and the culture within the Protestant Reformed community which it produced.'[95]

Such a conclusion chimes with Hume's assertion that 'the Orange Institution is the common thread in the fabric of the Protestant community. It unites people from all backgrounds. It is national and international.'[96] One member concurred, noting that 'we – the various countries – come out and celebrate the idea of Protestant folk.'[97] This noted, the extent to which a common Britishness is seen to continue to extend beyond the UK through membership of the Orange Order is questionable. There was no mention of a shared Britishness in public notices of the Imperial Orange Council gathering in Belfast, and although Hume acknowledges that in modern Britain there are many people from the Commonwealth who 'are part of our identity and culture now',[98] British identity is seen primarily as something linked with the UK state.

The promotion of a common Ulster-Scots heritage has though encouraged the establishment of a narrative that emphasises the common radical anti-statist credentials of Orangeism, particularly in the UK and North America. Hume has noted that he is 'from the Presbyterian community, which rebelled against the King for good reasons in 1776 in America' and argues that it was Ulster-Scots who 'helped stage and win the American Revolution'.[99] The Grand Lodge of Ireland has also sought to develop their role as ambassadors for cultural tourism in Northern Ireland, particularly the 'tremendous potential in distinct geographical areas of North America where the Scots Irish or Ulster Scots tradition is strong'.[100] For many members, the strongest ties were also associated with North America. One noted that 'we look to the internationalism of the Order, particularly in America.'[101]

The Commonwealth continues to provide an important link for Orangeism. The *Orange Standard* noted in 2008 that 'there is still a deep-seated respect and admiration for the Commonwealth and all that it stands for, especially those countries who have close ties with Northern Ireland.'[102] Links with overseas Orange associations are construed within ethnic and religious contexts. In Canada, New Zealand and Australia, for example, the emigration of 'Ulster folk' is seen as the principal tie, thus prioritising ethno-religious commonalities. Links with African Orange associations are however primarily the result of the work of Ulster missionaries or Orange brethren in Togo and Ghana and the Orange Order has been keen to draw attention to their multi-racial composition.

Concerns about the Commonwealth tie into broader issues about the dilution of identity and the role of the crown in defining a British community. The Orange Order has highlighted that it has members in 'many Commonwealth nations' and that the Commonwealth 'is an institution which has the support of all true Britons'. Unlike European countries, 'most of whom have no history of special ties with the British', the Order suggests that 'Ulster people who have had the privilege of visiting Canada, Australia, New Zealand and other nations will know just how proud the peoples of these great countries are of their British ancestry and heritage.'[103]

The role of crown as head of state of sixteen countries across the Commonwealth is also seen as important in limiting the possibility of the UK government revising the Act of Settlement with regard to Catholic succession. The Orange Order has noted that changes to the constitutional position of the monarchy would not just affect the UK and would therefore require consent from the parliaments of the other states where the crown remains head of state.[104] The ability of the Orange Order in other countries to respond to such a threat in a uniform manner was however doubted. One member summed up such uncertainties, noting that 'the Orange Order in Northern Ireland is probably a lot different in its background to the Orange Order in Australia or the Orange Order in Canada.'[105]

CONCLUSIONS

Many Orange Order members see British society, particularly English society, as markedly different to that found in Northern Ireland. Issues of identity, community, multiculture and religion were often conflated but there was a pervading sense that, although citizenship was defined by the common ascription to the crown and other institutions, Britain was a place apart. It was evident that members shared concerns about the potential of Scottish separatist nationalism and a distinctive cosmopolitan Anglo-Britishness to undermine the cohesion of the UK state and a shared British national identity. Some members clearly viewed such developments through the prism of a defensive Britishness that underpinned their understanding of issues in Northern Ireland. This was tempered by an accommodation of pluralism. Many members' understanding of politics and society on the 'mainland' indicated a layering of citizenship and identity which reflected the multi-national and multicultural nature of the UK state.

The complexities of Northern Irish Orangeism are most evident when understood within transnational contexts. Ireland was rarely considered within civic terms and it played no role in how those interviewed understood their citizenship or national identity. Although some members acknowledged an often latent sense of Irishness, the symbols of the Irish state were rejected out of hand as being in any way representative of their various identities. Faith and, to a much lesser extent, crown provides a common but somewhat diffused framework for the Orange Order across several countries to celebrate a shared 'global' Orangeism. Attempts to define the complexities outlined in this chapter were best represented in an Orange Hall in Armagh one cold January morning. One member sought to resolve many of the tensions by noting:

> There's hopefully more Protestants in the world than just those claiming to be British. I don't think that you would need to be British, or you don't need to be British to be an Orangeman. There's plenty of other countries in the world that have Orangemen.

Such complexities have distinctive interpretations in Northern Ireland and are strongly linked to a desire to maintain the union. It is this affiliation with a British state that is most often viewed with suspicion that distinguishes Northern Irish Orangeism and ensured that the focus of those interviewed and the Grand Lodge that represents them rarely left Northern Ireland. When it did, it painted a view of a Britain that many who live there would struggle to recognise.

NOTES

1. D. Bell, 'Acts of Union: Youth Sub-Culture and Ethnic Identity Amongst Protestants in Northern Ireland', *The British Journal of Sociology*, 38, 2, (1987), pp.158–83, at p.176.
2. See, for example, D. Bryan, 'Rituals of Irish Protestantism and Orangeism: The Transnational Grand Orange Lodge of Ireland', *European Studies*, vol. 19 (2003), pp.105–23; C. Kinealy, 'The Orange Order and Representations of Britishness', in S. Caunce, E. Mazierska, S. Sydney-Smith and J.K. Walton (eds), *Relocating Britishness* (Manchester: Manchester University Press, 2004), pp.217–36; E. Kaufmann, *The Orange Order: A Contemporary Northern Irish History* (Oxford: Oxford University Press, 2007).
3. Editorial, *Orange Standard*, April 1999.
4. HMSO, *The Agreement: Agreement Reached in Multi-Party Negotiations* (Belfast: HMSO, 1998).
5. *Belfast Telegraph*, 'Orange Parades have a place in a United Ireland, says Adams', 15 July 2009, p.4.
6. J. Coakley and L. O'Dowd, 'The Transformation of the Irish Border', *Political Geography*, 26, 1 (2007), pp.1–12.
7. S. Cohen, 'Winning While Losing: The Apprentice Boys of Derry Walk their Beat', *Political Geography*, 26, 8 (2007), pp.951–67.
8. Bryan, 'Rituals of Irish Protestantism and Orangeism', p.115.
9. Interview with the authors, 25 January 2008.
10. *Orange Standard*, 'False Information Being Spread', June 2008.
11. Hume, Speech at Grangemouth, 2008.
12. Interview with the authors, 25 January 2008.
13. Interview with the authors, 26 January 2008.
14. Interview with the authors, 25 January 2008.
15. A. Aughey, 'From Declinism to Endism: Exploring the Ideology of British Break-Up', *Journal of Political Ideologies*, 15, 1 (2010), pp.11–30.
16. Interview with the authors, 25 January 2008.
17. Interview with the authors, 26 January 2008.
18. Interview with the authors, 25 January 2008.
19. A. Boyd, 'The Orange Order, 1795–1995', *History Today*, 45, 9 (1995), pp.16–23.
20. D.M. MacRaild, *Faith, Fraternity and Fighting: The Orange Order and Irish Migrants in Northern England, c. 1850–1920* (Liverpool: Liverpool University Press, 2005), p.3.
21. P. Day, 'Pride Before a Fall? Orangeism in Liverpool Since 1945', in M. Busteed, F. Neal and J. Tonge, *Irish Protestant Identities* (Manchester: Manchester University Press, 2007).
22. Kinealy, 'The Orange Order and Representations of Britishness', p.226.
23. J. Coakley, 'National Identity in Northern Ireland: Stability or Change?' *Nations and Nationalism*, 13, 4 (2007), pp.573–97.
24. Interview with the authors, 25 January 2008.
25. F. Neal, *Sectarian Violence: The Liverpool Experience, 1819–1914* (Manchester: Manchester University Press, 1987); R. Waller, *Democracy and Sectarianism: A Political and Social History of Liverpool, 1868–1939* (Liverpool: Liverpool University Press, 1981); S. Bruce, T. Glendinning, I. Paterson and M. Rosie, *Sectarianism in Scotland* (Edinburgh: Edinburgh University Press, 2004).
26. Channel 4, 'Billy Boys', Tribes series, 1990.
27. 'Alexei Sayle's Liverpool', available at http://www.bbc.co.uk/programmes/b00c3qss/episodes/2008; accessed 6 May 2011.
28. *Orange Standard*, 'Liverpool Still an Orange Citadel', October 2006, p.8.
29. Day, 'Pride before a Fall?'; T. Birtill, 'A lighter shade of Orange', *Irish Post*, 27 January 1996, p.12.
30. http://www.heraldscotland.com/news/home-news/glasgow-has-more-parades-than-belfast-and-londonderry-combined-1.823788; accessed 6 May 2011.

31. http://www.orangeorderscotland.com/news.html; accessed 6 May 2011.
32. D. Hume, 'The Orange Order and Britishness', speech as part of the 'New Perspectives on Britishness' seminar series, University of Huddersfield, 4 March 2010.
33. C. Farrington and G. Walker, 'Ideological Content and Institutional Frameworks: Unionist Identities in Northern Ireland and Scotland', *Irish Studies Review*, 17, 2 (2009), pp.135–52. The authors note that devolution has actually enhanced Northern Ireland's position in the union as has provided a means for integration and formal recognition rather than being considered an anomaly.
34. S. Bruce, T. Glendinning, I. Paterson and M. Rosie, 'Religious Discrimination in Scotland: Fact or Myth?' *Ethnic and Racial Studies*, 28, 1 (2005), pp.151–68.
35. T. Devine (ed), *Scotland's Shame? Bigotry and Sectarianism in Modern Scotland* (Edinburgh: Mainstream, 2000); J. Bradley, 'Orangeism in Scotland: Unionism, Politics, Identity and Football', *Éire-Ireland*, 39, 1/2 (2004), pp.237–61.
36. L. Paterson, 'Sources of Support for the SNP', in C. Bromley, J. Curtice, D. McCrone and A. Park (eds), *Has Devolution Delivered? The New Scotland Four Years On* (Edinburgh: Edinburgh University Press, 2006), pp.46–68.
37. N. McKay, 'Orange Order's threat to take up arms: Catholic and SNP outrage', *Sunday Herald*, 8 July 2001, p.3.
38. *Orange Standard*, 'Orange Lobby at Westminster over Act of Union', December 2008.
39. *The Scotsman*, 'Orange Order ignites SNP over Union', 19 October, 2009. This is a shift away from earlier calls by Jack Ramsey, former grand secretary in Scotland, who suggested Orangemen would turn to paramilitarism if independence was enacted (*Sunday Herald*, 8 July 2001).
40. *News Letter*, 'SNP "scaremongering" over Orange parade', 10 June 2010, p.7.
41. D. Hume, Speech at Grangemouth, *The Orange Chronicle*, 28 June 2008, http://www.orange-order.co.uk/chronicle/?item=david-hume-s-speech-at-grangemouth-scotland; accessed 6 May 2011.
42. K. Stapleton and J. Wilson, 'A Discursive Approach to Cultural Identity: The Case of Ulster-Scots', Belfast Working Papers in Language and Linguistics no. 16 (Magee: University of Ulster, 2003), pp.57–71.
43. N. Morag, 'The Emerald Isle: Ireland and the Clash of Irish and Ulster-British Nationalisms', *National Identities*, 10, 3 (2008), pp.263–80. Morag highlights the strong similarities.
44. *Orange Standard*, 'Orange Stands for the Union', July 2008.
45. D. Officer and G. Walker, 'Protestant Ulster: Ethno-History, Memory and Contemporary Prospects', *National Identities*, 2, 3 (2000), pp.293–307.
46. Interview with the authors, 3 November 2007.
47. Interview with the authors, 26 January 2008.
48. Interview with the authors, 2 November 2008.
49. M.N. Craith, 'Politicised Linguistic Consciousness: The Case of Ulster-Scots', *Nations and Nationalism*, 7, 1 (2001), pp.21–37.
50. Bradley, 'Orangeism in Scotland: Unionism', pp.256–8.
51. E. Kaufmann, 'The Dynamics of Orangeism in Scotland: Social Sources of Political Influence in a Mass-Member Organization, 1860–2001', *Social Science History*, 30, 2 (2006), pp.263–92.
52. Interview with the authors, 26 January 2008.
53. Interview with the authors, 3 November 2007.
54. Interview with the authors 2 November 2007.
55. Interview with the authors, 26 January 2008.
56. L. Colley, *Britons: Forging the Nation, 1707–1737* (New Haven, CT: Yale University Press, 1992); N. Southern, 'Britishness, "Ulsterness" and Unionist Identity in Northern Ireland', *Nationalism and Ethnic Politics*, 13, 1 (2007), pp.71–102.
57. Hume, 'The Orange Order and Britishness', 2010.
58. G.K. Peating, 'Unionist Identity, External Perceptions of Northern Ireland, and the Problem of Unionist Legitimacy', *Éire-Ireland*, 39, 1/2 (2004), pp.215–36.
59. Interview with the authors, 3 November 2007.
60. Interview with the authors, 26 January 2008.
61. Interview with the authors, 25 January 2008.
62. Interview with the authors, 2 November 2007.

63. Interview with the authors, 25 January 2008.
64. For evidence of the Anglo-centric focus of debates about 'British' multiculturalism, see B. Parekh, *Rethinking Multiculturalism: Cultural Diversity and Political Theory* (London: Palgrave Macmillan, 2000); T. Modood, *Multiculturalism* (London: Polity, 2007). Politicians also often overlook the distinctiveness of debates about multiculturalism outside of England. See, for example, T. Blair, 'The Duty to Integrate: Shared British Values', 8 December 2006, http://www.number10.gov.uk/Page10563; accessed 6 May 2011; D. Cameron, 'PM's speech at Munich Security Conference', 5 February 2011, http://www.number10.gov.uk/news/speeches-and-transcripts/2011/02/pms-speech-at-munich-security-conference-60293; accessed 6 May 2011.
65. P. Geoghegan, 'Multiculturalism and Sectarianism in Post-Agreement Northern Ireland', *Scottish Geographical Journal*, 124, 2 (2008), pp.185–91.
66. M.N. Craith, *Plural Identities, Singular Narrative: The Case of Northern Ireland* (Oxford: Berghahn Books, 2002), p.5.
67. S. Thompson, 'The Politics of Culture in Northern Ireland', *Constellations*, 10, 1 (2003), pp.53–74.
68. J. Todd, N. Rougier, T. O'Keefe and L. Canas Bottos, 'Does Being Protestant Matter? Protestants, Minorities and the Re-making of Ethno-Religious Identity after the Good Friday Agreement', *National Identities*, 11, 1 (2009), pp.87–99.
69. Interview with the authors, 3 November 2007.
70. Interview with the authors, 2 November 2007.
71. D. Hume, 'Orange Order Condemns Racist Attacks', Speech in Ballykilbeg, County Down, 18 June 2009, http://www.orange-order.co.uk/chronicle/?item=orange-order-condemns-racist-incidents; accessed 6 May 2011.
72. Interview with the authors, 25 January 2008.
73. Interview with the authors, 3 November 2007.
74. Ibid.
75. Interview with the authors, 2 November 2007.
76. Interview with the authors, 26 January 2008.
77. Ibid.
78. Interview with the authors, 25 January 2008.
79. Ibid.
80 Ibid.
81. Interview with the authors, 26 January 2008.
82. Interview with the authors, 3 November 2007.
83. Interview with the authors, 25 January 2008.
84. See S. Howe, *Ireland and Empire* (Oxford: Oxford University Press, 2000).
85. R. Dudley Edwards, *The Faithful Tribe: An Intimate Portrait of the Loyal Institutions* (London: HarperCollins, 2000); B. Kennaway, *The Orange Order: A Tradition Betrayed* (London: Methuen, 2006).
86. D.M. MacRaild, 'Wherever Orange Is Worn: Orangeism and Irish Migration in the 19th and Early 20th Centuries', *Canadian Journal of Irish Studies*, 28, 2 (2002), pp.98–117; D.A. Wilson, (ed.), *The Orange Order in Canada* (Dublin: Four Courts Press, 2007).
87. Kaufmann, *The Orange Order*, p.3.
88. Grand Lodge of Ireland, 'Orange Expansion', undated, http://www.grandorangelodge.co.uk/history/Orange_Expansion.html; accessed 6 May 2011.
89. Interview with the authors, 25 January 2008.
90. See, for example, R. McLaughlin, 'Irish Nationalism and Orange Unionism in Canada: A Reappraisal', *Éire-Ireland*, 41, 3 (2007), pp.80–109.
91. Interview with the authors, 25 January 2008.
92. Interview with the authors, 26 January 2008.
93. Interview with the authors, 25 January 2008.
94. Ibid.
95. *Orange Standard*, 'Renewal is the Order of the Day', August 2009.
96. Hume, 'Orange Order Condemn Racist Attacks', 2009.
97. Interview with the authors, 2 November 2007.
98. Hume, 'The Orange Order and Britishness', 2010.
99. Hume, speech at Grangemouth, 2008.

100. Grand Lodge of Ireland, 'Orange Order Working with Tourism Chiefs', 22 November 2007, http://www.grandorangelodge.co.uk/press/PressReleases-2007/071122orange_order _working_with_tourism_chiefs.htm; accessed 6 May 2011.
101. Interview with the authors, 25 January 2008.
102. *Orange Standard*, 'Commonwealth Has A Valued Role To Play', September 2008.
103. Ibid.
104. *Orange Standard*, 'Tampering with the Constitution', November 2008.
105. Interview with the authors, 26 January 2008.

CHAPTER THREE

Culture and Identity in Contemporary Orangeism

We, those names are hereunto subscribed, who have now joined the Prince of Orange for the defence of the Protestant religion; and for the maintaining of the ancient government and the laws and liberties of England, Scotland, and Ireland, do engage to almighty GOD, to His Highness, The Prince, and to one another; to stick firm to the cause in the defence of it, and never to depart from it till our religion, laws, and liberties are so far secured to us in free parliament that they shall no more be in danger of falling under popery and slavery.[1]

Although compared with previous decades Orange Order membership has declined dramatically, and while today association with Orangeism is unlikely to offer direct patronage or reward, it would be wrong to think that the Orange Order no longer features prominently in structuring religious, social and political life for many Protestants. Core to this is the construction of the cultural politics of Orangeism reflecting the shared values and norms held by the membership. It is through the strength of this shared sense of social identification that the group builds its sense of collective social identity.

As van Dijk indicates, such identities are often constructed around answers to key questions surrounding issues of uncertainty for the group, including, who *are* we? what do we *do*? *why* do we do this? (aims); and concerns surrounding the group's position in society and how they relate to other groups.[2] Woodward expresses a clear overview, explaining that:

Identity involves aligning ourselves with one group of people; saying that we are the same as them, as well as marking ourselves out as different from other groups of people. We can have a collective identity, at the local or even at the global level, whether through culture, religion or politics, as well as having an individual identity, as a mother, father or worker.[3]

WHO ARE THE ORANGE ORDER?

All social identities must, of course, be contextualised. Identity is not just about constructing meaning for those self-categorised as part of a group, but also the relationship of that group to others and the wider social structure. Before our survey, reliable information on the composition of the Orange Order membership had been difficult to come by. Broadly, the Order is cross-denominational: almost half of its members are Presbyterian, around one-third belong to the Church of Ireland with a further 7 and 4 per cent respectively belonging to the Methodist or Free Presbyterian churches. Although historically, Free Presbyterianism was not associated with Orangeism, those respondents interviewed raised few theological objections.

Objectively, the Order is mainly, but not overwhelmingly, a working-class organisation, with 56 per cent of members self-identifying as working class. Some 17 per cent view themselves as middle class,[4] while one quarter of the membership do not regard themselves as a member of any social class whatsoever. Few (less than 10 per cent) of Orange Order members in Northern Ireland are drawn from the unskilled working class; it is more than six times more common for a member to be a skilled worker. A substantial number, around one in five members, are self-employed, higher than the Northern Ireland average of 15 per cent.

Around one quarter of members attended grammar school, and while 15 per cent are university graduates, twice that number, around 30 per cent, possess no educational qualifications. The vast majority of members are homeowners (90 per cent), while the median income of members is in the £15,000–£25,000 range (incomes generally are around 20 per cent lower in Northern Ireland than elsewhere in the UK). Although often presented in the media and by opponents as predominantly elderly in its make up, the median age range of the current membership is 45–54.

While politics are not *in isolation* a major motivation for joining and the vast majority of members see the institution as a cultural rather than a political organisation, we shall see that this carries a particular meaning for Orangeism. Further, Orange Order members tend to be highly politicised. A substantial majority (84 per cent) claim to be interested in politics and only 5 per cent of members admitted to not voting in the 2005 general election. Broadly, the interviews conducted support the view of Kennaway that the present generation of Ulster Protestants look at their religion through political eyes.[5]

Moving beyond this membership profile this chapter considers how Orangeism manifests as a social identity, how some of the core tenets of Orangeism are constructed and how this identity translates into action and behaviour. Orangeism as a collective identity draws on four overlapping pillars. These include the formal and informal rules that define membership; the goals that are shared by members of the group; the way it regards and relates to other social groups; and the worldviews and social and political understandings that are shaped by this identity.[6]

ORANGE IDENTITY

Crucial to understanding Orange identity is not just the identification of the norms, interests and values upon which it rests, but also a recognition of how these values are passed on through the generations by drawing on collective memories, which gives Orangeism its distinctive worldview. The parameters that frame this worldview may be accessed through the resolutions that are adopted annually at 12th of July demonstrations across Northern Ireland. These resolutions are categorised under three headings – 'faith', 'loyalty', and 'state' – which are addressed at all demonstrations across Northern Ireland by various elements of the Orange hierarchy. Thus, politicians tend to speak to the resolutions on 'state', clerics on 'faith' or members of the upper levels of the organisation on 'loyalty'.[7]

Resolutions are seen by the Order as annual public reaffirmations of its core beliefs and values. Take these indicative examples from the mid-1990s:

> The Orange Institution is set for the defence of Protestantism ... the political philosophy of the Orange Institution has been stated precisely, and constantly. It is unionist. The culture of Orangeism is so obviously British that there can be no doubt of its commitment to the Union ... We resolve to support vigorously the unionist cause as proper, legitimate and beneficial for this country.[8]

We can again see these main beliefs reflected if we consider the following extracts from resolutions carried on 12 July 2010:

THE FAITH: As members of the Loyal Orange Institution, a Christian organisation, we affirm our belief in the one true sovereign God – Father, Son and Holy Spirit. We believe that there is only one Mediator between God and man, Jesus Christ, the eternal Son of God, the only King and head of His church ...
LOYALTY: ... in commemoration of the 320th anniversary of the Battle of the Boyne [we] do hereby reaffirm our devotion and loyalty to the Throne and Person of Her Most Gracious Majesty Queen Elizabeth II, Queen of the United Kingdom of Great Britain and Northern Ireland and Her other Realms, Defender of the Faith.
THE STATE: As an Institution we celebrate the anniversary of the Battle of the Boyne in 1690, which established Civil and Religious Liberty and allowed the evolution of modern constitutional democracy ... The Union provides all the people of the United Kingdom with stability and opportunity and is a heritage worthy of being passed down untarnished to future generations. To further the cause of the Union, we call on our political representatives to work for and seek a common voice on the central issue that matters to the unionist people, the constitutional security of Northern Ireland.[9]

By drawing on these key themes in differing ways, the Order plays a vital role in orientating the reactions of members and influencing broader sections of the unionist community to contemporary social and political events. At an everyday level, the influence of the Order is most obviously seen throughout the rural areas of Northern Ireland, where the majority of villages with any significant Protestant population have an Orange Lodge, and the Orange Hall remains 'at the heart of many Protestant communities'.[10] These Halls provide 'a focus for many and varied activities from dances and socials to religious meetings, aerobics classes'; moreover, they also often provide a repository for 'events important to the folk-memory of the community'.[11]
One rural-based member gave the following example:

> We used to be a small village, a very close knit community ... now it's an extra large village, but the Orange Order is still central ... the Lodge do a lot of work that's never mentioned, raising money for charities. Take as an example the Queen's Golden Jubilee, we held a street party for that.[12]

Another explained what he saw as the place of the Orange Hall in the local community:

> The community can see that at the Hall you're doing things for the community, and then they're interested, and they come along and some will ask to join, just for the simple reason that you're involving them in the community, doing things for the community. So it's, it's not just, you know, we're the Orange and that's it ... you bring the people that live in your community around you and do things for them. We have helped pensioners in different ways, doing gardens, fitting security locks on their doors, you know, things like that there.[13]

This member expressed it as follows:

> I think that the Orange Order in the rural areas are much – how would I describe it – there's much more friendliness, much more openness and a much more family orientation towards their activities. Well, if you've ever been or seen the Twelfth in the country – that's an entirely different, an entirely different set up. I mean ... the whole thing in the country, it's a family day out.[14]

This led another member to speculate directly concerning the differences between rural and urban Orangeism, and to further emphasise the position of the Orange Hall in rural social life:

> Well I would say it's a different ... there's two Orangemen, there's the rural Orangeman and there is the urban Orangeman. A rural Orangeman would ... he will identify with his Lodge, and they'll leave the Orange Hall on the Twelfth morning. In Belfast ... in the majority of cases, he leaves the Worshipful Master's house to go to the Orange Hall and it's a different type of Orangeism that you'll find ... There is a more social side to the rural Orangeman. They will have their harvest dance, they will have their May dance, they will have different things you'll not see in an Orange Hall in urban Belfast. In rural areas most, well a lot of, Lodges will have an Orange Ball once a year and they'll come from miles around just to go to that one particular event ... they will have social events more than what the urban Orange man would, you know.[15]

While the importance of the social networks built around the Order may sometimes be less visible in urban areas, the continuing strength of the social relationships bound up with Orangeism and its importance within civil society should not be under-estimated. Across Northern Ireland members continue to regard the institution as core to their individual and collective identities, looking to the Order to represent them on major social, political and sometimes moral issues of the day and recognising Orangeism as 'a nerve that runs right through the heart of the Protestant community'.[16]

To fully understand this demands an exploration not just of how Orange identity is constructed, but also how this is conveyed from generation to generation of Orange members. Broadly, processes of political socialisation involve the transmission of an identifiable political culture to new generations in a given society.[17] Most often this occurs through the reproduction of collective memories and political myths used to develop strong senses of social categorisation and long-term differences in cultural learning. Processes of socialisation take place overtly through the transmission of what are seen as legitimate cultures and values, through ritual forms of behaviour (the most obvious in this context being the Orange parading tradition), and through less obvious informal influences such as the family or other social networks within the community.

This is in no way unique to Northern Ireland; indeed, in most developed societies the passing across generations of an identifiable set of values that reinforce existing political identities and social structures is noteworthy.[18] In the case of highly divided societies such as Northern Ireland, it is important to recognise that political culture remains extremely contested and political socialisation is highly fragmented.[19] More often than not socialisation and identity formation is limited almost exclusively to the reproduction of the core values of respective political communities, protecting the certainties of that group and reinforcing distance from the 'other'.[20]

Across the Orange Order membership it is important to identify continuities and flexibility within the processes by which such social and political values are transmitted and how responses of Orange Order members to their everyday situations are shaped by both the forces of political socialisation, subjective orientations and senses of collective identity (and the interactions between them). This chapter focuses on some of the key locations for Orange identity, followed by Chapter 4 which highlights the discourses that bind and direct Orangeism.

Within Orangeism, cultural learning is most readily experienced through the reproduction of a recognisable and divergent sense of Orange history, identity and heritage, which draws directly on its own historical reference points, mythology and folklore. Through the repetition of these cultural expressions Orangeism reinforces central aspects of the group's self-perceived identity. Orange rituals, for example, commemorate continuity and communicate a sense of durability and permanence for the group. In turn this helps shape a communal narrative and memory, revealed at a populist level in the recounting of particular events in Orange history, most obviously, for example, those surrounding the siege of Derry in 1689, the Battle of the Boyne in 1690, or the Battle of the Diamond in 1795.[21]

The significance of these communal reference points is reproduced both through this Orange narrative and the production of material artefacts – banners, badges, flags, commemorative medals and so on, all of which seek to represent the experiences of Orangeism. The importance of such objects should not be under-estimated. Drawing on the works of Smith[22] and Cohen,[23] Cairns and Smyth remind us that:

> Symbols, ceremonies and customs make up the cultural matrix of nations, groups and social movements. Manifested in symbolic form, accessible to all members, the basic rationale of the group – its ideology and identity – is made concrete by the use of iconic materials.[24]

For many within Orangeism material culture is seen to provide 'an authentic link to the past'[25] and a direct means of linking the past to the present. Thus when the Order moved into new headquarters in 2001 it was at pains to point out that the new building would include a display of certain objects, including:

- King William's saddlecloth, presented to Thomas Coningsby, his quartermaster general;
- King William's gloves;
- A Victorian Orange flag from Sandy Row in Belfast;
- A pre-1770 Williamite toasting glass;
- The minute book of Fort Edward 'Body of Orangemen' Lodge, 1798;
- The Grand Lodge minute books from 1798 to date;
- Small collarette worn by George Best when carrying the banner strings as a young boy in the Cregagh estate;

- The metal plate used as part of the process of printing the 1912 Ulster Covenant;
- Shrapnel from a car bomb used by the IRA to blow up the House of Orange in Belfast in the 1970s.[26]

Such artifacts are read and understood so as to place Orangeism at the centre of Protestant heritage in Ireland, to give Orangeism its core political and social orientations and to link the past with the contemporary. This occurs at many different levels. Take for example the following from a pamphlet issued at 1995 Larne District to celebrate 100 years of Orangeism in that area. The foreword by the Rev. Martin Smyth is instructive in demonstrating how Orange history and narrative is constructed. Smyth commends the booklet as follows:

> In an age which appears rootless it is encouraging to discover those who seek to retrace their roots. In this Bicentennial Year of the Battle of the Diamond and the subsequent reforming of the Orange Institution as we know it today, Larne is provided with an excellent probing of the roots of the Orange Tree ... With a clear place in history in the 1914 Gun-Running for the defence of Ulster at a time of an earlier attempted betrayal of the British – especially Protestant – people of Ireland ... It is important therefore that the role of the Orange family be properly presented. This is so that those who ... wander from the Faith and betray our heritage by carelessness may be better informed of our Reformed heritage and British convictions. Though others may fail, may we stand fast and maintain such a heritage for the future.[27]

Within Orangeism the transmission of cultural values has both formal and informal dimensions. At one level, processes of socialisation often involve the more or less unconscious conduction of particular values. At another, more available, level it takes place through the ritualisation of particular forms of behaviour as expressions of identity, and even more formally through educational publications[28] and programmes run by the Order, which also has an increasing internet presence.[29] The physical objects of Orangeism and the paraphernalia of Lodge and parade also generate powerful cultural reference points and messages about the group. Often these are used to symbolise and reinforce group identity and to directly augment the narrative of Orangeism.[30]

Together these provide the building blocks for the creation and reproduction of Orange culture, constituted through the closed meetings, identifiable rituals, symbolic actions and cultural objects unique to Orangeism. These expressions of culture work in turn to enhance group solidarity, strengthen Orange identity and to communicate core ideas, values and goals, both to those outside of Orangeism and across the generations within it.

Orange culture does not, however, somehow float free from politics, economics, or the other social institutions that configure social relationships in Northern Ireland and beyond. Rather Orange culture is interwoven with an array of political and social factors that exist within (and in part creates) the contemporary social structure. Processes of socialisation are therefore of central significance in understanding the views of the Orange Order membership and Orange identity. Socialisation remains a complex process through which individuals become aware of, and form, political and social values throughout the life cycle.[31] Political socialisation has been understood in a variety of ways,[32] but crucially involves the transmission from generation to generation of the political culture of a group, understood as a group's predominant beliefs, attitudes, ideals and values, alongside sentiments and evaluation about the political system.[33]

There are several different conduits for the transmission of Orange culture, but for many the notion of 'family tradition' remains at the heart of membership. Of those surveyed, a large majority (over 83 per cent) joined the Order through direct associations with family or friends, a large majority of those joining over the past two decades giving primacy to 'family connections' as their main reason for joining. Copies of the official publication of the Order, the *Orange Standard*, more often than not display an array of photographs of family compositions involving several generations, those present ranging from young members of junior Lodges to those with long-service awards, for a quarter of a century, or longer, of continued membership.

Hence the following from members outlining their reasons for taking up Orange membership:

> It was like sort of ... very much family orientated ... you know, sort of in the family blood.[34]

> I have 50 years' membership ... it's a family tradition ... I knew that my father, my grandfather were Orangemen and my grandmother was an Orangewoman. My great grandfather was an Orangeman. So it was, it was part of my family heritage and also part of my culture of course.[35]

When you came to that certain age, you followed your fathers and your uncles and so forth [into the Lodge].[36]

Family tradition, father, grandfather, grandmother, great grandfather, brothers, so [joining] was very much something that was within the family.[37]

My great grandfather was an Orangeman and my father and several of his brothers. So it was, it was part of my family heritage and also part of my culture of course.[38]

The Lodge that I joined, there was an association ... my father had an association with the Lodge ... it happened to be my grandparents' Lodge on my mother's side of the house.[39]

I am from a country Lodge. Our warrant was given to us in 1823 and every generation of my family has been Master of that Lodge since 1823. We can trace it ... my father, my grandfather and my great grandfather, and my great, great grandfather, right back to when the Lodge was formed.[40]

For me, its just something I've grown up with ... the whole family connection around the Orange Order. My Dad was in the Orange Order and we used to go to the Orange Hall and things like that.[41]

While it is certainly not the only reason for joining, the importance of family bonds to Orangeism cannot be overstated, nor the significance of family connections to the structural and ideological longevity of the Order underplayed. Family environment is seen to influence deeply the political views and values of most individuals through both the behaviour and the expression of beliefs they experience in that setting. Witness, for example, the evidence presented by writers such as Connolly and Maginn[42] and Lanclos,[43] indicating how from a very early age children in Northern Ireland develop a sense of social difference between Protestant and Catholic and begin to apply negative characteristics to the other group. Orange family links represent a 'remarkable bridging of the generations', and within Orangeism huge 'pride is taken in handing on the tradition from father to son to grandson'.[44]

Members of the Order are accessible, found across the Protestant community; hence others, while having no direct line of family membership, have joined through connections with friends and acquaintances. Such experiences are reflected in the following:

From a personal point of view, there's a generation gap in our family. My father always turned out to watch the parade and I thought why watch when you can take part in it and it was as simple as that. So I, er ... contacted a person I knew over the internet.[45]

I [saw a Lodge] that took my fancy ... in East Belfast, No 6 District ... it struck me, I knew a few of the personalities in the Lodge ... so that was the one I went for, and never looked back.[46]

My Dad never had anything to do with it, although one of my granny's family was in it and just, you know, my mum and my granny always took me down to watch our Battle of the Somme Parade, and our 12th of July Parade. I was always busting to walk when I was a wee kid, and my mum would never let me. My dad had a few friends in it and they put me in touch with our Lodge, and I joined that when I was seventeen, and I just got more and more involved in it.[47]

These men, both of whom were longstanding members (for over fifty years), told of related biographies, which drew strongly on several of the above elements, highlighting community, family and friendship patterns, as all having some influence on their decisions to join:

I joined the Junior Movement in 1939 ... because all the wee fellas around me were joining the Junior Movement. So I suppose it was social, a social thing even at that age. Then the war broke out and, and everything of course went a bit dead you might say, there was no parades, there was nothing, and then in 1944, I was knocking about with a few lads, one of them had a connection through his brother with a Lodge outside the town of Newtownards ... and their tradition, because there was no parading, they held a, a dinner or tea on the 12th of July.

He continued:

... between the 12th of July and I suppose September, some of the boys approached me: 'would you not join up here?' so I simply joined. It was a, basically, a social thing again. I was there for three or four years and, but my father had belonged to a Lodge in Newtownards, the one I'm in at the present, and in 1948, he says to me: 'I don't the heck know why you're going away up to the country to the Lodge, why don't you come to the Lodge I'm in?'

He'd been in it since the '20s. So I simply transferred down there and I've been there ever since.[48]

The other longstanding member also spoke of family, friends and community all having some influence in his decision to join:

... the Lodge I'm in is actually [an] ex-Service Lodge ... formed like most of them just after the First World War. I'd friends that were actually in [the Lodge] at that time. So I used to watch them parading to Finaghy, as it was in those days, and they said that was for me too, so I joined. At that time everybody, the followers, the Lodges formed all lived in the same area, the ex-Services' houses on the Cregagh Road ... I was born in Somme Drive, along with my brother and he was in. So that's why I joined.[49]

Despite the largely positive views outlined above, some did show an awareness of a contracted membership base and some of problems facing the Order, suggesting that this was because the 'Order has drifted away from too many ... of its basic principles'.[5] Those still in membership highlighted what they saw as the most common reasons for decline in membership. These included lack of time, movement to another area, or the closing of a Lodge. Other reasons also emerged, such as personality clashes and disagreement with Lodge policies, but the bulk of reasons offered can be located within the notion of wider societal changes that have had broader implications beyond the Order in terms of diminished social capital and geographical dislocation. These members expressed the following views:

I look for the future, I do think that it's going to be the social drift which will have a bigger influence on the Orange Order than the Order itself, or what the Order itself does. You go to a Scout group, numbers are a mere shadow of what they used to be, the Boys' Brigade, the Girls' Brigade, all the youth organisations, they are finding it so hard to attract membership, young membership. I think that ... whereas years ago membership of organisations was almost a must ... belonging to an organisation is not within the psychic of today's generation, and for probably the future generation, as it was previously.[51]

Previously, the Orange Institution was ... men went there to the Lodge, as much because of the, the social aspect as anything else ... it was a Gentlemen's Club, as it were, and ... it was part of your, the, the social structure of your life. But I think society has moved away from that, and therefore I think that the Orange Order will probably struggle in the future.[52]

The perception that the Order has weakened in the contemporary period is held much more strongly in urban areas, notably in Belfast, where respondents were far less sanguine concerning the future of the Order than their colleagues in more rural locations, perhaps reflecting the deeper integration of Orangeism in rural society indicated in the interviews above. Overall, fewer than twenty respondents claimed that their private Lodge numbers had increased over the previous decade, and our quantitative data showed that 85 per cent of members had joined prior to 1998, often long before this date. Approaching half (46 per cent) of members believe the Order is in decline, while 36 per cent disagreed. Social mobility, the decline of the extended family, a continuing Protestant exodus, the movement of young Protestant students to university in other parts of the UK, and the competition for interests within a more secular society were all highlighted as issues. As one respondent put it, 'stocks are not being replenished.'[53]

PROMOTING ORANGE IDENTITY

Thus, the active promotion of Orange identity and culture has become increasingly relevant in the ideological reproduction of Orangeism as the Order struggles to promote its values within an increasingly secularised society. In tandem with this are issues concerning the decline in membership numbers and making the Order relevant to the current generation of Protestants.

While family traditions and friendship networks are crucially important, some people join because they feel attachment and attraction to what Orangeism says or as a response to increasing concerns found across the Protestant community about the re-setting of the political structure in Northern Ireland. Many unionists believe that post-Agreement society has seen the erosion of the central cultural values of Protestant unionism and that it is the riposte of Orangeism to this that best articulates and communicates their political and cultural identity. In steadfastly expressing this position, many see the retort of Orangeism simply as the expression of the most sectarian bastion of unionism.[54]

In opposition to such views of the organisation, a consistent claim from members is that they are opposed to the doctrines of the Roman Catholic Church rather than hostile to Roman Catholics as individuals. Observance of the Protestant religion does remain for many, however, at the Order's core, as does religious observance. A large majority of members (68 per cent) claim to attend church weekly and 91 per cent of members attend at least monthly. Most within Orangeism see themselves at the forefront of the defence of Protestantism, but this is seen as inseparable from the struggle to keep Ulster British. Almost all interviewees regarded Protestantism and Britishness as deeply intertwined, as the following member makes clear:

> I mean Protestantism is part of being British ... you know there is a connection there ... you know, most Protestants are going to say, you know, I'm British ... I think that's partly because ... a sort of ... strength in numbers, you know, you're gonna want to remain strong and loyal to your, your sort of support, so you'd want to identify with being British and Protestant.[55]

Such views are deeply imbued, many within Orangeism which regards Protestant unionism as under direct challenge, and subject to a 'campaign against Ulster ... being waged on many fronts'.[56] The Order has largely positioned itself in terms of a constitutional response to that perceived threat. Indeed, throughout the conflict the Orange leadership encouraged members to join the security forces rather than loyalist paramilitaries, and aside from a brief period in the early 1970s when some Orange members had a flirtation with paramilitarism through the formation of the Orange Volunteers,[57] the Order has had no structural links with militant loyalism. Indeed, the Orange leadership has consistently and unequivocally condemned political violence no matter what the source.

That does not mean that Orangeism sees itself as uninvolved in political issues, or that the leadership and individuals do not engage in political organisation. Indeed, the Orange leadership has sought to position the Order directly in relation to wider political issues by calling upon all brethren to 'work unceasingly' to recruit many of their co-religionists who are 'either unaware of, or apathetic to, the campaign being waged against loyal Ulster and its people'.[58] One member expressed this as follows:

It is very very important because good religion creates good politics and our people need to be advised and with the disintegration and the dividing up into various Unionist parties where once there was only one our people need to be advised. I am speaking of the Unionist population at large who are not in the Orange Order. We feel that we can be a guide to them in politics yes, but even more importantly in religion on a day when, well, Christianity is under attack in Britain right from the Parliament down. That's the way we see it.[59]

Orangeism is framed and maintained by the strength of narratives that emphasise links with communal cultural memories and much broader political positions (see next chapter). In turn these are seen to legitimise a particular set of social and power relations. Central here is that growing body of literature linking the role of symbolic displays in defining collective identity.[60] Orange symbolism and artefacts demonstrate and communicate representations of cultural values and social and political messages through specific physical objects and other public displays. Thus, for example, parades link the Orange Order with the wider Protestant community. As these members explained:

... we can't be set apart from the ... support that we receive from the wider Protestant community, you just have to look at the 12th of July, and you see maybe twenty, thirty, forty thousand people gathered around to support, you know that includes Orangemen, bandsmen, wives and wider family circle and thousands and thousands of ordinary people.[61]

Those people who come out [on the 12th of July] and identify themselves with that cultural identity, that cultural or religious way of thinking, they all come out and support and are keen to sit on the side of the road on their deckchairs, or keen to sit at the side of the platform, or come in their cars and have their picnic in the field, and people do take part, maybe not partaking in the sense that I take part, but they are taking part in their own way.[62]

I express my identity by parading, by marching with the band, or walking with the Lodge. But for folk to come along and sit at the side of the road and be able to identify themselves with that, that's cultural identity.[63]

DISPLAYING ORANGE IDENTITY

Undoubtedly the Orange Order is most recognisable through its public displays and parading tradition. Parading (often referred to as walking or demonstrating within the Order) remains at the heart of Orange activity and is seen as a core expression of Orange identity, regarded by the Order as 'traditional and a distinct part of our cultural, social and political heritage'.[64] The following expands on this perspective:

> Orange Parades are commemorative. Various events in the history of the people are commemorated by parades that take different forms. These range from solemn remembrance of the Fallen at the Somme to the cultural extravaganza that is the 12th July commemoration of the Glorious Revolution secured at the Battle of the Boyne. Those who glibly dismiss the Boyne Commemorations would do well to think of the benefits that flowed from the Glorious Revolution, benefits which enrich all our citizens irrespective of religion or politics.[65]

The number of parades and length of the 'marching season' has steadily increased in recent decades, to the point where there are now more than somewhere over 3,000 loyalist organised parades held across Northern Ireland each year.[66] These parades take a variety of forms and these have been usefully categorised in a typology of nine discrete categories, each based on the parade's main purpose.[67] These are: (a) main commemorative parades; (b) local parades; (c) feeder parades; (d) Church parades; (e) Arch, Banner and Hall Parades; (f) social parades; (g) occasional parades; (h) competitive band Parades; and (i) commemorative band parades.[68]

Of the parades directly under the remit of the Orange Order in Northern Ireland,[69] the main events in the calendar remain those organised annually on or around the 12th of July (the parade is never held on a Sunday) to commemorate and memorialise the victories of King William III (William of Orange) in the religious wars of the late seventeenth century. Parades are held across Northern Ireland, but the largest is usually held in Belfast. The July 2007 demonstration, for example, is representative of recent years when the demonstration consisted of 134 Lodges supported by 69 marching bands and two floats.[70] There, and elsewhere across Northern Ireland, many thousands of spectators lined the routes to watch Orange members who marched to twenty different venues.

As Jarman rightly reminds us, loyalist marching bands[71] are an 'essential ingredient at the major public commemorations and celebrations'[72] associated with the Orange Order. Over the past forty or so years the culture of 'blood and thunder' (or as they were initially known, 'kick the pope') bands has found increasing popularity and following among sections of working-class Protestant youths.[73] Bryan argues that the development and growth of blood and thunder bands marks the most distinctive development in loyalist political culture since the 1960s,[74] such bands offering alternative forms of social organisation, based on networks and largely reflecting working-class experiences.

The resulting sub-culture that has developed has become increasingly oppositional to mainstream unionism and Orangeism, a trend first noted in the late 1980s. The origins of such bands, Bell suggests, rest in loyalist reaction to growing societal conflict and large-scale deindustrialisation experienced in the 1980s. One consequence was the increasing marginalisation of many young working-class Protestants from the wider society.[75] Part of this manifested in a crisis of gender identity for working-class teenage males, the response to which manifested in the formation of 'tartan gangs' and, somewhat later, through the organisation of blood and thunder bands. Both were expressions of a belligerent masculinity and ethno-sectarian identity[76] as sites of resistance to existing authority (such as police and Orange leadership), an expression of identity within yet marginal to mainstream unionist culture.[77]

There is continuing evidence that some young loyalists understand and experience marching bands as much more active and authentic expressions of social identity than that offered by the Loyal Orders.[78] This makes bands more attractive to younger disaffected groupings within the Protestant community.[79] One well-placed commentator described the developments as follows, suggesting loyalist youths:

> ... couldn't join the Orange; it's too much hassle to join the Orange because you have to get proposed and seconded at a meeting, and in a lot of areas to this day, you'll not get into the Orange if you're not a regular church attendee. So from a youth perspective, this is what they found and people were searching for another way, and what better way to show people what is felt than to get on the road in a band?[80]

Bands are independent and self-organising, highly proletarian in their composition, they participate in parades and competitions, offering a style which is often highly militarised and whose image often includes paramilitary, or pseudo-paramilitary symbolism displayed on uniforms, drums and on the flags and bannerettes that accompany the band. The social and political arrangements involved in Orange parades are multifaceted, within which Jarman suggests marching bands hold a highly equivocal position; representing a coherent understanding of one faction of contemporary unionism, but existing almost entirely outside the jurisdiction of the Loyal Orders.[81]

There are differing views concerning how deeply embedded blood and thunder culture is within the wider Protestant/unionist/loyalist community and the functions it plays in working-class areas. Bell, for example, sees the bands as an alternative to paramilitary activity and much of the posturing of the bands based on 'bravado',[82] while Dudley Edwards argues blood and thunder bands have acted as a safety valve for young men, stopping them joining loyalist paramilitary organisations.[83] Jarman, however, suggests that the relationship of the bands to loyalist paramilitarism is much closer.[84] What both Bell and Jarman are agreed upon, however, is that for the most part key sections of disenchanted working-class loyalists see the Order as irrelevant to their everyday experiences and have abandoned any thought of looking to it for leadership, or as a form of cultural expression.[85]

While not denying the importance of bands to loyalist popular culture,[86] or that they are 'the most important agency in the reproduction of populist loyalism across the generational divide',[87] they are structurally disconnected from the Orange Order; the vast majority of bands have no formal allegiance to Orangeism (although individual members may belong to both band and Order). Loyalist bands remain separate from mainstream Orangeism with their own social dynamics and cultural practices[88] and at times they offer a counter and alternative culture to Orangeism rather than being part of it.[89]

Indeed, blood and thunder popular culture is largely alien to, and increasingly problematic for, mainstream Orangeism and its deeply respectable aura. In particular there is growing concern in Orange ranks not just with the bands but with their followers, often called in interviews 'the blue bag brigade', referring to the alcohol they carry in bags served by local off-licences. These band followers are seen as bringing parades into disrepute and to be wrongly seen as under the direct influence of the Order.

Moreover, the actions of band followers is seen to run counter to a core goal of Orangeism as it seeks to retain significance by exhibiting solidarity across key sections of the Protestant community. Although there are differences of emphasis within the Order dependent on age – some younger Belfast members interviewed, for example, readily acknowledged they were more attracted by the band culture – there have been sometimes overt culture clashes between the Orange and band leaderships.

In response the Grand Lodge has introduced an extremely tight set of regulations on band conduct at all types of parades with which the Order is involved; church, commemorative or celebratory. Limitations on marching bands also include requirements that only hymns are played at church parades; the prohibition of alcohol; strict dress codes and stipulations regarding flags and banners.[90]

Orange members largely see such regulations as positive and the following comment is typical:

> A lot of the trouble maybe comes from, what some of the nationalist community were seeing as paramilitary displays by bands. Now that ... there's been more control in that now, and these paramilitary emblems have started to disappear, and the Orange Order has, to me, has clamped down on, on hiring these bands.[91]

Moreover, many Orange members associated blood and thunder bands directly with paramilitary support and saw one of the Order's roles as being in direct competition with loyalist paramilitary groups for the allegiance of young people. As one member put it:

> ... throughout the course of the Troubles we were a competitor to paramilitarism. So you know, for an organisation, which is more attractive for the young person growing up in the inner city of Belfast? Was it to join the Lodge who worked for the community or was it to progress into paramilitarism who were about corruption and money making ... I think that young people have realised the value now and that their identity is much more important to them. I think young people have realised that once and for all that their identity can be expressed with themselves and they don't have to resort to violence, they don't have to resort to criminality in order to do that ... there's no need to do that at all.[92]

One member outlined what he believed should be the consequences of paramilitary affiliation, recalling the following account of clashes between Orange and band cultures:

> If there were concrete evidence to the fact that there were members of the Orange Institution who were involved in paramilitary activity, I'd kick them out – no question, just simply kick them out. They have no place within Orangeism, no place within Orangeism whatsoever. In fact if I were in the situation where in my own local area there were known members of paramilitary organisations and they weren't being kicked out, then I would, I would walk out, I would walk away. Even after 50 years [membership].[93]
>
> I know that, for example, there was a band, which was going to take part in, in our parade, and it was brought to my notice that they were carrying a Red Hand Commando flag. So I went to the chief marshall, and said I understand this band is carrying a, a Red Hand Commando flag, which of course just isn't acceptable, and to cut the story short, that band has been actually excluded. Oh yes, totally excluded ...

But (and suggesting that Jarman may well be closer in his assessment of the relationship between band and paramilitary than Bell or Dudley Edwards) the same member was aware that seeking to exclude a blood and thunder band may well bring consequences:

> ... the [Worshipful] master, and the district master ... when we discussed this in district, he was saying, well part of the problem is ... who is going to be the one to put himself on the line in confronting these people, because they, they were all paramilitaries, and he said that, he said I can tell you quite clearly that I'm reluctant to do it as district master because of the threat. Because I could end up with a bullet in the back of my head, or my knees gone, he said, and as a married man with a family, I am not prepared to put myself on the line to do this.[94]

While undoubtedly participants have an assortment of reasons for taking part in parades, including religious, political and social motives,[95] parades remain a major means of coupling individuals and groups with the collective memory of Orangeism. Such public demonstrations symbolise and exemplify notions of history and tradition for those taking part. Jarman suggests this personifies the tradition through the uses of flags, banners and bannerettes, all of which go to form a vital 'material repository of the Orange tradition.'[96] Moreover, Orange parades allow the leadership to present the institution in its traditional role as a unifying force across the Protestant unionist community: politically through the promotion of party unity (see Chapter 5) and culturally as demonstrated through the public unity of parades, combining elements of community, religion, history and politics on the streets.

DRUMCREE AND ORANGE IDENTITY

As we have noted, public display (and in particular the parading tradition) remains central to the culture and identity of Orangeism. Recent times have seen a number of sometimes violent clashes surrounding the routes taken by Orange and loyalist parades. In an attempt to limit the impact of such disputes the Parades Commission was formed in 1998 as a quasi-judicial public body with responsibility for determining the routes and behaviour of those parades deemed as particularly controversial or provocative. As a result restrictions have been placed on several parades, particularly those that are routed through interface districts between Catholic and Protestant areas, or even occasionally in some areas where Catholics are in a majority. In response, Orange concerns around parading have stretched far beyond merely protests over routes, or presenting a positive public display of Orangeism to the world. Rather, the issue has become a point of engagement with the perceived cultural attack on Orangeism, the erosion of Northern Ireland's Protestant heritage and assaults on the unity of the Protestant and unionist community.

Of the many parades held in Northern Ireland, few (perhaps around fifteen) are highly disputed. Among these 'Drumcree' ranks highly. Issues surrounding the parade by the Portadown District Lodge to and from the Church of the Ascension at Drumcree on the Sunday morning before the 12th of July celebrations came to international attention in the mid to late 1990s.

The conflict emerged when, amid strong protests from nationalist residents, the Portadown District Lodge insisted on exercising its right to take its 'traditional' route on the way back to its parish church, which, following demographic changes, now included the predominantly nationalist Garvaghy Road district. The resultant confrontation led to annual disorder and violence, albeit on a lessening scale, for the remainder of the decade. The situation remains unresolved and the

Orange Order continues to offer symbolic (albeit sometimes token) resistance to the banning of the parade.

Some explanation is necessary regarding why one of the more obscure of several thousand Orange parades annually became international news and central to the political agenda of the Orange Order. As one commentator expressed it, 'how did a dispute about nothing so quickly become a conflict about everything?'[97] Even the then chair of the Parades Commission, Alistair Graham, described it as 'the touchstone, the litmus test, the line in the sand' (albeit for very different reasons from the Orange Order).[98]

From a nationalist viewpoint, the parades in Portadown convey and display a simple concoction of sectarianism and provocation,[99] wrapped in Orange triumphalism. For the Orange Order, however, the opposition of Catholic residents (and the rulings of the Parades Commission) flaunt contempt towards its culture and traditions and provide move evidence of government bias against Protestant unionism. Moreover, the Orange Order sees the opposition as largely motivated by a political campaign organised and motivated by Sinn Féin and its supporters. The following from the *Orange Standard* summarises this well:

> Marching has become an even greater focus of attention in recent years because republicans have decided that, having spent 35 years slaughtering members of the Protestant community with the gun and the bomb, they have now moved into the next phase of the plan to break Protestant resistance so as they can achieve their end goal – the destruction of Northern Ireland as part of the United Kingdom.[100]

Most important perhaps was the fear that Drumcree would set in train a 'domino effect'. As one leading unionist commentator put it, 'if Orangeism lost this particular battle in the heartland of Orangeism, routes all over Northern Ireland would come under attack.'[101] The position was clearly supported by the Rev. Ian Paisley, then leader of the DUP, who declared at one protest rally during the initial Drumcree crisis in 1995: 'If we don't win this battle, all is lost. It is a matter of life or death. It is a matter of Ulster or Irish Republic, it is a matter of freedom or slavery.'[102]

Although the intensity of confrontation and public concern around Drumcree has ebbed since the mid-1990s it has remained central to the political agenda of the Order. This was made clear by Darryl

Hewitt, the Portadown district master in the following statement on 4 July 2010, during that year's protest march:

> Once again we find ourselves standing in front of this barrier preventing us from completing our traditional route ... We will not be walking away from this place and I can assure you that we will continue to work hard to achieve what we desire ... It seems as though there is one law for the Nationalist/Republican community and another for the Unionist community.[103]

Another leading Orangeman expressed his view, declaring that attempts to ban parades involved

> ... draconian legislation contrary to the principles of civil liberty and there is nothing in this legislation which appeals to the Orange Institution. It is undoubtedly aimed at curtailing Parades organised by the Loyal Orders. It is a direct attack on both our faith and our culture bearing in mind our Parades to and from Church are an extension of our public witness ... There is no meaningful recognition in the legislation that our Parades are traditional and a distinct part of our cultural, social and political heritage.[104]

Several writers have suggested that overall the impact of Drumcree proved disastrous[105] and debilitating[106] for the Orange Order. As one leading internal critic put it, the confrontations that emerged over parades 'did a disservice to both Orangeism and Unionism'.[107] While for some it was a battle that Orangeism could simply not be seen to lose, other more moderate voices within the Order recognised that the insistence upon unfettered rights to march was provocative and took little account of changing demography. Many recognised it as a touchstone for contemporary Orangeism, but conceded that the affair had done little to enhance the standing of the Order across the world.

Overall, Drumcree caused discontent among both liberals and traditionalists within the Order, precipitating the resignation of members of both groupings. While the views of those interviewed were not uniform, the majority (57.9 per cent) were in favour of the 'right to march' through nationalist areas. Many, however, expressed concern surrounding members' willingness to engage in direct confrontation with the security forces, feeling it reflected an unhealthy new militancy within an organisation that had lost much of its religious grounding and guiding principles.[108] As this member put it:

There were, there were those who were prepared to stand up and face down the security forces at Drumcree. There were those who done it, there were those who threw bottles and stones and bricks and petrol bombs, but the vast majority of our membership thought no, we are opposing our own people.[109]

Another suggested that it was this paradox of loyalism that had eventually forced the Orange Order to 'throttle back on the protest'. He continued:

It wasn't a point of withdrawing from a situation of intimidation by republicanism. It was out of respect and acknowledgement that here we are as a body of people, who very openly support all that's good about Britishness and all that's good about, you know, respect for, for the Queen and constitution.[110]

Others like this member simply saw themselves in a 'no-win' situation:

You can't march here, OK, so we'll go away, or else the other situation is, you know, you can't march here, well we're gonna march anyway. In which case you can't win, because if you shy away, you'll lose your own support for not standing your ground. And if you do march down the road, you know, you're gonna get it from the other side, you know, again look at these bigots, they just storm through here and, you know, basically they're acting the aggressor.[111]

That said, the notion of placing any restrictions on Orange parades has long been sensitive,[112] and even most moderates interviewed thought that the Order was not 'going to resolve something out there by shying away'.[113] This needs some exploration. Many within the Order believe that any impositions upon the Order's rights have come following an orchestrated campaign by 'Sinn Féin/IRA residents' groups' and the 'cultural fascists' of the Parades Commission.[114] As this member explained:

... to us it's a sort of orchestrated thing by Sinn Féin ... clearly they were bringing people in just to basically get in the face of the Orange supporters and block them off. Whether they were seeking confrontation or what, I'm not sure. Probably to entice the Orangemen, the Orange supporters to probably, you know, provoke one of them into throwing a blow or something, and then the media come along and say, you know, look at these people, look what they're doing.[115]

The idea that 'Orange parades are now top of the republican hit list' and that the parades dispute has been manufactured as part of a 'carefully prepared and thought-out plan of action by Sinn Féin/ IRA'[116] is commonplace across the membership. The following views were typical:

> The truth is that the Provisional IRA have orchestrated an offensive against Traditional Parades. In parallel they attack every other aspect of our Protestant and British way of life ... Everything green and Irish is to be promoted; everything Orange, Crimson and British is to be demonised. ... The pan-nationalist front with the assistance of their friends within the media have sought to peddle the doctrine that Orangemen and Apprentice Boys must seek and receive the approval of nationalist residents, in any area their parades pass-by in order to exercise their right to march.[117]

Such views often culminate in the belief that what is being attempted is the dilution of Protestant identity and rights. Hence the following:

> The basic controlling principle is that together with all other law abiding citizens Orangemen possess certain inalienable rights. Among these is the right of free assembly and that necessitates the right to proceed in a peaceable and orderly manner to and from the place of assembly, whether it be a church or other venue. There can be no question of one group of free citizens having to ask permission from any self appointed authority to walk the public highways of our land. No one community owns the roads of Ulster.[118]

In recent times these views have found strongest expression in the 'Spirit of Drumcree' group, which has represented perhaps the most uncompromising voice of Orangeism, particularly in relation to the issue of parades. The perspective, however, is articulated across Orangeism, such as in the following statement:

> All roads should be open to all law-abiding citizens. No community owns any road, particularly if that road is the most direct route to a town or city centre. No group has any right to impede or harass any other group in the peaceful exercise of their civil rights.[119]

PARADES COMMISSION

From within the Orange Order particular ire and indignation is directed towards the Parades Commission, established in 1998 to adjudicate upon the routes of contentious marches. Since then the Commission has consistently applied restrictions upon certain parade routes and implemented a code of conduct for those who take part in public processions,[120] especially at sensitive and interface areas.[121] These restrictions include a ban on paramilitary clothing and paramilitary symbols on flags and musical instruments with paramilitary markings, and the playing of commonly understood sectarian songs (only hymns are to be played at church parades).

There remains within the Orange Order considerable antagonism to the Commission. As one leading Orangeman put it, 'the sooner the Parades Commission is dissolved the better – tomorrow would do!'[122] Hostility is widespread; some 87 per cent of members believe the Parades Commission should be immediately abolished, see any form of engagement with the Commission as futile and believe that essentially it addresses an anti-Orange and anti-Protestant agenda. Take this member's view:

> We have proved beyond a shadow of a doubt, no matter how much talking you do, who to, and anything else, it makes no difference. The Parades Commission have got an agenda, you have to come up with an agreement with your opposite side ... the Parades Commission used to say, you have to talk, you have to talk. These talks have taken place, but because there's no agreement, they're still saying you have to talk and you have to get an agreement. So therefore if I don't want you to do anything, all I have to say to you is no, and the Parades Commission seem to be hell bent on taking that side of the fence. And if I say no, you're not getting what you want ... that's it. We have discovered that, we have discovered the Parades Commission wasn't formed to help us, it was actually formed to hinder us, and it still is like that today.[123]

While another expressed this view:

> Really to my mind the Parades Commission was created for the police to hide behind. In my view the police were making the decisions all along but they didn't want to be seen as making those decisions – 'oh its not the police it's the Police Commission' –

and that's how it was because it really was pathetic the lack of knowledge that they had of different towns and some of the things that they come out with. You know, they didn't know the names of streets, hadn't bothered reading the forms correctly when putting in applications.[124]

The refusal for many years by the institution to even recognise, let alone engage with, the Parades Commission – dismissing it as 'an unelected quango ... that adopted a dogmatic and condescending approach without fear of rebuke or correction'[125] – meant that the Order fared badly in determinations on parades. Essentially many within the Order still hold that 'freedom to walk the Queen's highway' is not a privilege to be negotiated, arguing that in a 'democratic society there must be the right to peaceful procession by law abiding citizens along traditional routes'.[126] In this respect, the Order appeared at odds with mainstream Protestant opinion, where 61 per cent of 'ordinary' Protestants (and 96 per cent of Catholics) believe that the religious mix of an area ought to be considered by parade organisers prior to a decision to march.[127]

There is some evidence to suggest that enmity to the Commission is not universal within Orangeism. Around one third (31 per cent) of the membership are reasonably pragmatic, believing that the Orange leadership should (or in some cases has little option but to) negotiate with the Commission. One reason for this is the recognition that the image (and creditability) of the Order has been severely damaged by events surrounding disputed parades. This has come to a head especially following the disorder and violence that has intermittently broken out around parades (although not necessarily carried out by Orange members).[128] This has led some to review the overall position of the Order:

> When Drumcree kicked off, we realised ... we probably came onto the world stage ... where we had never been before, and we didn't know how to handle it, simply because we never have had to sell ourselves before, we never had to proactively, you know, promote ourselves or advertise ourselves. We had no experience of doing that sort of thing ... I think we have learned a lot of hard lessons ... but it's been a tough learning curve.[29]

This self-critical stance has led to developments such as an outreach educational programme and initiatives such as Orangefest (see Chapter

6). While there is continued uncertainty about such developments within the institution, there is also the recognition that among key sections of the broader population Orangeism is increasingly thought of with derision and denigration. This is especially true of sections of the Protestant middle class[130] who, once fully integrated into the Order, now largely regard 'membership as beneath them'[131] and have over the past forty years steadily broken the link with Orangeism. Within the contemporary Order fewer than one in five now consider themselves as middle class.[132] This loss of middle class social investment has also been reinforced by the changed social, economic and political structures, which have meant that the scope of the Order to play the role of benefactors and sponsors has dramatically reduced, at best.

ORANGE IDENTITY: STILL UNDER SIEGE?

For many members the parades issue is indicative of the notion that 'Orange culture is under attack',[133] seen as part of a wider offensive on the British identity of the Protestant unionist population. This has been expressed directly by the leadership of the Order as follows:

> ... the battle for the hearts and minds of the people will be fought with greater intensity than ever. Let no-one be under any illusions. The campaign by republicans and nationalists to erode the British identity of Northern Ireland will be stepped up in many ways, and the Orange Order will need to be in the vanguard of resistance to this latest phase in the strategy of the republican–nationalist alliance to try and achieve their objective.[134]

This idea and the belief that Orangeism must accommodate resistance to an organised republican drive has begun to gain wide currency within the Orange community. As this member put it:

> I think we have to ensure that we don't hide under the bushel, we've got to always maintain our level of publicly who we are and what we do. You know, the whole idea of banning of parades and objection to parades, it's, it's not just about, you know Orangemen marching, but it's suppressing, suppressing the identity, and suppressing it in such a way that they've got government support and government backing. And that's why, you know, organisations such as the Parades Commission were brought into view. Now, why was the Commission brought in ... it was a body

of people set up to suppress, monitor and keep Protestants at bay and I think that we've got a cultural warfare on our hands.[135]

Evidence of the onslaught on Britishness is seen almost everywhere, witnessed for example in recent events such as the

... axing of the RUC with its proud Royal prefix, the ban on traditional Orange parade routes, the removal of the Crown and Royal insignia from courthouse buildings, and the release of so many convicted terrorists who served only a fraction of their sentences for terrible crimes.[136]

Some even express the view that the Orange Order is at war, 'not a war of bombs or bullets but a subtle battle of words, of media manipulation and of skilful propaganda'.[137] Thus, the 'shooting and bombing war' is seen as having been replaced by 'a cultural war being waged against unionism and Orangeism'.[138] One member put it as follows:

The Institution is addressing education ... making sure that our culture is not suppressed, within a context of Ireland, if you like. The culture that comes from there is very strongly promoted across the world. I think that the Institution will give a voice to our culture in Northern Ireland.

At its utmost level some express the view that what is being witnessed is a campaign of de-Protestantisation and 'ethnic cleansing pursued by rampant republicanism'.[139] This theme that 'for over 30 years republican terrorists did their utmost to bomb and shoot [Ulster Protestants] into a united Ireland, and in many parts of the Province indulged in the most vicious form of ethnic cleansing'[140] developed during the conflict and for some continues today, as this interviewee makes clear:

Republicanism ... may not have won the war in Northern Ireland with arms, and they haven't. They didn't beat the Ulster people. The Ulster people were quite resistant to the IRA, they stood up against them. We have lost about 320 members of the Institution to Republican violence. Now it's a culture war, yeah, in the cultural world.

As we have seen, Orange identity is built from a range of narratives and understandings. Central to this is the construction of a communal knowledge of 'who we are'. In turn, this rests on a common 'imagined past' and a shared comprehension of the dangers currently faced by Orangeism. Drawing on Connerton, it is possible to point to how, for Orangeism, the past influences the present, but also how the present also determines what we see as, and how we understand, the past.[141] This is linked directly to a view of a common past that emphasises the group's strength of community and shared culture, which in turn goes to construct a group definition inclusive of communal memories to reinforce a collective identity through accepted cultural meanings that

> ... are embedded not in formal rules and laws but in all the informal aspects of cultural life that are taken for granted: customs, habits, daily rituals, unwritten social code ... feelings for the landscape and collective memories [in which] shared symbols play a crucial role in constructing and maintaining the idea of ... an imagined community. They not only express solidarity but also construct a solidarity that was not there before.[142]

CONCLUSIONS

As the main inter-denominational Protestant organisation, the Orange Order plays a significant role within that community. Belonging to the Order is still often part of a local socialisation process, with over four out of every five joiners being asked to sign up by family or friends. This joining process is important in reinforcing the ideological unity of the Orange movement.

The importance of collective identity is central to Orangeism, creating frameworks through which individuals not only articulate subjective identities but which allow them to make sense of their relationships with other individuals and groups, how they define legitimacy, political leadership, and the distance between themselves and other social groups. That social distance is reinforced by the belief held by many members that Orange identity is under attack and by 'the general loss of confidence and alienation within the Protestant community' underpinned by the feeling that within the Protestant unionist community 'there is a lack of education and understanding ... and this leads to lack of confidence in expressing "ourselves".'[143]

Hence, of primary concern to many members is the desire to stop what they see as the erosion of the symbols of British faith and culture.

Many Orange Order members regard themselves as engaged in a culture war to halt the retreat of Protestant unionist identity brought about in part by 'official' government policy and in part by a concerted campaign by the republican movement. The fears and concerns of Orangeism have coalesced around parades and disputes concerning the right to march. The resulting dispute over parade routes, perceived as a primary point of attack on Protestant cultural identity, has become a watershed in the assertion of Orange culture.[144]

Importantly, as Ross reminds us, such conflicts 'are not fundamentally about freedom of speech or religion or protection from intimidation, but about the threatened identities of people in the region'.[145] In the next chapter we examine in more detail how the specific discourses that frame Orangeism, and Orange discourses constructed through narratives and communal memories, are used by members to make sense of their social and political worlds.

NOTES

1. Declaration drawn up by Bishop Burnett, and signed at Exeter Cathedral, England, in November 1688, by William III and his supporters shortly after they landed in Torbay.
2. T.A. van Dijk, 'Discourse, Ideology and Context', *Folia Linguistica*, XXX, 1–2 (2001), pp.11–40.
3. K. Woodward, *Social Sciences: The Big Issues* (London: Routledge, 2003), p.20.
4. While our own findings would seem to confirm Kaufmann and Patterson's proletarianisation thesis, the absence of time series data means we cannot confirm longer-term trends. The presence of a significant middle-class membership would also appear to distinguish the Orange Order in Northern Ireland from its almost exclusively working-class counterparts in Scotland and Merseyside.
5. B. Kennaway, *The Orange Order: A Tradition Betrayed* (London: Methuen, 2006).
6. See R. Abdelal, Y.M. Herrera, A.I. Johnston and R. McDermott, 'Identity as a Variable', in R. Abdelal, Y.M. Herrera, A.I. Johnston and R. McDermott (eds), *Measuring Identity: A Guide for Social Scientists* (Cambridge: Cambridge University Press, 2009), pp.17–32.
7. C. Stevenson, S. Condor, and J. Abell, 'The Minority–Majority Conundrum in Northern Ireland: An Orange Order Perspective', *Political Psychology*, 28, 1 (2007), p.110.
8. Grand Orange Lodge of Ireland, 'Resolutions', GOLI press release, 12 July 1995.
9. Grand Orange Lodge of Ireland, '12th July 2010 Resolutions', GOLI press release, 12 July 2010.
10. M. Fealty, T. Ringland and D. Steven, *A Long Peace? The Future of Unionism in Northern Ireland* (Wimborne: Slugger O'Toole, 2003), p.34.
11. G.W. Montgomery and J.R. Whitten, *The Order on Parade* (Belfast: Grand Orange Lodge of Ireland Education Committee), p.9.
12. Interview with the authors, 3 November 2007.
13. Ibid.
14. Interview with the authors, 25 January 2008.
15. Ibid.
16. *Orange Standard*, August 2004.
17. G.A. Almond and S. Verba, *The Civic Culture* (Princeton, NJ: Princeton University Press, 1963).
18. P.L. Hammack, 'Identity as Burden or Benefit? Youth, Historical Narrative, and the Legacy of Political Conflict', *Human Development*, 53, 4 (2010), pp.173–201.
19. See, for example, D.E. Cosgrove, *Social Formation and Symbolic Landscape* (Madison, WI:

University of Wisconsin Press, 1998); P. Devine-Wright, 'A Theoretical Overview of Memory and Conflict', in E. Cairns and M.D. Roe (eds), *The Role of Memory in Ethnic Conflict* (Houndmills: Palgrave Macmillan, 2003), pp.9–33; R.E. Hassner, *War on Sacred Grounds* (Ithaca and London: Cornell University Press, 2009).

20. B. Murtagh, 'Social Activity and Interaction in Northern Ireland', *Northern Ireland Life and Times Survey Research Update*, no. 10, February 2002.
21. P. Connerton, *How Societies Remember* (Cambridge: Cambridge University Press, 1989).
22. A.D. Smith, *National Identities* (Harmondsworth: Penguin, 1991).
23. A. Cohen, *Two-Dimensional Man* (London: Routledge, 1974).
24. D. Cairns and J. Smyth, 'Up off our Bellies and unto our Knees: Symbolic Effacement and the Orange Order in Northern Ireland', *Social Identities*, 8, 1 (2002), p.1.
25. A. Jones, *Memory and Material Culture* (Cambridge: Cambridge University Press, 2007).
26. Grand Orange Lodge of Ireland, 'All About the Order: Schomberg House'. Available at: http://www.grandorangelodge.co.uk/parades/schomberg_house.html; accessed 6 October 2009.
27. D. Hume (ed.), *'When Brethern are Met in their Order so Grand': A Brief History of Orangeism and Orange Lodges in Larne District* (Larne: Vermont Press), p.1.
28. See, for example, D. Hume, J. Mattison and D. Scott, *Beyond the Banners: The Story of the Orange Order* (Holywood: Booklink, 2009).
29. See N. Ó Dochartaigh, 'Building New Transnational Networks Online: The Case of Ulster Unionists', http://topic.developmentgateway.org/ict/rc/ItemDetail.do~346057; accessed 17 February 2006, and 'Reframing Online: Ulster Loyalists Imagine an American Audience', *Identities: Global Studies in Culture and Power*, 16, 1 (2009), pp.102–27. Importantly Ó Dochartaigh highlights that the focus of Orange-based websites is far from uniform. In those URLs hosted by US lodges, for example, there is little or no reference to contemporary political events in Northern Ireland. Elsewhere, however, sites maintained by Orange lodges and individual members of Orange lodges in Scotland and England show a strong interest in contemporary events surrounding Northern Irish politics.
30. See M. Jess, 'So, what really happens behind lodge doors ...', *Belfast Telegraph*, 22 May 2007.
31. See L. Powell and J. Cowart, *Political Campaign Communication: Inside and Out* (Birmingham: University of Alabama, 2003).
32. R.M. Merelman, 'The Family and Political Socialization: Toward a Theory of Exchange', *The Journal of Politics*, 42, 2 (1980), pp.461–86.
33. Almond and Verba, *The Civic Culture*.
34. Interview with the authors, 3 November 2007.
35. Ibid.
36. Ibid.
37. Ibid.
38. Ibid.
39. Ibid.
40. Ibid.
41. Ibid.
42. P. Connolly and P. Maginn, *Sectarianism, Children and Community Relations in Northern Ireland* (Coleraine: Centre for the Study of Conflict, University of Ulster, 1999).
43. D. Lanclos, *At Play in Belfast: Children's Folklore and Identities in Northern Ireland* (London: Rutgers University Press, 2003).
44. G. Quigley, *Review of the Parades Commission* (Belfast: Northern Ireland Office, 27 September 2002.
45. Interview with the authors, 3 November 2007.
46. Ibid.
47. Ibid.
48. Interview with the authors, 25 January 2008.
49. Ibid.
50. Interview with the authors, 3 November 2007.
51. Interview with the authors, 26 January 2008.
52. Interview with the authors, 3 November 2007.
53. Interview with the authors, 26 January 2008.

54. See, for example, M. Farrell, *The Orange State* (London: Pluto, 1980).
55. Interview with the authors, 3 November 2007.
56. *Orange Standard*, April 1999.
57. The Orange Volunteers were formed in the early 1970s. There is no evidence to suggest that the paramilitary group was sanctioned by the leadership of the Orange Order. Although the Orange Volunteers were active during the Ulster Workers' Council strike of 1974 and supported the loyalist strike of 1977, the grouping was believed to have ceased to exist during the 1980s. They should not be confused with the dissident loyalist paramilitary group using the same name that emerged in the late 1990s and which claimed responsibility for a number of attacks on Catholics and Catholic property. This new grouping was most likely comprised of former members of the Loyalist Volunteer Force (LVF) and the Ulster Freedom Fighters (UFF) opposed to the peace process and Belfast Agreement. Another grouping using the name emerged in 2009 issuing threats to Catholic-owned property, seemingly in reprisal to attacks on Orange Halls. Their claims were roundly condemned by Orange Order grand secretary Drew Nelson, who claimed the Orange Volunteers 'besmirched the name of Orangeism' and called on all concerned to demonstrate 'restraint and civic responsibility' (see 'Orange Volunteers' threat condemned', *News Letter*, 12 July 2009).
58. *Orange Standard*, April 1999.
59. Interview with the authors, 3 November 2007.
60. See, for example, K. Simpson, *Unionist Voices and the Politics of Remembering the Past in Northern Ireland* (Houndmills: Palgrave Macmillan, 2009); K. Simpson, *Truth Recovery in Northern Ireland: Critically Interpreting the Past* (Manchester: Manchester University Press, 2009).
61. Interview with the authors, 3 November 2007.
62. Ibid.
63. Ibid.
64. Grand Orange Lodge of Ireland, 'On Parade: The Case Against the Parades Commission' (press release).
65. Grand Orange Lodge of Ireland, *The Millennium Book: A History of Orangeism in County Armagh* (Belfast: GOLI Publications, no date), p.255.
66. Bryan, *Orange Parades*.
67. N. Jarman and D. Bryan, *Parade and Protest: A Discussion of Parading Disputes in Northern Ireland* (Coleraine: Centre for the Study of Conflict, University of Ulster, 1996).
68. See also N. Jarman, *Material Conflicts: Parades and Visual Displays in Northern Ireland* (Oxford: Berg, 1997); N. Jarman, *On The Edge: Community Perspectives on the Civil Disturbances in North Belfast, June–September 1996* (Belfast: CDC, 1997); N. Jarman, *Drawing Back from the Edge: Community-Based Responses to Violence in North Belfast* (Belfast: CDC, 1999).
69. Beyond Northern Ireland there are a number of small demonstrations to mark the Twelfth. The major demonstration outside of Northern Ireland is in Scotland (reflecting the largest membership outside of Ireland), alongside a demonstration in north-west England (normally held before that in Northern Ireland) attracting members and sometimes entire lodges from the province. Elsewhere, although they have lessened significantly in size and impact, the 'Twelfth' is still celebrated in the Republic of Ireland in public displays, as well as in Canada, New Zealand and the USA, although there has been a growing tendency in recent times in these places to move towards more community-based events, such as those family barbeques found in Canada, or the gala days celebrated in the US.

The situation varies considerably by country. After decades of a rapidly declining membership there are reports that Orangeism is experiencing a moderate increase in support in parts of Ontario (see C. Martin, 'Orange Lodge gets new life', *London Free Press* (Ontario), 4 September 2009). Membership in the US has also been in freefall in recent years, although it was recently reported that in Chicago a new lodge (LOL 229 'Protestant Defenders') was founded on 17 April 2010. R. Sweetman, 'Towards a History of Orangeism in New Zealand', in B. Patterson (ed.). *Ulster–New Zealand Migration and Cultural Transfers* (Dublin: Four Courts Press, 2006) provides a useful review of New Zealand Orangeism, as does B. Patterson, '"Be you an Orangeman, you shall meet Orangemen": New Zealand's Ulster Plantation Revisited', in L.M. Geary and A.J. McCarthy (eds), *Ireland, Australia and New Zealand: History, Politics and Culture* (Dublin: Irish Academic Press, 2008). Those interested in Canadian Orangeism should read D.A. Wilson (ed.), *The Orange Order in Canada* (Dublin: Four Courts Press, 2007).

70. *Belfast Telegraph*, 13 July 2007.
71. Marching bands are also commonplace in the parades in Scotland and England. In Scotland the Twelfth is celebrated in a series of parades on consecutive weekends. In 2010, for example, the Glasgow march saw 182 lodges, accompanied by almost 100 bands, in the parade based in Greenock, 78 lodges and 50 bands from Ayrshire, Renfrewshire and Argyll took part, while on Saturday 10 July, 123 lodges and 90 bands from Lanarkshire and Stirlingshire gathered at Wishaw (see Grand Orange Lodge of Scotland, http://www.orange-orderscotland.com/news.html; accessed 26 September 2010). The largest march in England usually takes place in July in Southport, where in 2010 an estimated 3,000 people took part (see 'Liverpool Orange lodge marches in Southport', BBC News, http://www.bbc.co.uk/news/10603208; accessed 26 September 2010).
72. D. Bryan, *Orange Parades: The Politics of Ritual Tradition and Control* (London: Pluto Press, 2002), p.159.
73. D. Cooper, 'On the Twelfth of July in the Morning ... (or the man who mistook his sash for a hat)', *Folk Music Journal*, 8, 1 (2001), pp.67–89.
74. Bryan, *Orange Parades*.
75. D. Bell, *Acts of Union: Youth Culture and Sectarianism in Northern Ireland* (Basingstoke: Macmillan, 1990).
76. D. Bell, 'Acts of Union: Youth Culture and Ethnic Identity Amongst Protestants in Northern Ireland', *British Journal of Sociology*, 38, 2 (1987), pp.158–83.
77. See D. MacDonald, *Blood and Thunder: Inside an Ulster Protestant Band* (Cork: Mercier Press, 2010).
78. K. Radford, 'Drum Rolls and Gender Roles in Protestant Marching Bands in Belfast', *British Journal of Ethnomusicology*, 10, 2 (2001), pp.37–59.
79. J.W. McAuley, 'Peace and Progress? Political and Social Change Among Young Loyalists in Northern Ireland', *Journal of Social Issues*, 60, 3 (2004), pp.541–62.
80. Quincey Dougan of the Ulster Bands Forum, cited in MacDonald, *Blood and Thunder*, p.23.
81. N. Jarman, 'For God and Ulster: Blood and Thunder Bands and Loyalist Political Culture', in T.G. Fraser (ed.), *The Irish Parading Tradition: Following the Drum* (Basingstoke: Macmillan, 2000).
82. Bell, *Acts of Union*.
83. R. Dudley Edwards, *The Faithful Tribe: An Intimate Portrait of the Loyal Institutions* (London: HarperCollins, 2000).
84. Jarman, 'For God and Ulster'.
85. See J.W. McAuley, 'Peace and Progress?', pp.541–62 for a review of the situation of young people in loyalist communities in Northern Ireland.
86. Cooper, 'On the Twelfth of July in the Morning' provides an excellent overview of the history and development of Orange music.
87. Bell, *Acts of Union*, p.125.
88. K. Radford, 'Drum Rolls and Gender Roles in Protestant Marching Bands in Belfast', pp.37–59.
89. A.J. Witherow, '"No Hope Here": Youth Subcultural Theory and a Loyalist Flute Band in Protestant Working-Class East Belfast', unpublished PhD thesis, School of Sociology, Social Policy and Social Work, Queen's University Belfast, 2010.
90. Bryan, *Orange Parades*, p.125.
91. Interview with the authors, 5 June 2008.
92. Ibid.
93. Interview with the authors, 3 November 2007.
94. Ibid.
95. British–Irish Inter-Parliamentary Body (2001), 'The Cultural Significance of Parades' (2001). Available at: http://www.biipb.org/biipb/committee/commd/8102.htm; accessed 16 September 2010.
96. See N. Jarman, *Material Conflicts: Parades and Visual Displays in Northern Ireland* (Oxford: Berg, 1997); and N. Jarman, 'Material Culture, Fabric of Identity', in D. Miller (ed.), *Material Cultures: Why Some Things Matter* (London: UCL Press, 1998), pp.121–45.
97. B. Bland, 'Marching and Rising: The Rituals of Small Differences and Great Violence', *Contagion* (November 1996), pp.1–21.
98. BBC News, 'Orangemen vow to defy Drumcree decision', 29 June 1998. Available at: http://news.bbc.co.uk/1/hi/events/northern_ireland/latest_news/122515.stm; accessed 10 June 2008.

99. Meath Peace Group, 'Orange Marches in Portadown: The Garavaghy Road Residents' Perspective', St Columban's College, Navan, 13 November 1995.
100. *Orange Standard*, August 2004.
101. Gordon Lucy, chair of the Ulster Society, *Irish Times*, 13 July 1996.
102. Ian Paisley, quoted in M. Brennock 'Portadown March Outcome Claimed by Senior Unionist Figures as Victory', *Irish Times*, 12 July 1995, p.7.
103. Grand Orange Lodge of Ireland, 'Speech by District Master Darryl Hewitt at Drumcree on Sunday, July 4, 2010', press statement, 4 July 2010.
104. John McCrea, grand secretary of the Grand Orange Lodge of Ireland, speaking at the Installation of Officers of Aghanloo LOL 656, Limavady on 19 January 1998.
105. Ruth Dudley Edwards suggests that by the time of the second dispute at Drumcree in 1996 the parades issue had become not just a public relations disaster for the Orange Order but had also polarised the two communities and led to more militant elements joining the dispute. See Dudley Edwards, *The Faithful Tribe*.
106. C. Ryder and V. Kearney, *Drumcree: The Orange Order's Last Stand* (London: Methuen, 2001).
107. B. Kennaway, 'All Change But No Change: Can We Learn Lessons from the Past?', IBIS Working Paper no. 101 (University College Dublin: Institute for British–Irish Studies, 2010), p.7.
108. Kennaway, *The Orange Order: A Tradition Betrayed*.
109. Interview with the authors, 3 November 2007.
110. Ibid.
111. Ibid.
112. E. Kaufmann, *The Orange Order: A Contemporary Northern Irish History* (Oxford: Oxford University Press, 2007).
113. Interview with the authors, 3 November 2007.
114. Grand Orange Lodge of Ireland, 'Belfast Orangemen Call on All Unionists to Stand Firm Against Cultural Fascists', press statement, 9 July 2004.
115. Interview with the authors, 3 November 2007.
116. *Orange Standard*, August 2000.
117. 'The Right to March', speech by Alderman Peter D. Robinson, MP to a Right to March Rally in Portadown, DUP press release, 31 July 1996.
118. Grand Orange Lodge of Ireland, press statement issued at the Portadown district's mini Twelfth parade on Saturday 12 June 1999.
119. Loyal Orange Institution of Ireland, 'The Case Against the Parades Commission', (no date; no publisher).
120. Parades Commission, 'Public Processions and Related Protest Meetings: A Code of Conduct' (Belfast: Parades Commission, no date).
121. Parades Commission, 'Public Processions and Related Protest Meetings: A Code of Conduct', Appendix B (Belfast: Parades Commission, no date).
122. Grand Orange Lodge of Ireland, 'Speech By District Master Darryl Hewitt at Drumcree on Sunday, July 4, 2010', press statement, 4 July 2010.
123. Interview with the authors, 3 May 2008.
124. Ibid.
125. Grand Orange Lodge of Ireland, 'The Case Against the Parades Commission'. Available at: http://www.grandorangelodge.co.uk/parades/parades_commission_against.html; accessed 14 October 2010.
126. Grand Orange Lodge of Ireland, 'The Tradition of Parades'. Available at: http://www.grandorangelodge.co.uk/parades/tradition_parades.html; accessed 10 October 2010.
127. Independent Review of Parades and Marches in Northern Ireland [The North Report] (Belfast: HMSO, 1997).
128. K. Smith, 'Northern Irish riots reveal deep-seated Protestant malaise', Reuters News (Dublin), 13 September 2005.
129. Interview with the author, 3 May 2008.
130. Kaufmann, *The Orange Order: A Contemporary Northern Irish History*.
131. A. Pollak, 'Drumcree exposes depth of unionist alienation and anger', *Irish Times*, 13 July 1996.
132. McAuley and Tonge, 'For God and for the Crown'; J.W. McAuley and J. Tonge, 'The

Contemporary Orange Order in Northern Ireland', in M. Busteed, F. Neal and J. Tonge (eds), *Irish Protestant Identities* (Manchester: Manchester University Press, 2008), pp.289–302.
133. *Orange Standard*, August 2000.
134. *Orange Standard*, July 2007.
135. Interview with the authors, 3 May 2008.
136. *Orange Standard*, February 2004.
137. Ken Wilkinson, cited in M. Hall (ed.), *Orangeism and the Twelfth: What it Means to Me* (Newtownabbey: Island Publications, 1999), p.10.
138. D. Hume, *News Letter*, 13 July 2007, p.35.
139. *Orange Standard*, March 1999.
140. *Orange Standard*, December 2002.
141. Connerton, *How Societies Remember*.
142. B. Parekh, *Report of the Commission on the Future of Multi-Ethnic Britain* (London: Profile Books, 2000), p.20.
143. Grand Lodge of Ireland, *Submission to the Secretary of State for Northern Ireland* (Belfast: GOLI Publications, 9 February 2007).
144. See Bryan, *Orange Parades*; D. Bryan, T. Fraser and S. Dunn, *Political Rituals: Loyalist Parades in Portadown* (Coleraine: Centre for the Study of Conflict, University of Ulster, 1995); Jarman, *Material Conflicts*; Jarman and Bryan, *Parade and Protest*.
145. M.H. Ross, 'Psychocultural Interpretations and Dramas: Identity Dynamics in Ethnic Conflict', *Political Psychology*, 22, 1 (2001), p.158.

CHAPTER FOUR

Orange Discourse, Memory and Traditions

Unfurl the Orange Standard, men, the foe are in the field,
To arms, ye warriors once again, make heartless Rebels yield,
Shoot down the foe with musket ball, give chase with flashing
blades,
Arm! Arm! Your country loudly calls For Protestant Brigades.
Unfurl the Standard of the Blue, the Green is waving now,

Flock to our ranks ye brave and true, and breathe your battle vow,
For alters, homes and truth to fight, if need be for to die,
So do not sheath your swords tonight, give forth our battle cry.

Yes, let the Orange and the Blue, fly proudly out again,
Before the anxious, longing view, of all true hearted men,
Yes let it wave high in the skies, for Orangemen to see,
Let's gain Religious Liberty, and make our country free.[1]

Being a member of the Order offers an identifiable form of cultural engagement and political involvement across Northern Irish society. The institution constantly seeks to mobilise to influence policy and governance in directions that are seen to best benefit Protestant unionism. Thus, Orange membership remains a key marker of social identity; 'that part of an individual's self-concept, which derives from his knowledge of his membership of a social group (or groups) together with the value and emotional significance attached to that membership.'[2]

This chapter highlights many of the key discourses and central narratives within contemporary Orangeism. Drawing directly on interviews, public announcements and writings produced by the Order, we consider the ways in which Orange discourse and narrative communicates common understandings of the past and links these with the contemporary moral, political and social beliefs of Orangeism. The chapter also indicates how this discourse is constructed to frame the possibilities for social change and, importantly, how it influences the actions taken by the Orange Order.

The major narratives of the Grand Orange Lodge of Ireland reflect the organisation's core goals. These are that:

- civil and religious liberty is maintained in Ulster, that the Christian faith, Reformed and Protestant, will be preached and taught here;
- the British connection is maintained;
- every effort is made to make our country happy, prosperous and outward looking, a good place for everyone who lives there;
- the Protestant religion must be a self-propagating faith whilst not denying the same rights to other religious persuasions.[3]

As the previous chapter has indicated, induction into this particular worldview rests on the perceived primacy of a range of ideas and understandings that integrate Protestantism with unionism[4] to present a position that is 'unashamedly Protestant and Unionist'[5] and 'unyielding on the key principle of Ulster being British'.[6] These particular expressions of Orangeism are reinforced by discourses that make certain behaviour more legitimate, more plausible and perhaps even more necessary than others. This finds cultural and political expression through the promotion of the sense of Protestant unionist identity outlined in previous chapters, and through a focus on resistance to anything that is seen to loosen the attachment of the union or erode a sense of Britishness.

Elsewhere, we have identified the central importance within the Order of the overarching discourses of crown, faith and loyalty as markers of social belonging[7] and ethnic identity[8] across contemporary Orangeism. Within these broad frames there are several other significant organising discourses and narratives around commemoration, memory, tradition and sacrifice. These narratives are continually reproduced in ways that suggest that it is impossible to differentiate between the security of the union and the guarding of Protestantism. As one leading member, Nelson McCausland put it:

> ... the Orange Order represented all the things that I felt very strongly and passionately about ... For me the qualifications for

being an Orangeman are things I would totally identify with. It expresses for me not only religious conviction but also a strong political conviction, in that here is something, which down the years has served as a bulwark for the British community here in Ulster and against any move towards a United Ireland. These are things, which I felt very strongly about and for me joining the Orange Order seemed the natural thing to do.[9]

Orangeism shares an ideology expressed through a discourse that provides explanations for events often by way of commonsense and everyday narratives that make it, in McCausland's words, 'the natural thing to do'. Such narratives often contain powerful messages, including judgments about the actions and motivations of both one's own group and those of opponents and also present guidelines that may be seen as the best actions open to one's own group and the interpretation of the acts of others.

These discourses are constructed in ways that bond Orangeism and which help produce a sense of collective identity, and expression of an 'interpretive community',[10] offering particular cues and reference points so that members can make sense of the world around them and react in relevant ways. The narratives of Orangeism are often emotionally powerful, but like many other political and social narratives they are not necessarily straightforward or consistent.[11] For example, while core to Orange discourse is a narrative that projects the Order as strong and steadfast, it is also common alongside this to find a parallel discourse that sees the Order as vulnerable and under direct threat.

DISCOURSES OF ORANGEISM

Orange discourse and narratives function to maintain and preserve the ideological position of the group and to frame what are, and what are not, seen as legitimate responses to particular circumstances. They also in part outline idealised futures and indicate the possibilities for change, or at least the likely boundaries for change. As with other collectives, Orange discourse helps bound and safeguard a distinct sense of historical integrity and provides the frame within which contemporary events are interpreted, providing, for example, the justification for positions taken by the leadership on particular issues, or how members react to more everyday matters.

Thus, discourse can act to both shape common sense beliefs and to collectively reinforce (or sometimes transform) existing ideologies.[12] Although the concept of discourse[13] is widely used across a variety of disciplines,[14] essentially, as Stuart Hall reminds us:

> Discourses are ways of referring to or constructing knowledge about a particular topic of practice: a cluster (or formation) of ideas, images and practices, which provide ways of talking about forms of knowledge and conduct associated with a particular topic, social activity or institutional site in society.[15]

Here we take a wide-ranging view that links discourse with ideology, recognising that while discourses can enable, they can also restrict and inhibit social and political developments.[16] Discourse finds meaning in particular narratives, which are found in spoken and written words, artifacts, expressions of shared experiences and even sometimes in the physical environment by way of monuments and memorials. Through this narrative and memory Orangeism reinforces identity, and constructs and draws upon a collective memory, which becomes 'the content and context for what they will jointly recall and commemorate'.[17]

ORANGEISM AND COLLECTIVE MEMORY

Central to this construction of collective memory is the selection from the past and the creation of a common viewpoint, interpretation and understanding around it. In reviewing the notion of collective memory, Hunt suggests the following:

> Memory is interplay between events, time, society and the individual. Memories are manipulated to fit our life history, our own views about ourselves. They are also manipulated by society ... none of these interpretations of the past are objectively true. They are true for individuals, and for groups of people within a given society. But then memory is not about truth, it is about interpretation. In order to understand memory we must understand the interplay between individual and collective memory, how our own narratives (memories) develop through this interplay.[18]

Past events involving the actions of individuals and groups are thus highlighted, brought to the fore and then into shaper focus when considering the present. This explains why many outsiders simply see the Order as archaic or stuck in the past. While Orange group narratives do consistently refer to the past, they do so in a particular way and are much more than, and different from, a mere history of the group.[19] Drawing on the works of Halbwachs and his concept of collective memory it is possible to distinguish between what are seen as the facts of history and the formation of collective memory, which is a reading of the past that constructs a core part of our social identities.[20] As Olick and Robins express it, 'collective memory is the active past that forms our identities.'[21]

The way in which the 'active past' is interpreted by Orangeism is marked by the social production of memory as a 'collective production in which everyone participates'.[22] Building on processes outlined in the previous chapter, this identity is reinforced and in turn reinforces strong self-perpetuating political frames of reference drawing on collective narratives, memories and understandings and processes of remembering and forgetting. Further, the connections with the past often help structure beliefs about what is to be done in the present.

Hence, Orangeism relates past events to the contemporary in particular ways by demonstrating the continuing relevance of the past to the group's self-identity and current position supporting the creation and wherewithal of individual and group identities.[23] From an Orange perspective history is far from mere details of the past drawn from academic study; rather it is usable in forming plausible explanations and accounts of the experiences of shared cultural identities and the possibilities of continuity and change for the group.[24]

Essential factual accounts of the history of Orangeism are fixed; there is little notion of historical revisionism with the Order's accounts. Of more importance here is the use of history by Orangeism involving both the politics of remembering and how the Order remembers.[25] It is clear, for example, that the emphasis placed by Orangeism upon specific events can change over time. Roe and Cairns note, for example, how the celebration of the Battle of the Boyne altered to become much more significant in the nineteenth century.[26]

Orange additions to narratives have emphasised links between the past and present in particular ways and have 'claimed' individuals as their own. An example can be found in the Grand Lodge's promotion of a 'heroes from history' project.[27] Those highlighted as Orangemen include John A. Macdonald (1815–91), the first prime minister of Canada; rifleman Robert Quigg (1885–1955), winner of the Victoria Cross at the Somme in 1916; the newspaper proprietor Sir Robert

Baird (1855–1934); and William Ferguson Massey (1856–1924), who
became prime minister of New Zealand in 1912.[28]

All are hailed as historical 'Orange heroes', members of the institution
who had much wider societal influence and whose history it is
understood should still exert authority today. By so 'placing the present
in the context of the past and of the community, the myth of descent
interprets present social changes and collective endeavours in a manner
that satisfies the drive for meaning'.[29]In turn this emphasises that
memory cannot exist without people executing the act of remembering
through collectively shared representations and understandings of the
past.

Another example of explanation of the active can be found in the
presentation of the 'Ulster-Scots' as central to Orange identity. The
endorsement and elevation of an Ulster-Scots culture has become
pronounced among sections of Ulster Protestants.[30] It is projected as
the basis for a distinct identity, within which the strongest narrative is
one that links contemporary Orangeism directly through the 'Scottish
connection', by way of the plantation, or even through the creation of
alternative myths of origin around the existence of pre-planter Scots in
Ulster.[31] The resulting connections are understood as having physical,
cultural, social and genealogical aspects,[32] while one of the primary
aspects of the movement has been the promotion of a distinct
language.[33] In many ways the identity is constructed as ballast to what
is perceived as self-confident modern Irish nationalism, but has
nonetheless been taken on board enthusiastically by large sections of
Orangeism, which actively promotes Ulster-Scots culture and identity
through its publications.

ORANGE NARRATIVES

Orange narrative focuses on those events that are seen to carry the most
emotional, political and social significance. Broadly, themes include:
the continued 'rejection of the themes of the Roman Catholic
Church';[34] the history of Protestantism in Ireland; the origin and
development of the Order; past threats to the group and how these
have been successfully resisted; and the relevance of the Order to the
contemporary world.[35] Often the Orange narrative develops around
conflict with enemies, and the extolling of the survival of the group and
successful leadership of the Orange Order through periods of trauma.
Thus, in reviewing a century of Orangeism, the Order asserted:

Orangeism is still the great guardian of Protestant, Unionist and British values in Northern Ireland, and even more so than ever, as recent events have proved. The Protestant churches no longer speak with one voice on issues like Orangeism, Unionism, or even loyalty to the Crown. Unionism too is divided as never before, which leaves the Orange Order as the one Institution which has remained unbroken and unyielding in its defence of Ulster Protestantism.[36]

A clear signifier of these themes can be found in the public displays of Orangeism. When the Ulster Society sought to categorise Lodge banners they classified them under the following main headings: biblical; buildings; home rule; historical personalities; reformation; royalty; troubles; old flags and banners; Williamite; world wars and industrial.[37] These physical expressions of collective memories offer a shared identity and the understanding of direct links between past and present that enable the framing of contemporary needs in the context of historical continuity.

Collective memory differs from more specific activities involving historical and academic reconstruction of the past. Collective memory is not a preservative for bygone events, but instead reconstructs it through memory shaped by broader social forces, including commemorative displays and ritual.[38] In the words of Halbwachs' ground-breaking study, 'the mind constructs its memories under the pressure of society [moreover this] causes the mind to transfigure the past'.[39] Indeed, Connerton has forwarded the useful notion of 'collective autobiography',[40] while Halbwachs suggests remembrance and commemoration may well act to fill breaches in personal memory.[41]

TRADITION, MEMORY AND IDENTITY

Commemoration and tradition are inextricably linked to the construction of social and collective identities. The importance of this to group formation is made clear through the concept of 'invented tradition', set out as:

> ... a set of practices, normally governed by overtly or tacitly accepted rules and of a ritual or symbolic nature, which seek to inculcate certain values and norms of behaviour by repetition, which automatically implies continuity with the past.[42]

Thus, remembering the past and the formation of memory and tradition take place within a social context that links the individual to the group. While certain memories of history are relegated or ignored, others are given primacy. These are transferred to the imagined community through specific actions, events and narratives and the construction of group tradition and memories.

The discourse of tradition and the notion of a coherent past are deeply imbued across Orangeism. As one leading member of the Order put it, 'the strength of tradition cannot be underestimated.'[43] This is reflected in different ways across the membership. The following assertions of Orange Order members confirm this:

> I think the Order still maintains its very traditional ethos, which I would like to think we'll always maintain there. You know, that strong commitment to the biblical principles ... the notion that there is some kind of fairness, or some kind of route attached to the scriptures ... we should never wander away from those core principles. I like the traditional aspect in being who we are, how we profess who we are, how we identify ourselves in the community.[44]

> ... the main role of the institution is to maintain that notion of ... preserving one's identity as being Protestant. You know we reflect back to the period of the Boyne ... we passionately look back to 1690, where King William crossed the Boyne and the battle that surrounded that. But what, what does the Boyne ... mean for me? You know it wasn't just, you know, historically it wasn't a battle about Protestant versus Catholic ... it was the securing and the preserving of a way of life. It provided for me ... the constitutional democracy that we all enjoy today.[45]

The intensity of Orange identity draws its strength from collective memory and cultural reproduction. Within this there is a heavy accent on continuity, in terms of both the membership (see previous chapter) and in the reproduction of cultural values. If again we turn to Parekh we find a useful summary of the processes involved in the construction of a dominant narrative and the creation of shared identity through reference to a collective history, the purpose of which:

> ... is not to give an accurate historical account but to enable individuals to position their personal life-stories within the larger, more significant national story. Identification not knowledge is its raison d'être. It allows individuals to identify with something

outside, and greater than, personal experience. It binds individuals into a broader interdependence ...[46]

It is also important to recognise how Orange discourse links to a 'grand cultural unionist narrative'.[47] Within the process of self-identification with Orangeism reference to collective memories and a common history remain core in constructing social and political identities and in understandings of everyday events. The reproduction of Orange discourses helps members of the Order explain, relate to, and position themselves in the wider social world[48] and through drawing on collective memories strengthen senses of identity, choosing to prioritise those that best allow for expression of endurance of fundamental beliefs.[49]

Membership of the Order is of course a voluntary act, a decision in the context of Northern Irish society that acts as a primary point of political identification. This is reflected in the perceptions evident throughout our interviews with members who see the Order as the most important promoter of a broad British-Protestant way of life.[50]Further, many see the cultural-religious form of Britishness expressed by Orangeism as under continuous threat and that the Order represents the best mechanism to defend against these alarms.

Orange Order membership is also an expression of political identity and support for unionism.[51] In what are still regarded as indeterminate times the Order continues to project itself as an instrument of stability, a bastion within the Protestant unionist community for unifying the 'unionist family'.[52] Calls for political unity across unionism have become central to much of the public expression of Orangeism and draw upon longer-standing discourses within Orangeism concerning the lack of unionism to mobilise its members in a coherent manner, political marginalisation and the entry of the enemy within the gates in the form of Sinn Féin in government (see Chapter 5).

The Orange leadership, in its consistently expressed belief that the Belfast Agreement cannot 'bring about a just and lasting peace'[53] and has 'failed unionism',[54] has also reflected such views. This was underpinned by an understanding that the British government entered into a policy of appeasement with the republican movement, the result of which (Sinn Féin in government) has eroded democracy[55] and undermined the union.[56] Such perspectives are apparent in the following argument:

[T]he representatives of terror are now received for tea and biscuits by ministers who appear to be totally insensitive to the effect that appeasement on this scale has on the victims of terrorism. Protestations on the part of government ministers about feeling sorry for the victims of IRA terrorism are meaningless when the evidence on all sides is that violence has paid and the perpetrators of horrendous crimes are free and back in society, while the families of victims continue to suffer. No apology has been forthcoming from the IRA and other republicans for their crimes, no pledge that the violence has ended forever, matched by a handover of the weapons of death ... What a travesty of a 'peace' which has not been founded on a complete renunciation of violence by the IRA and other groups as a means of pursuing political objectives.[57]

THREATENED IDENTITIES: DISCOURSES OF CULTURAL DEFENCE

It is important to identify another consistent discourse underscored above, namely that Orangeism must demonstrate eternal vigilance against all those seeking to chip away at the core tenets of Protestant unionism in general and in particular Orangeism, which represents that 'part of a community that has been constantly under attack for 400 years'.[58] A vital part of the Orange narrative, therefore, is to allow the institution to take a leadership role at the heart of the cultural defence of Protestant unionism.

This is not to suggest that the Orange leadership is able to exert undue control over its members, nor to lose sight of the role that human agency plays in social organisations. All groups, however, seek to exert some level of conformity on members, among whom common interpretations of events often develop. Further, these pressures are often greatest in conflict situations, when the social forces structuring the construction of the 'Other' intensify, and blame for the conflict is levelled directly at the other group(s).[59]

While creating their own social identity of Orangeism people also influence the wider social context. One manifestation of this is a set of understandings that see the Order as deliberately misunderstood, misinterpreted, vilified and subject to a campaign of negative propaganda.[60] This finds expression as part of a broader crusade to demonise the Orange Order and all that it stands for.[61] Such a concern can be clearly seen in the following statement issued by the Grand Orange Lodge in the late 1990s:

This has been a period when we have been blamed for events that we had no part in nor would ever condone. It has also however been a time when, despite the best efforts of our detractors we have remained constant in defence of civil and religious liberty for all, when we have consistently sought accommodation not segregation.

We have been demonised partly because it is now fashionable to ridicule those who have principles. We have also however been demonised through a concerted effort to break an organisation committed to the Protestant faith and the Union of Great Britain and Northern Ireland.[62]

The Orange Order often sees evidence of a coherent strategy, a 'vicious smear campaign against Orangeism'.[63] Further, those groupings engaged are seen as widespread, involving:

> ... government 'spin doctors' and a largely compliant news media ... used to try and demonise the Orange Order ... which portrayed the Orangemen as heartless bigots ... The hate campaign launched in the media against the Protestant people has been unrestrained and sustained. Newspapers have shamefully vied with each other to come up with some new angle to blacken the Ulster Protestants.[64]

Indeed, for the Order this has reached the point whereby 'no Orangeman is in any doubt that the media treats him, and the Orange Institution, with little understanding and less sympathy.'[65]

The view that the Orange Order are unfairly treated by the media is widely held across the membership. The views of this member are representative of wide sections of the Order when he says:

> ... any media coverage you would see, it's usually, you know look at these people throwing stones, or look at these people doing this. There's no media coverage, you know, of, like, the Grand Master's Charity Support, you know, it's only in, like, the *Orange Standard* you'd actually hear about these things, you know. You wouldn't hear about, you know, the events run in any of the sort of regular media. It's always very anti-Orange.[66]

Particular indignation is directed towards the television coverage of the 12th of July parades. While opponents suggest that such programmes are 'insulting and a waste of public money',[67] the perceived lack of time allocated to showing the events by the BBC and Ulster Television (see also Chapter 6) brings constant criticism from members, as the following claim makes clear:

> ... coverage of the Twelfth, I think has been diminished over this past number of years ... When you think about the amount of people that are out on the Twelfth day and the amount of support it does get, the coverage is very poor.[68]

These broad feelings that the Protestant unionist experience is not understood or represented fairly in the media often are encompassed in a wider narrative concerning the outsmarting of Orangeism. This is contrasted with the coherent strategy devised and implemented by Sinn Féin in seeking to denigrate and undermine the status of Orangeism. As this longstanding member put it:

> I actually think that, that the likes of Sinn Féin are very good in what they do. They're very organised, you know, and they sort of have a clear idea of what they want to do and I think they have corroded away the image of the Orange.[69]

This notion that Orangeism is losing out in a cultural and media struggle with Sinn Féin is commonplace. Take the following:

> ... I believe that the Orange Order and the Twelfth have now become the focus of attention for our enemies. In particular, if you look at the way Sinn Féin, having campaigned to push individual Protestants out of their homes, have openly admitted that in various areas of Northern Ireland they are now also trying to prevent Protestants, wholesale, from expressing their culture and their Protestantism through the Orange Order.[70]

SACRIFICE AND SUFFERING

In seeking to refute the voices of opponents the Order turns to other consistent counter-narratives. Central is the notion of sacrifice and suffering by Protestants, which is located in a series of collective memories grounded in an understanding that 'ever since the formation of the Order in 1795 members have played their part in the defence of their country and the great principles of freedom and democracy'.[71] The Order highlights how thousands of members have worn the uniform of their country's forces and many have paid the supreme sacrifice.

While the centrality of events such as the Battle of the Somme has been firmly established in the formation of loyalist identity, for Orangeism this is but one link in the chain of continuing commitment, evidenced through loss of life through military service in two world wars and via the loss of over a thousand Belfast citizens who died in the German air raids of 1941.[72]

Such memories connect Orangeism to the broader political collective of unionism by linking historical narratives to contemporary senses of loyalism and identity. Thus, it is not uncommon to directly associate the loss of life experienced by the 36th Ulster Division during the Somme campaign of the First World War to those who died in the Second World War, to those who lost their lives during the Troubles, through to those who have died in more recent conflicts such as Iraq or Afghanistan.

These strands of collective memory, based upon notions of loyalty and continued sacrifice, are clearly represented in the following editorial from the *Orange Standard*, which claimed:

> It will be generations before the suffering and the grief experienced by innocent Ulster people during the 30 years of the 'Troubles' is eased. Certainly, the anguish will never be forgotten by their families, and one has only to bear in mind that 80 years from when the guns ceased at the end of the 1914–18 War bereaved families still mourn the loss of men who left Ulster and died in Flanders and France.[73]

As the Order express it, their 'memory remains with us today and we pledge ourselves to remember those who gave their lives and hold their memory for future generations so that their loyalty, courage and sacrifice will never be forgotten'.[74] This is linked directly to recent conflict in Northern Ireland through the following:

> Unfortunately it has not only been in the various theatres of war that members of the Order have laid down their lives. Hundreds have been murdered or maimed in successive terrorist campaigns in this island and specifically over the last eighty years in Northern Ireland.[75]

Of primary contemporary importance to the Orange Order is the commemoration of those members who lost their lives during the Troubles.[76] Of the 300 RUC officers killed during the conflict, for example, around one in five were members of the Orange Order, many off-duty when targeted. From a nationalist viewpoint, the sizeable number of Orangemen within policing ranks merely provided further evidence of the sectarian, partisan nature of the security forces, offering the basis for collusion with loyalist paramilitaries and mistreatment of the Catholic population. From the perspective of the Order, however, the figures plainly demonstrate the selfless service Orangemen offered in defence of their country. Moreover, within Orangeism, there is some perception that the majority of Protestants were killed because the 'IRA used any excuse to target Protestants'[77] and 'some were murdered because they were Orangemen.'[78]

For the Order 'the Protestant community ... has been unwilling to publicly tell the story of terrorism's impact on it over the decades.'[79] In seeking to counteract this, the Order has in recent years used the annual International Day of Peace (21 September) organised by the United Nations to highlight 'the cost of terrorism'. In 2009, for example, the Order marked the day by transporting a group of 'opinion formers' to Tullyvallen Orange Hall in south Armagh, scene of one of the worst atrocities of the Troubles in September 1975 when five members of the local Lodge (LOL 630) were shot dead while attending one of their regular meetings.

In 2010, the event took place in County Tyrone, where, among others, representatives of the Equality Commission, Chinese Welfare Association, Alliance Party, Democratic Unionist Party and Department of Foreign Affairs were invited to listen to stories from the local Protestant community about the Troubles. There has been an increasing stress from the Order on the need for 'innocent victims of the Troubles to be recognised by the State in terms of compensation and counselling'.[80]

Although the overt conflict has subsided and in many ways Northern Ireland can be termed a post-conflict society, low-level everyday sectarian violence remains a reality. Indeed, the recording year 1 April 2009 to 31 March 2010 saw the number of sectarian incidents reported to the PSNI increase by 15 per cent on the previous year, and a rise in the number of sectarian-motivated crimes by almost a quarter (24 per cent) to 1,264.[81]

One manifestation of this has been attacks on the public displays of Orangeism. The last two decades, for example, has seen numerous incidents of vandalism and arson attacks on Orange Halls. Indeed, between 1994 and 2002 more than one-quarter of the 800 Orange Halls across Northern Ireland were either damaged or destroyed.[82] These attacks continue unabated, figures released by the PSNI in April 2009 showing that there had been over seventy attacks on Orange Halls in Northern Ireland during the previous twelve months.[83]

While Sinn Féin has condemned such attacks,[84] these have largely served merely to buttress loyalist scepticism over the 'non-sectarian' claims of Irish republicans and to reinforce the idea of a sustained campaign waged against the Order. As one leading Orangeman put it, 'We feel there is no doubt whatsoever that there is an organised campaign against Orange halls',[85] while the Ulster Unionist peer Lord Laird described the events as 'fascist attacks carried out by ignorant people'.[86]

Such attacks are widely perceived by Orange Order members as demonstrating a loathing of their very existence and carry significance far beyond damage to individual properties. It was Halbwachs who first suggested that the acquisition of memories is a societal phenomenon and that it is also in society 'that they recall, recognize, and localize their memories'.[87] Consequently he goes on to argue that individuals cannot in any coherent way remember outside of the context of their group. It is the group that provides the mechanisms and context for the individual to recall some events and to forget others.

Perhaps most importantly, collective memories are used to construct an understanding whereby the differences between physical attacks on the group and symbolic or cultural attacks on its identity are seen as marginal. Both are seen as part of the same process, both invoke feelings of vulnerability, and both are seen as seeking to achieve the same goal. The 'attacks' on Orangeism and unionism provoke a weary and frustrated response:

> ... the people of this Province are being subjected to a daily diet of 'Irish' events and every effort is being made to try and make British Ulster people feel more Irish than British. It will not succeed, as Ulster people's loyalty goes far deeper than that and they will not transfer their allegiance from Her Majesty the Queen to the President of the Irish Republic, or exchange membership of the United Kingdom for that of Éire. But it is irritating that so many people of influence seem to believe that if they keep on trying to remind Ulster people of their Irishness it will somehow dilute their pride in being British.[88]

DISCOURSES OF RESISTANCE

For many within the Order there is a continual need to recognise and counter enemies within and without who continually endanger the core values of Orangeism. The deep sense of loss and anger on the part of families and friends of those murdered in Northern Ireland is compounded by the presence of Sinn Féin in government, opposed on political and moral rationale (see also Chapter Six):

> I don't think Sinn Féin should be in government, no, because they've murdered our people. Well, maybe not them personally, but they are the political wing of the republican movement, and that organisation has murdered and maimed our people for years, not just during the course of the Troubles.[89]

As the Order sees it:

> Republicans have decided that, having spent 35 years slaughtering members of the Protestant community with the gun and the bomb, they have now moved into the next phase of the plan to break Protestant resistance so as they can achieve their end goal – the destruction of Northern Ireland as part of the United Kingdom.[90]

In the Orange worldview, it is 'the traditional enemies of Protestantism and Unionism' – Irish nationalism and republicanism – which are spearheading this attack on Northern Ireland's loyal ethos.[91] These 'enemies' share a common goal of 'the ultimate incorporation of the Province in an all-Ireland in which British, Protestant, Orange and Unionist culture and identity would be swamped and eventually eradicated'.[92]

The Order places itself at the heart of Protestant unionist resistance in responding to contemporary events. As this member put it:

> We have a long history of protecting all that's British ... we are an organisation that are very proud of our British identity and our attachment to the ideology of the British crown. We for many years and in many ways are the organisation that can maintain the link with Britain ... we are still Her Majesty's most loyal subjects.[93]

It has been suggested that a continual sense of siege is a 'central reality of Northern Protestant society'.[94] This encompasses fears about physical security but also less concrete, although no less valid, concerns surrounding the destruction of the group and the obliteration of its cultural icons and sites. At its end point this manifests in claims that Orangemen, particularly in border areas, were subject to a republican campaign of ethnic cleansing,[95] 'pursued by rampant republicanism' and causing areas to 'become republican dominated'.[96]

This is seen as part of a more general process involving attempts to 'sweep away symbols held dear by the unionist community'[97] and strategies aimed at the 'de-Protestantisation' and removal of Britishness from Northern Ireland.[98] As one member asserted:

> ... for years they [republicans] have actively pursued policy to remove Protestants from Ireland. They've successfully tried to do it in the Republic of Ireland, and they've made folk shift to Northern Ireland, forcefully. And they tried to do it here as well and yes, they nearly succeeded, but thankfully, the resistance of our people stood up to them. This is our, this is our homeland.[99]

While most members recognise that the 'shooting and bombing war' is over, Orange members now see themselves involved in a 'Culture war we must win'.[100] As the *Orange Standard* expressed it:

> ... the battle for the hearts and minds of the people will be fought with greater intensity than ever. Let no-one be under any illusions. The campaign by republicans and nationalists to erode the British identity of Northern Ireland will be stepped up in many ways, and the Orange Order will need to be in the vanguard of resistance to this latest phase in the strategy of the republican-nationalist alliance to try and achieve their objective.[101]

The prominence of 'anti-Orange' activity is observed as another direct challenge to Protestant cultural identity, part of a extensive plan 'carefully prepared and thought out ... by Sinn Féin/ IRA'.[102] Such views are directly reflected in these perspectives offered by members on the roles played by Sinn Féin and those mobilised by them:

> ... the shock for me was that there were so many Roman Catholic nationalist people were prepared to go out and vote for Sinn Féin. They were aligning themselves with people who were actively out to shoot, bomb and murder. I couldn't believe it ... cos it wasn't that they didn't have an alternative, they had an alternative in the SDLP, they chose not to take it. So you know, it had an influence

on me that there, I thought, you know, what's motivating these people to go and vote for people who have butchered people, butchered them for 30 years.[103]

You know, somebody once said ... if you go back far enough they're the same you know. I still have to say to you genuinely that I think Martin McGuinness and Gerry Adams ... you know, they've other strategies in place, you know, and there would still be suspicion out there for me.[104]

Well actually to me it's more of a sort of orchestrated thing by Sinn Féin to try and get ... I'm not sure whether it was to try and get, you know, to get more support, or, or what the motive there was, but it was clearly they were bringing people in just to basically get in the face of the Orange supporters and block them off.[105]

These broad concerns of the membership are reflected in the views of this leading figure within Orangeism:

I see Sinn Féin as the other side of the IRA coin, and in spite of what may have been said with regards to the IRA, their err, renunciation of violence and all the rest, I still see the organisation as having the potential if it ever needed to, to pick up its arms again, and there's always been the big question mark as to what extent all the arms were decommissioned and destroyed. There's always going to be a big question mark over that ... there wasn't ever the opportunity for people who would have been very sceptical and most stringent in their demands with regards to verification, and the IRA refused the whole way down the line to allow these critical, very sceptical people to see what was going on.[106]

This concern that Orangeism is under coherent and structured attack is readily identified around parading, which, it is claimed, is at the top of an Irish republican 'hit list'.[107] While, as we have seen in the previous chapter, the symbolic content of Orange parades has changed considerably since the 1960s, Bryan is surely correct in arguing that such events continue to provide a ritual through which the public arena may be occupied, perhaps even dominated .[108] Connerton suggests that participation in commemorative ceremonies is one way of understanding how the present is, in part at least, shaped by way of the past sustained by ritual performances.[109]

Orange parades have adapted changing narratives reflecting the altered social and political circumstances of Orangeism, but in turn have reinforced a more cohesive narrative based directly upon the legitimisation of tradition and a sense of shared history, which both informed and reinforced the sense of collective identity.[110] One member makes such views clear:

> ... the parading season, or processions, or marches ... our public witness, that's who we are as a community, that's who I am as an individual, that's why I subscribe to being a member of the institution. It's because I am afforded the right to put on my collaret or my identity badge ... my insignia and that allows me to stand out from the crowd and say look I am a member of the Orange Institution and we hold dearly to the following principle, that is the principles of the reformed faith, and ... it also gives me that opportunity to identify myself as being part of a very strong Protestant ethos.[111]

(RE)BRANDING ORANGEISM

Fears and uncertainties surrounding continuing assaults on Protestant unionism remain unabated across Orangeism. In direct response to the 'culture wars', one of the current goals of the Grand Lodge has been to re-brand Orangeism, to make it more accessible to, and to seek to draw new people to, the institution.

Moreover, there is a growing recognition, particularly at the leadership level, that the Order must act to ensure it is seen as relevant in a society experiencing a 'rapid slide into secularism and materialism and the decline in religion'.[112] This must be done, however, without alienating its current members, or losing its essence or sight of its core values and beliefs. In response, the Order has sought to engage more fully across civil society and to address its public image, which is often less than sanguine, especially around the issue of disputed routes for parades.

As part of this retort Orangeism has sought to set in place educational programmes and cross-denominational school visits, and to encourage younger people into the movement it has introduced the Orange cartoon 'superhero' Diamond Dan, intended specifically to appeal to young children. Further, under the direction of a cluster of modernisers, a new young and often highly educated grouping within the formal leadership has set about re-branding the 12th of July commemoration as Orangefest, promoting it as 'one of Europe's largest cultural festivals with music, marching and street pageantry' undertaken in a 'carnival atmosphere'.[113] (For the religious debate over Orangefest see Chapter 6.)

All of this is seen as essential weaponry in securing victory in the culture war. The public relations campaign involves a programme of Ulster Scots and traditional Orange music, highland dancing, local bands, poetry, drama and storytelling. The cultural battle around Orangefest is, however, far from won even among Orange members, where views remain largely supportive but mixed:

> ... there's a difficulty in my mind. If you turn it into a carnival, which I certainly don't want, I don't see how it improves our image, or improves anybody's reflections on the Orange Institution, to see people going about with silly hats on, which seems to become very popular.[114]

> ... the week's festival of different events is a way to celebrate the Twelfth ... but this idea of somehow trying to turn the 12th of July parade into ... the big one in South America, you know where everybody gets dressed up in silly clothes ... to my mind, that is not what the Orange Institution is trying to portray.[115]

Some saw Orangefest as relaxing the rules so as to encourage those members who were only seen to participate in Orange events on 12 July. Such members were particularly badly thought of by more active members:

> ... there are those in the organisation who come out of the woodwork just for the 12th of July. I don't have a lot of time for them to be quite honest, I don't think anybody here does have, because they're the ones that tell you what you should be doing, but they're never there when you need to say how you should be doing it.[116]

Others expressed much more positive views:

> ... with Orangefest, I have to say, we have had an outreach to the community and we have provided in the field, different entertainment for kids and so forth, particularly for kids. There were some very large kids, who seem to get great enjoyment out of it too and we have a good way to promote the Orange.[117]

I like Orangefest in Belfast [because] it is not just about the 12th of July. The 12th of July is the core of Orangefest and there's no doubt about it and that's what we're about. But there's other times of year that we should also be commemorating ... we have actively looked at possibly a week next year, which we are going to celebrate, and it will not be in July ... we aim to have lectures, to have exhibitions ... to have entertainment for everybody that wants to come to it.[118]

... we attend different events and promote Orangeism, and we seem to be doing it quite successfully through Orangefest. We have engaged with children at the moment in an art competition for which we got funding from the Arts Council, and we also, in conjunction with the *News Letter*, did a story competition not that long ago.[119]

NARRATIVES AND MEMORIES OF THE FUTURE

Collective memory and the socialisation of cultural meaning provide generational continuity across the Order's membership. Orange discourse and narratives offer overt guidance to individuals as to how their personal and public lives should be conducted. These narratives include the central place of religiosity, respect for authority and a strong political, albeit non-party, discourse. Such narratives are framed by the strength of discourses promoting the union, Britishness and the monarchy.

While most who join the Order sign up because they already sympathise with the longstanding Orange worldview through the conduit of strong family and friendship networks, this does not mean these processes are static. Collective memories provide the platform to draw on a usable past for the legitimisation of beliefs, attitudes and needs in the present.[120]

Despite the widespread changes in the political panorama of Northern Ireland, many of those interviewed still openly expressed high levels of anxiety and apprehension for their future. This theme was evident in the initial public stance taken by Edward Stevenson who was elected grand master of the Orange Order following the resignation of Bobby Saulters in 2010.

Stevenson made clear that he had little intention of changing the direction of the organisation, declaring that the Order would still not engage with the Parades Commission and that he had no intention of meeting with any 'Sinn Féin-fronted residents' group'.[121] Further, as part of the justification for this decision he drew directly on parts of the collective memory outlined above when he added, 'one in ten victims of the Troubles were members of the Orange Order, but Sinn Féin have never said sorry to them, nor have they shown any remorse, and until that happens I will not engage with them.'[122]

Social identification, remembering and forgetting alongside the use of accessible artifacts and a particular understanding of tradition combine to enable Orange members orient themselves in their social world. While members emphasise different elements and discourses, for many, politics and religion remain about the existence of the state. Indeed, many of the more recently joined members interviewed had been attracted by the discourse of consistent opposition to what are seen as the many negative consequences of the post-Agreement period for unionists.

Others seek to modernise the organisation and make it relevant in an increasingly secular and globalised society. What is clear, however, is that the overarching discourse is that all of these elements can only be guaranteed by the continuance of the union between Northern Ireland and Great Britain, and the core belief that the Order must act as a bulwark to ensure the maintenance of the constitutional link that remains primary. There remains widespread suspicion towards the 'other' community, even within the new political era and with a working devolved Assembly, and a discernable level of distrust of those unionist politicians willing to work with Sinn Féin and of the intentions of the British government.

CONCLUSIONS

For Orange Order members the institution remains positioned at the 'core of the Protestant community'.[123] Orange discourse continues to be centred upon its longstanding core elements: the Protestant faith and Christian principles; and loyalty to the crown and to a state that guarantees civil and religious liberty. These reflect constants in Orange ideology, and the contemporary narratives that are constructed around these elements allow Orange members to make sense of current events in circumstances that are still seen to be uncertain. As such, Orange discourses:

> ... are more than ways of giving meaning to the world, they imply forms of social organisation and social practices which structure institutions and constitute individuals as thinking, feeling and acting subjects ... it signifies forms of knowledge, ways of constituting the meaning of the world, which take a material form, have an institutional location and play a key role in the constitution of individuals as subjects.[124]

Orange Order members draw on pre-existing narratives and collective memories to provide support and justification for actions in the contemporary arena. They do not of course draw on obtainable discourses in uniform or mechanistic ways, but collective memories do help shape experience and patterns of thought 'in terms of past, present and future'.[125] Within Orangeism memory takes on narrative forms to become central to 'meaning-making' processes by providing the tools through which people make sense of their everyday lives.[126]

As Gillis puts it, what one remembers is defined by the identities one assumes.[127] Further memories:

> ... 'feed' group or social identities, but, in turn, they are also determined by people's membership of particular groups. Above all, narrative represents the most basic and ubiquitous form of organization of human experience and provides 'conceptual' or 'mental' tools for people to engage in the processes of remembering, forgetting, representing and identifying.[128]

Recognising the breadth of the Orange experience, one leading commentator has argued that the Orange Order 'has to decide if it is religious, cultural, community or political or some combination of these'.[129]

This, however, is to misunderstand how Orange identity is made up. For many within Orangeism, such differentiation is impossible. For most members preservation of the union is essential to the defence of Protestantism, and the defence of Protestantism is fundamental to the safeguarding of the union. Collective memories reinforce the idea that civil and religious liberty is protected through the protection of Protestantism and that the overarching identity of Britishness must be gazed through a Protestant lens. Hence, as this member put it, the Order is:

> ... traditional, cultural, historical, political, religious. It can be each of one of those things, it can be all of them to each

individual. Somebody might join because they're politically active and they want to get involved in the political scene. Others want the fellowship of going to church services and so on with the Orange. But others want to learn more of the cultural, but they can be a mix of all three.[130]

NOTES

1. 'Orange Standard', traditional Orange song.
2. H. Tajfel, *Human Groups and Social Categories* (Cambridge: Cambridge University Press, 1981), p.255.
3. Grand Orange Lodge of Ireland, 'What does Orangeism Stand for Today?', available at: http://www.grandorangelodge.co.uk/parades/orangeism_stand.html; accessed 25 June 2010.
4. It may be useful here to review the formal face of Orangeism as stated by the institution itself: 'Members of the Orange Institution are pledged to uphold the Protestant faith and liberty under the law ... The Orange Order is fundamentally a Christian organisation. The institution stands in the Reformed tradition as the various statements contained in the "Qualifications" illustrate: LOVE OF GOD – a sincere love and veneration for his Heavenly Father. He should never take the name of God in vain; FAITH IN CHRIST – steadfast faith in Jesus Christ, the Saviour of mankind; AUTHORITY OF SCRIPTURE – he should honour and diligently study the Holy Scriptures and make them the rule of his faith and practice.' Available at: http://www.grandorangelodge.co.uk/parades/orangeism_stand.html; accessed 3 February 2010.
5. *Orange Standard*, October 1999.
6. 'Ulster Protestants as Resolute as Ever', *Orange Standard*, May 1999.
7. J. McAuley and J. Tonge, 'The Old Order Changeth – or Not? Modern Discourses within the Orange Order in Northern Ireland', in K. Hayward and C. O'Donnell (eds), *Political Discourse and Conflict Resolution: Debating Peace in Northern Ireland* (London: Routledge, 2010), pp.109–25.
8. See J. McAuley and J. Tonge, '"For God and for the Crown": Contemporary Political and Social Attitudes Among Orange Order Members in Northern Ireland', *Political Psychology*, 28, 1 (2007), pp.33–52.
9. Cited in M. Hall (ed.), *Orangeism and the Twelfth: What it Means to Me* (Newtownabbey: Island Publications, 1999), p.10.
10. S. Fish, *Is There A Text in This Class?* (Boston: Harvard University Press, 1980), pp.147–74.
11. S.J. Kaufman, *Modern Hatreds: The Symbolic Politics of Ethnic War* (London: Cornell University Press, 2001).
12. A. Doane, 'What is Racism? Racial Discourse and Racial Politics', *Critical Sociology*, 32, 2–3 (2006), pp.255–74.
13. Central to all contemporary debates around discourse, of course, is an engagement with the works of Foucault, particularly through his arguments that the subject is constructed through discourses of power and knowledge (see M. Foucault, *The History of Sexuality, Volume 1: An Introduction*)(London: Penguin, 1977) and *Discipline and Punish* (London: Tavistock, 1979) and that discourses are 'practices that systematically form the objects of which they speak', *The Archaeology of Power* (London: Routledge, 1989), p.49.
14. See C. Sutherland, 'Nation-Building through Discourse Theory', *Nations and Nationalism*, 11, 2 (2005), pp.185–202; S. Zizek, *Interrogating the Real* (New York: Continuum, 2005).
15. S. Hall, 'Introduction', in S. Hall (ed.), *Representation: Cultural Representations and Signifying Practices* (London: Sage, 1997), p.6.
16. See S. Hall, 'The Rediscovery of Ideology: The Return of the Repressed in Media Studies', in J. Storey (ed.), *Cultural Theory and Popular Culture: A Reader* (London: Pearson, 2006), p.101.

17. D. Middleton and D. Edwards, 'Introduction', in D. Middleton and D. Edwards (eds), *Collective Remembering* (London: Sage, 1990), p.7.
18. N. Hunt, 'Book Review: *Voices of Collective Remembering* by James Wertsch', *Human Nature Review*, no. 2 (2002), pp.528–30.
19. P. Nora, 'Between Memory and History: Les Lieux de Mémoire', *Representations*, no. 26 (Spring 1989), pp.7–24.
20. See M. Halbwachs, *On Collective Memory* (Chicago: Chicago University Press, 1992).
21. J.K. Olick and J. Robbins, 'Social Memory Studies: From "Collective Memory" to the Historical Sociology of Mnemonic Practices', *Annual Review of Sociology*, vol. 24 (1998), p.111. See also J.K. Olick, 'Collective Memory: Two cultures', *Sociological Theory*, 17, 3 (1999), pp.333–48; J.K. Olick, '"Collective Memory": A Memoir and Prospect', *Memory Studies*, 1, 1 (2008), pp.23–9.
22. Popular Memory Group, 'Popular Memory: Theory, Politics, Method', in R. Johnson, G. McLennan, B. Schwarz and D. Sutton (eds), *Making History: Studies in History-Writing and Politics* (London: Hutchinson, 1982), p.207.
23. J. Wertsch, *Voices of Collective Remembering* (Cambridge: Cambridge University Press, 2002).
24. For a useful introduction to the literature addressing social change, see J. McLeod and R. Thomson, *Researching Social Change: Qualitative Approaches* (London: Sage, 2009).
25. R. Wodak and J.E. Richardson, 'On the Politics of Remembering (Or Not)', *Critical Discourse Studies*, 6, 4 (2009), pp.231–5.
26. M.D. Roe and E. Cairns, 'Memories in Conflict: Review and a Look to the Future', in E. Cairns and M.D. Roe (eds), *The Role of Memory in Ethnic Conflict* (Basingstoke: Palgrave, 2003), p.171.
27. See for example the 'Heroes from History' calendar issued in 2009.
28. Others highlighted include Thomas Henderson, MP (1877–1970); William Johnston of Ballykilbeg (1829–1902); Oronhyatekha [Peter Martin] (1841–1907); Sir Basil Brooke (1888–1973); Rev. W.F. Marshall (1888–1959); Rev. Dr Richard Rutledge Kane (1841–98); William Willoughby Cole [Lord Enniskillen] (1807–1886); Dr Thomas Barnardo (1845–1905).
29. A.D. Smith, *Myths and Memories of the Nation* (Oxford: Oxford University Press, 1999), p.62.
30. K. Stapleton and J. Wilson, 'A Discursive Approach to Cultural Identity: The Case of Ulster Scots', Belfast Working Papers in Language and Linguistics no. 16 (Belfast: University of Ulster, 2003), pp.57–71.
31. K. Stapleton and J. Wilson, 'Ulster Scots Identity and Culture: The Missing Voices', *Identities: Global Studies in Culture and Power*, 11, 4 (2004), pp.563–91.
32. BBC Northern Ireland has a weekly Ulster-Scots radio programme, 'A Kist o Wurds' which has been running since 2002. It hosts items concerning the history of Ulster-Scots, alongside a selection of music, poetry and literature deemed to be from within that tradition.
33. M. Nic Craith, *Plural Identities, Singular Narratives: The Case of Northern Ireland* (Oxford: Berghahn, 2002).
34. C. Smyth, 'Orangeism and the Union: A Special Relationship?', in R. Hanna (ed.), *The Union: Essays on Ireland and the British Connection* (Newtownards: Colourpoint, 2001), p.128.
35. 'Orangeism Lives On ...', *Orange Standard*, July 2000.
36. 'Looking Back on a Century of Orangeism', *Orange Standard*, August 1999.
37. D. Nelson, 'The Message of the Orange Banners', in *Grand Orange Lodge of Ireland: A Celebration, 1690–1990: The Orange Institution* (Belfast: GOLI, 1990), pp.56–7.
38. P. Connerton *How Societies Remember* (Cambridge: Cambridge University Press, 1989), pp.13–14.
39. Halbwachs, *On Collective Memory*, p.51.
40. Connerton, *How Societies Remember*, p.70.
41. Halbwachs, *On Collective Memory*, p.46.
42. E. Hobsbawm and T. Ranger (eds), *The Invention of Tradition* (Cambridge: Cambridge University Press, 1983).
43. D. Hume, 'Why I'm proud to walk the path my father trod', *Belfast Telegraph*, 12 July 2007.

44. Interview with the authors, 3 November 2007.
45. Ibid.
46. B. Parekh, *The Future of Multi-Ethnic Britain* (London: Profile), pp.16–17.
47. N. Porter, *Rethinking Unionism: An Alternative Vision for Northern Ireland* (Belfast: Black-staff, 1996).
48. J.W. McAuley and J. Tonge, '"Faith, Crown and State": Contemporary Discourses within the Orange Order in Northern Ireland', *Peace and Conflict Studies*, 15, 1 (2008), pp.136–54.
49. P. Novick, *The Holocaust and Collective Memory* (London: Bloomsbury, 2001).
50. 'Eroding of British Identity', *Orange Standard*, July 2007.
51. McAuley and Tonge, 'For God and for the Crown'.
52. *Orange Standard*, June 2000.
53. Grand Orange Lodge of Ireland, Press Statement, 1998.
54. 'Belfast Agreement has Failed the Unionists', *Orange Standard*, May 2001.
55. Rev. Martin Smyth cited in *Belfast Telegraph*, 12 July 2007.
56. 'The Union Must be Protected', *Orange Standard*, October 1998.
57. *Orange Standard*, April 1999.
58. Drew Nelson cited in 'Orange Order marches on but now it's a festival', *The Independent*, 8 July 2007.
59. See G. Kelly and M. Fitzduff, *Government Strategies on Victims in Post-Conflict Societies* (Coleraine: University of Ulster/United Nations University, 2002).
60. 'Tell the Truth and Not the Propaganda', *Orange Standard*, April 2007.
61. 'Unjust Criticism', *Orange Standard*, September 2000.
62. Press Statement issued by the Grand Orange Lodge of Ireland at Portadown District's Mini Twelfth Parade on Saturday 12 June 1999.
63. 'Vicious Smear Campaign Against Orangeism', *Orange Standard*, September 1998.
64. *Orange Standard*, September 1998.
65. *Orange Standard*, October 1998.
66. Interview with the authors, 3 November 2007.
67. Barry McElduff, Sinn Féin, MLA, cited in *Irish News*, 12 July 2004.
68. Interview with the authors, 3 November 2007.
69. Ibid.
70. Ibid.
71. Grand Orange Lodge of Ireland, 'In Memorium', available at: http://www.grandor-angelodge.co.uk/parades/in_memorium.html; accessed 15 November 2010.
72. See K. Brown, '"Our Father Organization": The Cult of the Somme and the Unionist "Golden Age" in Modern Ulster Loyalist Commemoration', *The Round Table: The Commonwealth Journal of International Affairs*, 96, 393 (2007), pp.707–23; B. Graham and P. Shirlow, 'The Battle of the Somme in Ulster Memory and Identity', *Political Geography*, 21, 7 (2002), pp.881–904; D. Officer and G. Walker, 'Protestant Ulster: Ethno-History, Memory and Contemporary Prospects', *National Identities*, 2, 3 (2000), pp.293–307.
73. *Orange Standard*, December 1997.
74. Resolution at the 12th July demonstrations in 2008 cited in *News Letter*, 12 July 2008.
75. Grand Orange Lodge of Ireland, 'In Memorium', available at: http://www.grandor-angelodge.co.uk/parades/in_memorium.html; accessed 15 November 2010.
76. 'Orange Victims' Tribute', *News Letter*, 7 April 2006.
77. W. Ross, 'IRA used any excuse to target Protestants', *News Letter*, 7 April 2006.
78. Grand Orange Lodge of Ireland, 'Orange Order Highlights 335 Members Murdered During The Troubles', Press Statement, 22 September 2010.
79. 'Orange order highlights 335 murders of members', *Londonderry Sentinel*, 23 September 2010.
80. 'Victims Deserve Justice', *Orange Standard*, March 2008.
81. Information available at: www.ofmdfmni.gov.uk/good_relations_indicators_-_2010_up-date.xls; accessed 12 January 2011.
82. N. Jarman, *No Longer A Problem? Sectarian Violence in Northern Ireland* (Belfast: Institute for Conflict Research, 2005).

83. 'Attack on Orange hall every five days', *News Letter*, 9 April 2009.
84. See 'Orange hall attacks: United front needed against hate crimes, say Sinn Féin MPs', available at http://aprnonline.com/?p=81736; accessed 20 January 2011.
85. Drew Nelson, Grand Secretary of the Orange Lodge in Ireland, cited in *News Letter*, 5 December 2007.
86. *News Letter*, 9 April 2010.
87. Halbwachs, *On Collective Memory*, p.38.
88. *Orange Standard*, December 1997.
89. Interview with the authors, 7 May 2008.
90. *Orange Standard*, August 2004.
91. *Orange Standard*, April 1999.
92. *Orange Standard*, September 1998.
93. Interview with the authors, 7 May 2008.
94. F. Wright, *Northern Ireland: A Comparative Analysis*, 2nd edn (Dublin: Gill & Macmillan, 1996). See also A. Finlay, 'Defeatism and Northern Protestant "Identity"', *The Global Review of Ethnopolitics*, 1, 2 (2001), pp.3–20.
95. *Orange Standard*, December 2002.
96. 'Protestants Felt Brunt of Ethnic Cleansing', *Orange Standard*, March 1999.
97. *Orange Standard*, March 2008.
98. *Orange Standard*, February 2004.
99. Interview with the authors, 3 November 2007.
100. *Orange Standard*, March 2008.
101. *Orange Standard*, July 2007.
102. *Orange Standard*, August 2000.
103. Interview with the authors, 7 May 2008.
104. Ibid.
105. Interview with the authors, 3 November 2007.
106. Interview with the authors, 7 May 2008.
107. *Orange Standard*, August 2000.
108. D. Bryan, '"Traditional" Parades, Conflict and Change: Orange Parades and Other Rituals in Northern Ireland, 1960–2000', in J. Neuheiser and M. Schaich (eds), *Political Rituals in Great Britain: 1700–2000* (Augsburg: Wisner-Verlag, 2006).
109. Connerton, *How Societies Remember*, pp.70–1.
110. See, for example, 'Standing Up for Orangeism', *Orange Standard*, August 2000; 'Heartbeat of Orangeism Will Not be Stopped', *Orange Standard*, August 2004.
111. Interview with the authors, 3 November 2007.
112. 'Increased Role for the Order', *Orange Standard*, February 2007.
113. Northern Ireland Tourist Board, 'OrangeFest08', available at: www.discovernorthernireland.com/product.aspx?ProductID=13131; accessed 10 June 2008.
114. Interview with the authors, 5 June 2008.
115. Ibid.
116. Ibid.
117. Ibid.
118. Ibid.
119. Ibid.
120. Wertsch, *Voices of Collective Remembering*.
121. D. Deeney, 'New Orange Order leader will not be meeting with Sinn Féin', *Belfast Telegraph*, 6 January 2011.
122. Ibid.
123. David Hume cited in Noel McAdam, 'Cultural war against us must end', *Belfast Telegraph*, 12 July 2007.
124. G. Jordan and C. Weedon, *Cultural Politics: Class, Gender, Race and the Postmodern World* (Oxford: Blackwell, 1995), p.14.
125. J. Brockmeier, 'Remembering and Forgetting: Narrative as Cultural Memory', *Culture Psychology*, 8, 1 (2002), p.21.

126. J. Bruner, *Acts of Meaning* (Cambridge, MA: Harvard University Press, 1990).
127. J.R. Gillis, 'Memory and Identity: The History of a Relationship', in J.R. Gillis (ed.), *Commemorations: The Politics of National Identity* (Princeton, NJ: Princeton University Press, 1996), pp.3–26.
128. M. Kuzmanić, 'Collective Memory and Social Identity: A Social Psychological Exploration of the Memories of the Disintegration of Former Yugoslavia', *Psihološka Obzrja/Horizons of Psychology*, 17, 2 (2008), p.7.
129. Roy Garland, *Irish News*, 14 March 2005.
130. Interview with the authors, 3 November 2007.

CHAPTER FIVE

The Politics of the Orange Order Membership

A century of formal alignment between the UUP and the Orange Order ended when the Order's leadership terminated the alliance in 2005. The parting of the ways came with little sadness or surprise to either organisation. Instead it reflected the changes which had occurred in both institutions. Above all, severance was an acknowledgement of the lack of political utility yielded by the relationship. The Orange Order's membership no longer saw the UUP as the natural repository of their political loyalty, while the Orange presence within the UUP had contributed to the UUP's structural and political difficulties. A majority of Orange Order members were voting for the DUP by the time divorce finally arrived. The DUP had enjoyed considerable electoral benefit from its opposition to the Belfast Agreement and from the divisions within the UUP over the Agreement. In addition to the specific Orange and unionist political anxieties generated by the early post-Belfast Agreement years, the demise of a once-symbiotic relationship between party and Order reflected broader social forces. Separation was partly a consequence of 'the pressure under which the conservative combination of Crown and Bible has now been placed and parallels the decline of the [Ulster] unionist Party itself.'[1] This chapter charts the termination of the UUP–Orange Order relationship and explores the modern political affiliations of the Orange membership.

THE WAY THEY WERE: THE ORANGE–UUP ALLIANCE

The Orange Order was an integral part of the Ulster Unionist Council (UUC) from the foundation of the Council in 1905. Indeed the UUP effectively emerged from the fusion of religion with politics encouraged by the Order in the creation of the UUC. One-quarter of the UUC's 200-strong original membership were drawn from the Order, recognition of its 'mobilising abilities and its history of political service to the Conservatives', who, until this point, had purported to represent unionist political interests.[2] The Order played a leading role in the mobilisation of the unionist population against plans for home rule for all of Ireland, preparing to use whatever resistance was required. The mainstream Orange Order was also seen by unionist politicians as a bulwark against labourist, left-wing tendencies, to which the much smaller Independent Orange Order, founded in 1903, was seen as more closely aligned. With the vast bulk of businesses locally owned (the first foreign-owned multinational firm did not arrive in Northern Ireland until 1959) it was important that unionist factory owners could rely on a loyal labour force. Orangeism provided social bonding across the class divide and the UUP reaped the political capital from the lack of class antagonism.

Until the collapse of direct rule in 1972, when tensions within unionism boiled over amid the diminution of unionist political authority, the Orange Order and the UUP enjoyed a productive relationship. The Order's influence consolidated the union as an entity based not merely upon the constitutional upholding of the unionist-weighted demographics which kept Northern Ireland within the United Kingdom. It also shaped the arrangement as one rooted in the primacy of the Protestant religion. While secularism and the decline of anti-Catholic sentiment elsewhere in the Kingdom rendered Protestantism of little interest, the Order's presence in the upper echelons of the unquestioned governing party in Northern Ireland infused constitutional arrangements with religious justification and theological ballast. Protestantism and unionism were inextricably linked; to be a Catholic citizen was to be a curiosity, an item attracting suspicion if allowed anywhere near decision-making structures. This conflation was most evident in the resistance encouraged by the Orange Order to the recruitment of Catholics into the UUP.

The importance of Orangeism for unionist political elites was epitomised in various ways. The Order influenced the selection of candidates by local unionist party associations. Orange delegates sat on the Ulster Unionist Council and the Executive Committee of the party. Only three members of the unionist cabinet were not members of the Order between 1921 and 1969. The assertion of Northern Ireland's first prime minister, James Craig, that he was 'an Orangeman first and a politician ... afterwards' emphasised where primary loyalty lay.[3] Craig's wartime successor as prime minister, John Andrews, was grand master of the Orange Order from the late 1940s until the mid-1950s and consolidated the alliance, using his position to urge all Orangemen to vote for the Unionist Party. This was perhaps the high-water mark for the unionist-Orange establishment, enjoying largely untroubled political hegemony in a peaceful Northern Ireland. In a deterministic conflation of religion with political outlook, the grand master of the Orange Order from 1959 to 1969, Sir George Clark, insisted that it was 'difficult to see how a Roman Catholic, with the vast differences in our religious outlooks, could be either acceptable within the Unionist Party as a member or, for that matter, bring himself unconditionally to support its ideals'.[4] Structurally, the religious-cultural-political fusion of unionism was evident in the Ulster Unionist Council, which brought together Grand Lodge and Unionist Party delegates in what was far more of a movement than a tightly regulated party organisation.

Tensions were episodically evident. Orange Order leaders occasionally complained that their members' interests were not sufficiently accommodated or were taken for granted by the UUP, the grand master of Belfast threatening to resign from the UUC on this basis in the 1930s.[5] The converse sometimes seemed true; a senior civil servant complained in 1935 of the Orange tail wagging the government dog.[6] Andrews' successor as prime minister, Basil Brooke, was obliged to defend the substantial level of state support for Roman Catholic schools to a sceptical Grand Lodge, which also complained of the lack of teaching of Protestant principles within state schools. While acknowledging the Order's continuing importance in delivering a core ethnic vote, Graham Walker has viewed the willingness of the unionist Party leadership to face down Orange opposition to the generous funding of Roman Catholic schools as:

> ... a watershed in the Order's relationship to unionism. Subsequent concessions on other matters aside, the Order never recovered the pressure-group clout it had demonstrated most notably over education in the 1920s and 1930s. Unionists of course still exercised firm control but there had at least been an alteration in the nature of their rule.[7]

Yet unionism remained tinged with Orangeism for so long as devolved one-party government endured beyond the interest of its unconcerned Westminster parent. Besides, Orange and non-Orange unionists accepted the right of Roman Catholic parents to educate their children in that faith; indeed such segregation suited Orange and Catholic interests, whatever the rhetoric to the contrary. While there was certainly Orange disquiet over the level of funding provided by the unionist government and annoyance over the comparative lack of religious ethos within non-Catholic schools, segregation in education – as in political life – was not seen as a major problem; indeed it had certain benefits in allowing schools with an overwhelmingly Protestant intake to have different curriculum emphases – mathematics, science and 'British' sports – from their Catholic counterparts.[8]

There were government versus Order rows over the banning of Orange parades in Dungiven in the 1950s, but these allowed Orange–UUP elites to marginalise and discipline those rebels critical of the minister for home affairs for prohibiting the parades. Orange unionists near the border provided a significant number of rebels prepared to question the authority of the UUP and Orange leaderships. There were also social class tensions and divisions within the unionist leadership between sectarian populists who believed public policy should be used to reward the Protestant working class and more cautious, prudent figures.[9] When Orange and UUP relations did become frayed, as in the row over Catholic education, sectarian legislation in other areas could offer compensation to hardline Orangemen. Thus the Flags and Emblems Act 1954 was largely pointless, but threw sectarian bones to the needy by allowing confiscation of the Irish tricolour.

Notwithstanding periodic tensions, the key feature of the Orange–UUP alliance was its firmness from the 1920s until the 1960s, when the arrival of Terence O'Neill as UUP leader heralded a modest change in political direction. Patterson and Kaufmann have noted two tendencies within the Orange relationship with the UUP; a rebel tendency often reluctant to accept the writ of political or Orange elites and a conservative, cautious group of Orangemen much more willing to submit to central authority.[10] This latter group could itself be sub-divided into politically oriented Orangemen who promoted Orangeism as an integral part of the Unionist Party and religious conservatives occasionally embarrassed when Orange demonstrations were used for the promotion of political, pro-UUP messages.

The advantage of the Orange Order to the UUP was that it demonstrated how the party straddled different social classes among Protestants, allowing the UUP to portray itself as the universal embodiment of Protestant–unionist–British will. This advantage diminished with the rise of the Northern Ireland Labour Party in the post-war era, but did not entirely vanish. The disadvantages of the Orange Order to the

UUP were two-fold. Firstly, it infused a sectarian flavour to unionist politics which became more difficult to justify to the wider world as parties became subject to increasing media and academic scrutiny. The UUP needed to be mindful of its other alliance, with the Conservative Party in Great Britain, although the insulation of Northern Ireland affairs ensured a lack of interest from that quarter in the internal affairs of unionism. Secondly, the UUP–Orange link was disconcerting for unionist political elites if the grassroots Orange Order membership could not always be controlled by the party. In eras of relative calm for Northern Ireland, the Orange Order's grassroots were less motivated by the basic issue of constitutional defence and more likely to indulge in criticism of their political elites, a trend which increased with the growing proletarianisation and class consciousness of the membership.[11] The rise of Paisleyism, the challenge of the civil rights movement and the patrician nature of the Orange–UUP elites combined to undermine Orange unionism as a politically homogeneous movement straddling an otherwise acute intra-unionist social class divide.

As grand master, Sir George Clark attempted to assuage Orange disquiet over O'Neill's meeting with the taoiseach, Seán Lemass, in 1965 and calm unrest over the prime minister's supposedly liberal attitude to nationalist commemorations of the Easter Rising during the following year. While O'Neill's major critics during the mid-1960s remained Paisleyites beyond the UUP–Orange orbit and thus marginal, this situation was not to survive beyond the crises precipitated by civil rights demonstrations and state responses towards the close of the decade.

By 1967, 12th of July resolutions praising O'Neill, who viewed himself as highly supportive of the Orange Institution, were jeered at some demonstrations. O'Neill's 'concessions' to nationalists were viewed as inappropriate by many within the Orange wing of his party and the Orange Order was at the forefront of opposition to the universal extension of the local authority franchise, fearing it would increase the number of nationalist councils. Liberals within the UUP became increasingly unhappy at the overtly sectarian 'principles' applied by the Order, which included the condemnation of unionist politicians attending Roman Catholic funerals. This criticism was echoed by the hitherto largely uncritical *Belfast Telegraph*, which insisted that 'either the Order alters its out-dated rules or surrenders its influence in party affairs'.[12] The Order was soon to be moved from the centre to the margins of a unionist party which itself was to be marginalised by the abolition of Stormont and replacement by British direct rule in March 1972. Yet the Order's marginalisation could not be assumed at the close of the 1960s. It was seen as a Protestant–unionist bulwark by many and the Order's membership peaked at 93,447 in 1968, up from 76,500 in 1948.[13] It was the decades of conflict, political marginalisation and increasing secularism which followed the rising tensions of the 1960s that cost the Order dear; by 2006, its membership was down to 35,758.[14]

Amid a deteriorating situation, the 1969 Stormont elections saw the UUP fractured into pro- and anti-O'Neill candidates, a faultline replicated within the Orange Order which could no longer mobilise its membership to maximise the unionist vote amid such fracture. Grand Lodge was sufficiently alarmed by O'Neill's modest reformism and his dismissal of the populist minister for home affairs, William Craig, to offer censure to Northern Ireland's prime minister. The influence of the Orange Order remained considerable and its loss of confidence in O'Neill proved important in his downfall. This marked the end of the alliance not in formal terms but in its traditional form, a seemingly inextricable link based upon warm empathy, political and religious solidarity and the shared wealthy, patrician background of party and Orange leaders. From this point, although the link remained important and a broad unity of purpose remained in resisting the republican armed campaign of the Troubles, the relationship between Order and party was more detached.

Declining as a force in Northern Ireland society from the 1970s onwards, the Order struggled to articulate its interests via the UUP, and the lack of utility of the arrangement was to become apparent. At the onset of the Troubles, the primary concern of the Orange Order appeared to be that its parades should continue. O'Neill's successor, James Chichester-Clark, provoked Orange wrath for banning all demonstrations for the second half of 1970, leading to a series of no confidence resolutions being passed by Lodges against the prime minister and provoking calls for severance of the link with the UUP. At this point, however, it was more militant members of the Orange Order who argued for maintenance of the link, arguing that it was UUP liberals who wanted the institution's removal.[15] Chichester-Clark took no action over the Orange–UUP link. However, he showed his distaste for the most blatantly sectarian implications of the alliance by providing the most unambiguous message yet that Catholics were welcome in the UUP and by appointing a minister for community relations (a member of the Orange Order, who resigned from the institution upon appointment).[16]

Although the electoral challenge of Paisley's DUP was held off for another three decades, the contribution of the Orange Order to delivering a cross-class UUP vote began to diminish. Some working-class Protestants were attracted to more militant organisations in resisting the threat to the union, as Vanguard, the Ulster Defence Association (UDA) and the Ulster Volunteer Force (UVF) all attracted recruits. Prior to Vanguard's eventual development as an electoral rival to mainstream unionism, it was possible, indeed common, for Orange Order members to be in that movement in addition to the UUP, even if Vanguard's leanings towards an independent Northern Ireland were probably not supported by most Orangemen. Given the Order's persistent condemnation of loyalist violence, belonging to the UDA (some of whose members were close to Vanguard) or UVF was incompatible with Orange membership, with Orange Order members encouraged to join the conventional security forces.

A new breed of non-patrician Orange leaders emerged, such as the Reverend Martin Smyth, who became grand master of the Order in 1972. Smyth was anxious that the religious aspects of the Order continued to achieve political outworking. Although some Order members demanded unionist unity this was politically impossible, and Smyth insisted:

> The only hope we have is of retracting into the old UUP with the Orange Institution taking an active part. Vanguard and the DUP are not happy to have Orange representation. There is no point in becoming like the Grand Lodges of England and Scotland with no political influence.[17]

From March 1972 onwards, the biggest problem facing both the UUP and the Order was their joint impotence, after their bitter opposition to the demise of Stormont was dismissed by the British government. The introduction of direct rule heralded a new militancy within the Order, which urged non-cooperation with the direct rule administration, seemingly unaware that a British government administering direct rule had little interest in the Orange cause. This struggle for relevance led the UUP under the leadership of Brian Faulkner (an Orangeman), despite many misgivings, to support the 1973 Sunningdale Agreement, to the chagrin of the Orange Order. In demanding a return to majoritarian government at Stormont and bitterly opposing the proposed Council of Ireland, the Order did much to ferment the already strong unionist opposition to the deal, even if the disdain for loyalist paramilitaries (reciprocated by loyalist militants who regarded the Orange Order as ineffective dinosaurs) meant the organisation played no role in the Ulster Workers' Council strike which finally broke the deal.

The arrival of James Molyneaux as UUP leader in 1979 shored up the Orange–UUP connection for the following sixteen years. Molyneaux's impeccable background as a sovereign grand master of the Royal Black Institution, the 'Orange elite', allied to his political outlook – outright rejection of power-sharing and any Irish dimension – was obviously in tune with mainstream unionist opinion, although his integrationist tendencies and accommodation with direct rule could irritate those Orange elements still hankering for a return to full devolved majoritarian government. While Molyneaux desired the return of a unionist Stormont parliament, he recognised this would not happen. Although the UUP and the Orange Order participated in the United Unionist Forum to try and achieve consensus on the mode of devolved government, any such plans – and there was much disagreement – were rendered redundant by the introduction of James Prior's ill-fated 'rolling devolution' plan in 1982. As secretary of state in Margaret Thatcher's Conservative government, Prior was cautious over the return of full powers to the province and his unwillingness to re-introduce majority rule annoyed unionists, while the absence of an all-Ireland dimension ensured nationalist disinterest.

Molyneaux struggled to restore his political credibility after the Anglo-Irish Agreement, a British–Irish intergovernmental concord which afforded the Irish government consultative rights on Northern Ireland, was thrust upon an unsuspecting unionist leadership in 1985. His trust in the Thatcher government to protect Northern Ireland appeared suspect to an Orange population believing (wrongly) that the 1985 deal heralded a staging post to Irish unity. From this point, the Order lacked faith in Molyneaux's integrationist tendencies and Orange unionist devolutionist sentiments were more pronounced than ever, as the means of removing 'Anglo-Irish Diktat'. Nonetheless, the unity of purpose evident in the combined UUP and DUP opposition to the Anglo-Irish Agreement in the early years after its introduction, allied to the consistency of Molyneaux's political views, ensured that the UUP remained the dominant political force within unionism and its relationship with the Orange Order remained intact. A vote among

Orange Order leaders in 1995 rejected disaffiliation. The end for Molyneaux came at the same time, however, ten years after the Anglo-Irish Agreement, when he again appeared to be caught unaware by the Conservative government's launch of the Joint Framework Documents, which advocated the linking of devolved power-sharing institutions to substantial all-island political arrangements.[18] There remains considerable doubt whether the government, bereft of a House of Commons majority and at times rudderless under the prime ministership of John Major, had any intention of proceeding with implementation of the documents, but for Molyneaux, already aged seventy-five, the furore they generated was sufficient incentive to step down. While not realised at the time, his departure and replacement by David Trimble precipitated the end for the Orange–UUP alliance.

THE 'LUNDY' TRIMBLE, ORANGE OPPOSITION TO THE BELFAST AGREEMENT AND THE MOVE TOWARDS DIVORCE FROM THE UUP

The final parting of the ways between the Orange Order and the UUP came towards the end of David Trimble's ten turbulent years as UUP leader. Ironically, Trimble, an Orangeman, had initially enjoyed strong Orange support, amid his very public backing for the Order's right to march down the contested Garvaghy Road in Portadown after a service at Drumcree parish church. Trimble's Orangeism had hitherto been less marked than at least one of his rivals, the Reverend Martin Smyth, and his party work was of a lower profile than the favourite in the contest, John Taylor. Smyth had failed to appear at Drumcree, however, and was criticised by some Orangemen within and beyond the UUP as too party-oriented at the expense of his Orangeism.[19] It seemed a strange criticism of a grand master of the Orange Lodge of Ireland for almost a quarter of a century (and UUP MP from 1982) and an odd reason for Smyth to be trounced as a party leadership candidate, but the Drumcree dispute created a fevered period for Orangeism and unionism.

Famously, Trimble had linked arms with Paisley, declaring that 'we are delighted to be back down the traditional route' after the march had been allowed to proceed, before the arrival of a seemingly interminable ban from 1998. The *Orange Standard* thus welcomed Trimble's election as an indication that 'unionism has chosen wisely' in selecting 'a cult figure among Portadown and Lurgan Orangemen ... rock-solid in his Protestant and Orange allegiance'.[20] Certainly Trimble's arrival did not necessarily herald a revision of the old association of party and

Order, who appeared as intertwined as ever in terms of shared affiliations. At the time Trimble ascended to the leadership of his party, eight
of the nine UUP MPs were members of the Order and the exception
belonged to the Apprentice Boys of Derry.[21] Indeed throughout the
UUP's history, 95 per cent of its parliamentary elected representatives
have belonged to the Order.[22]

There were moderates within the Order aghast at the efforts to
force through the Orange parade in Portadown. According to Brian
Kennaway, convenor of Grand Lodge's education committee from
1992 until 2000, 'the religious nature of the institution was undoubtedly compromised by the violence associated with the consecutive
Drumcree stand-offs', a blow from which he felt the Order might
struggle to recover.[23] Yet many Orange members bitterly opposed
compromise on the issue and viewed Trimble as someone who would
stoutly defend their interests. The Order had proletarianised[24] and
hardened. The comfortable compromises between UUP and Orange
elites had been replaced by a tougher, more militant edge and the
Orange Order expected the new UUP leader to help deliver unfettered
marching rights. This was not seen as a UUP or DUP issue, but one in
which it was essential for unionism to stand united. Moreover, by the
time of the Drumcree dispute, nearly two-thirds of Orange Order
members did not believe the Order should be affiliated to a particular
political party according to Grand Lodge's own internal survey.[25]

The Orange Order was divided three ways, between the militant
Spirit of Drumcree group demanding virulent assertion by Grand
Lodge of marching rights (and calling for the resignation of the Grand
Lodge leadership), a broader membership many of whom sympathised
with the ambitions, if not all the tactics, of the Spirit of Drumcree
group and an Orange leadership seemingly paralysed by the sheer scale
of Orange protests during the height of the Drumcree row. Although
the leader of the Spirit of Drumcree faction, Joel Patton, was eventually expelled from the Order, the group left its mark in helping harden
Orange opinion against compromise, reflected in consequent rejection
of the legitimacy of the Parades Commission's attempts to regulate
parades.

The backing of the UUP leadership for the 1998 Belfast Agreement
ripped asunder the fragile political consensus which had endured
between the Orange and liberal-civic brands of unionism. Rational
civics such as Trimble viewed the Belfast Agreement as a logical
defence of the union, in which inclusive power-sharing and a modest

all-Ireland dimension to political arrangements were reasonable concessions in return for constitutional guarantees – tacitly accepted even by Sinn Féin – that there could be no change in Northern Ireland's position in the United Kingdom without the consent of its people. Notwithstanding the swallowing of some painful medicine, notably the release of terrorist prisoners while their political allies sat in government, rational civics calculated that unionist self-interest lay in acceptance of the deal. Beyond political calculation, there was a modest element of reaching out to heal divisions and accept the legitimacy of the nationalist and republican traditions, reflected in Trimble's stated desire for Stormont to operate as a 'pluralist parliament for a pluralist people'.[26]

Orange sceptics included prominent UUP Orangemen such as Martin Smyth and the former leader Molyneaux, in addition to those outside the party and unsympathetic to the UUP link, such as the executive officer, George Patton. For this large group of opponents, the Agreement was entirely unsatisfactory on moral and political grounds. It was immoral having 'terrorists in government' and outrageous to witness 'the release of convicted republican and loyalist terrorists, criminals found guilty of the most heinous crimes'.[27] This aspect of the Agreement was seen as an insult to victims and politically dangerous, one which legitimised previous violence. Early release was seen as a betrayal of those citizens who had served in the security forces and an insensitive act against those families (including those of a sizeable number of Orangemen) whose grief remained permanent. Grand Lodge voted by nearly eight to one that it could not recommend support for the deal in the May 1998 referendum. However, the tradition that the Order did not tell its members directly who or what to vote for was maintained, in that the motion that the Grand Lodge 'says No' was defeated, by seventy votes to twenty-two. The Orange Order's 'petit non' left the issue to the conscience of its members but the distaste for the deal within Grand Lodge was apparent.

UUP representatives ought to have been bound by party policy, with the Agreement endorsed by over 70 per cent of the UUP Executive and the UUC. However, these ratifications cut little ice with internal opponents of the deal, some of whom stood in the June 1998 Assembly elections on platforms of opposition. Trimble responded in considerable detail to the concerns of the Grand Lodge secretary, John McCrea and acknowledged that the UUP 'share Grand Lodge's distaste for prisoner release', but highlighted in particular the satisfactory constitutional aspects , the replacement of the Anglo-Irish Agreement by local influence and the commitment to non-violence expressed by republicans.[28]

The *Orange Standard* was less circumspect in its opposition to the Agreement, the front page of its May 1998 edition carrying a huge 'NO', lest the brethren be in any doubt and insisting that this was a deal 'no Protestant in good conscience could support'.[29] Mandatory power-sharing with republicans, the creation of an all-Ireland Executive and the potential dismemberment of the Royal Ulster Constabulary under the proposed Patten Review[30] of policing were all unacceptable to Grand Lodge, which condemned the 'incessant wave of Government concessions to Irish nationalism and republicanism'.[31]

Anxious to try and sell the deal, the prime minister, Tony Blair, met an Orange delegation but, inevitably, no consensus was found. Patterson and Kaufmann put it neatly: 'The Order's moral philosophy was based on inviolable Kantian first principles while that of Blair was based on utilitarian results.'[32] Moral ambivalence on prisoners and constructive ambiguity on the politics of the deal were cornerstones of the arrangement. Other than conveying their displeasure to Blair, Trimble and the wider unionist community, the Orange Order could do little to resist the Agreement. The solitary institutional vehicle created by the Belfast Agreement which would at least have given the Order a voice was the Civic Forum, a non-executive and non-legislative 'talking shop' designed to afford representation to the most important interest groups in Northern Irish society. Bizarrely, the Order, one of the largest groups, was excluded from the Forum. Notwithstanding the Order's negativity towards the new political and institutional dispensation, their omission was a further reason why the Civic Forum lacked credibility from the outset, given its willingness to invite other much smaller and less significant associations.

There was considerable political and media pressure at the time of the Belfast Agreement referendum (May 1998) to back the deal, amid portrayals of the contest as one between progressives (pro-Agreement) and dinosaurs (anti-Agreement). Although a narrow majority of Protestants, 57 per cent to 43 per cent, supported the Belfast Agreement,[33] this was not the case among Orange Order members, of whom 29 per cent supported the deal, with 60 per cent voting against.[34] Nine years later, in the authors' survey, Orange Order members were still hostile, only 26 per cent saying they would vote in favour in the event of another referendum. Faulkner had failed to sell Sunningdale to Orangemen in the 1970s and his support for a deal had ended his political career; in the late 1990s and early 2000s Trimble was attempting a similarly ambitious task of selling a not dissimilar, yet even more ambitious, agreement to a sceptical grouping within his own party. Meanwhile, the DUP, with its then strident anti-Belfast Agreement stance, offered a tempting political outlet for Orangemen disaffected with the UUP's support for the deal. By 2002, as the Northern Ireland Assembly collapsed, it was reported that only one-third of Protestants still supported the Agreement.[35] Anti-Agreement Orange UUP members made common cause with the DUP and other refuseniks, but still had the problem of belonging to a pro-Agreement party.

By 2004, senior UUP figures such as Peter Weir, Nelson McCausland and Jeffrey Donaldson, each a member of the Orange Order, had given up the anti-Agreement struggle within the party and defected to the DUP. Despite completion of the release of prisoners, little progress on the decommissioning of paramilitary weapons was evident at this stage. The RUC was replaced by the Police Service of Northern Ireland, recruiting equal proportions of Roman Catholics and non-Catholics. Support for the UUP began to dissipate. By the time of the 2001 Westminster election, more Orange Order members (49 per cent) were voting for the DUP than for the UUP (45 per cent) even though the UUP still had an 8 per cent lead over its rival at this point. Only five years earlier it had been claimed that 'the vast majority of Orange Order members would be UUP supporters.'[36] As confidence in the Belfast Agreement collapsed among unionists, the DUP lead among Orangemen was to widen and extend to the broader Protestant population. By the 2005 Westminster election, the DUP was outpolling the UUP by two to one. Under a Downsian model,[37] the UUP would have switched to opposition to the Agreement, to place itself nearer the median Protestant voter, but Trimble was too associated with the deal for this to be a credible position. Yet despite his strong support for the Agreement and willingness to take risks and face down critics, Trimble struggled to portray himself convincingly as a civic unionist. While warning UUP delegates at their 2002 conference against a retreat into a sectarian laager, he denounced the Irish Republic in inflammatory terms as the 'pathetic, mono-cultural, mono-ethnic, sectarian state to our south'.[38]

Given his support for the Belfast Agreement, Trimble's good early press within Orangeism and unionism seemed a distant memory. By the time the political institutions collapsed in September 2002, Trimble was seen by many within the Orange Order as a 'Lundy', a traitor to an

Orange cause he had used to secure personal political advancement. Trimble was also blamed indirectly for the workings of the Parades Commission, which re-routed some of the most contentious Orange parades. He was also criticised by Orange zealots for attending Roman Catholic funerals. Even Trimble's political advisor, Stephen King, declared graphically that 'David is regarded as a cancer by the Orange Order.'[39] As Kennaway observed, declarations of support for Trimble had become 'the principal "mortal sin" within Orangeism'.[40] The Orange Order's contempt for Trimble was reciprocated by an increasingly beleaguered party leader.

Trimble was 'aware of who my enemies are' in the Ulster Unionist Council and a lot of them were Orange.[41] The UUP leader wanted to reform the chaotic, if democratic, structure of the Ulster Unionist Council. Its outdated, coalitional and federal organisation, essentially unchanged since 1946, allowed Orange delegates to help shape party policy alongside representatives from local UUP associations (many of whom were also Orangemen), Young Unionists (a majority of whom were in the Orange Order and were also largely hostile to the UUP leadership), the Ulster Unionist Councillors' Association and the Ulster Women's Unionist Council. The need to placate these various constituencies, notably the increasingly militant Orange tendency, diminished the capacity of Trimble to steer the ship.

The presence of County Grand Lodges within the UUP, formally recognised in the party constitution (unlike that of Grand Lodge, whose constitution did not mention the UUP) may have been of little significance in the years of broad consensus, but amid the political chasm opened by the Belfast Agreement, it was important. Along with other affiliated organisations, Orange delegates had voting rights within the UUC. County Lodges provided the 122 delegates who sat on the UUC. The delegates elected by their counties were supposed to be members of their local UUP branch, although little checking was apparent. Twelve Orange delegates, who were elected by County Lodges and sent by Grand Lodge Central Committee, also sat on the UUP's Executive Committee.[42] Of the total of 858 UUC members, approximately half also belonged to the Orange Order and for some, Orange loyalties ran deeper than party fidelity.

Thus, through a combination of formal structure and emotional attachment to Orangeism, the Orange input into the UUP was considerable. Modernisation of the UUP was an imperative regardless of the political situation, However, the repeated attacks upon Trimble and a series of cliffhanger votes within the UUC on his political strategy, which could be called at the behest of a mere sixty members but reflected the acute political divisions, made the task even more pressing, but no easier to enact. A majority of the Orange Order's delegates opposed Trimble's support for the deal, opposition particularly strong among those delegates most active within the Order and from those drawn from urban locations in Antrim and Belfast, where no Orange delegates backed the Belfast Agreement.[43] Anti-Agreement Belfast, which had lost much Orange membership in previous decades, was over-represented within the UUC, its twenty-four delegates more than double what it would have provided had UUC representation been proportionate to County Lodge Orange numbers, as was required under the UUC constitution.[44] Some element of rural deference towards the leadership remained and a majority of Tyrone delegates backed the Agreement, but this was the only County Lodge that did so and it held only eleven UUC delegates, with the urban, more proletarianised, sections of the Order demonstrating little faith in Trimble.[45]

This is not to suggest overwhelming homogeneity within the Orange wing of the UUP. Kaufmann and Patterson concur that UUC members who belonged to the Orange Order were mainly against the Belfast Agreement, but found that Orange delegates who were also prominent office-bearers within the Order (a large majority of those delegates) were far more likely to oppose the deal than Orange office-bearers who did not represent the bloc (i.e. those Orange Order members who attended the UUC as constituency delegates).[46] The county which these delegates represented was also important in respect of the pro- versus anti-Agreement faultline, more so than social class or education. Most pro-Agreement of all, however, were the non-Orange delegates (see below) and UUP Northern Ireland Assembly members, who tended to represent an elite more affluent than the broader unionist population. The backing of these sectors allowed Trimble to win, narrowly, all the numerous UUC votes on his political strategy.

The lack of support for Trimble within the Orange Order had been illustrated vividly in 2000, when the grand master from 1971 until 1996, Martin Smyth, launched a leadership challenge against the incumbent, despite claiming he had 'no real desire to be leader of the party'.[47] Smyth was particularly angered over what he viewed as Trimble's weakness in pressing for IRA decommissioning, even though the Executive and Assembly were already suspended at the time of the leadership contest because of Trimble's insistence that verifiable disarmament must begin. Smyth had polled only sixty votes when contesting the leadership during Trimble's 1995 victory and had been the first candidate to be eliminated. Given this, his support within the UUC at the outset of the 2000 event was rated at a mere 20 per cent by the *Belfast Telegraph*,[48] and only one UUP Assembly member publicly declared that he did not support Trimble. The 20 per cent calculation proved, however, a gross under-estimate as Smyth polled 43.2 per cent in the leadership vote, achieving 348 votes to Trimble's 457. It was hardly a resounding vote of confidence in the UUP leader, but these figures were to be repeated in favour of the leader – give or take a few per cent – on a range of policy votes within the UUC during the post-Agreement era. Given this, it is illuminating to analyse whether Orange Order membership was an influential factor in how UUC delegates voted, with Smyth highlighting his Orange credentials, pointing out that he had 'first been an Orangeman, then a politician'.[49] How the Trimble–Smyth vote broke down in terms of Orange Order membership within the UUC is shown in Table 5.1.

TABLE 5.1 VOTING IN THE ULSTER UNIONIST PARTY LEADERSHIP CONTEST 2000, BY ORANGE ORDER MEMBERSHIP (%)

	Voted for Trimble	Voted for Smyth
Member of the Orange Order	48.7	51.3
Non-member of the Orange Order	67.9	32.1

Table 5.1 indicates a strong Orange Order effect, in that the UUP leader was rejected by a majority of Orange Order members, whereas two-thirds of non-members of the Order were content to support Trimble. It is nonetheless noteworthy that nearly half of Orange Order members were prepared to back Trimble despite the lack of faith of the Orange leadership in the cornerstone of his political strategy, support for the Belfast Agreement. A logistic regression (Table 5.2) is needed to determine the significance of Orange Order membership relative to other variables of gender, age, income, occupation and county (east versus west of the province) residence. The dependent variable is the Trimble–Smyth vote in the 2000 leadership election, with support for Trimble coded '0' and backing for Smyth coded '1'. Table 5.2 indicates that Orange Order membership did indeed yield a significant independent effect in terms of preferred UUP leader, with Orange support leaning towards Smyth. Nonetheless, age (younger

TABLE 5.2 LOGISTIC REGRESSION OF TRIMBLE–SMYTH VOTING IN THE ULSTER UNIONIST PARTY LEADERSHIP CONTEST 2000[50] (0 = TRIMBLE; 1 = SMYTH)

	B	SE	Wald	P
Gender	.15	.23	.46	.50
Age			21.72	.00
15–24	2.59	1.07	5.84	.02
25–34	.76	.51	2.21	.14
35–44	-.22	.42	.26	.61
45–54	-.69	.38	3.28	.07
55–64	-.97	.33	8.66	.00
75+	-1.45	.46	10.03	.00
Orange Order membership	.46	.17	7.76	.01
Income.			6.91	.03
£40,000+	-.65	.26	6.34	.01
<£20,000	.49	.23	4.76	.03
Occupation			17.35	.01
Secretarial/clerical/trade	.82	.42	3.73	.05
Junior or middle manager,				
civil servant	.56	.27	4.20	.04
Farmer	-.26	.35	.56	.45
Professional	.88	.42	4.32	.04
Teacher/academic	-1.24	.51	6.00	.01
Senior management	-.43	.50	.76	.38
County of residence	-.18	.18	1.00	.32
Constant	-.38	.29	1.68	.20

Model _2 = 75.69, 17df.p<.001
Pseudo-R2 = .33

very anti-Trimble; older much more supportive), income (low income anti-Trimble) and occupation (teachers, academics and managers, but not other professionals, pro-Trimble) were also significant, indicating that Orange Order membership mattered – but the divisions within unionism during this fevered period had a demographic and structural basis, as well as assuming an Orange versus non-Orange flavour.

Despite their disagreements with UUP policy, most Orange delegates to the UUC did not want to sever their association with the party at this stage and Smyth supporters, in particular, were keen for the alliance to be preserved. Table 5.3 shows the raw attitudes on the retention of voting rights issue, according to leadership vote and Orange Order membership. Overall, the UUC was almost evenly divided on whether the Orange Order should remain affiliated.

TABLE 5.3 ATTITUDES TO ORANGE ORDER VOTING RIGHTS WITHIN THE UUC, BY ORANGE ORDER MEMBERSHIP AND UUP LEADERSHIP CONTEST VOTE, 2000

(+2 Strongly Agree with the Orange Order holding voting rights)
(-2 Strongly Disagree with the Orange Order holding voting rights)

	Member of the Orange Order?	
Voted for:	Yes	No
Trimble	-47	-1.03
Smyth	1.50	.93

As can be seen, Trimble supporters were against the Orange Order holding voting rights within the UUC regardless of whether or not they were Orange Order members themselves, but the degree of such hostility to such rights was much greater, at -1.03, among non-members of the Order, often the civic pro-Trimble progressives desirous of radical change. Among those voting for Smyth, there was very strong support for the Orange Order to continue holding a formal role within the UUP among Orange Order members. Despite bitterness towards the party leadership and its policy direction, the deepest Orange section of the UUP did not want to jump ship at this stage, whereas non-Orange Trimble-ites would gladly have seen the back of the Order. A further five years elapsed, with the UUP crumbling and the Belfast Agreement enduring protracted problems, before the County Lodges decided there was no longer any point in attempting to work within the UUP.

Table 5.4 uses a regression to show the independent effect of the Orange Order and leader preference variables. It shows that the divisions on Orange voting rights were not reducible merely to Orange membership. Such membership and the way UUC members voted on the leadership question *both* yielded a significant independent effect. Non-members of the Order who sympathised with Smyth were still happy to see it play a role, presumably as a bulwark against UUP backing for the Belfast Agreement. Orange Order Smyth supporters were nonetheless more intense than non-members over the need for Orange voting rights to be retained.

TABLE 5.4 OLS REGRESSION OF ORANGE ORDER VOTING RIGHTS ON THE ULSTER UNIONIST COUNCIL BY ORANGE ORDER MEMBERSHIP AND UUP LEADERSHIP CONTEST VOTE, 2000[51]

Dependent variable: 'The Orange Order should retain voting rights on the UUC'
(+2 Strongly Agree; – 2 Strongly Disagree)

	B (S.E.)	P
Member of Orange Order	.57 (.13)	.000
Voted for Smyth	1.97 (.13)	.000
Constant	-3.57 (.26)	.000

Adjusted R2=.481
Weighted N = 292

The Orange versus non-Orange faultline within the UUC was a jagged entity, with complicating demographic trends, notably the hostility of young UUC members to Trimble, and it would be unfair to say that Trimble versus Smyth in 2000 was reducible to a contest over ethnic Orange versus liberal and civic unionist in terms of the future direction of the UUP. There was a section of the UUP whose Orange membership was not a barrier to support for the Belfast Agreement and the UUP leader. Nonetheless, Trimble and Smyth were to some extent proxies for two broad tendencies within the UUP. The Orange sceptic adherents of Smyth opposed political change on a range of other indicators evident in the survey of the UUC conducted shortly after the leadership battle.[52] Trimble supporters favoured parallel consent for decision-making; Smyth backers opposed this. Power-sharing with cross-border bodies was accepted by Trimble adherents, whereas Smyth supporters were very strongly opposed to such political pluralism and bi-nationalism, their opposition reaching -1.4 on a scale where -2.0 was the maximum possible disagreement. The two wings of the UUC were united in opposition to the Patten Commission report on policing and on the early release of paramilitary prisoners, but the level of hostility to both was much greater among Smyth's backers.

The Smyth Orange wing of the UUC appeared to have abandoned the old devolution majoritarian dream and declared in favour of the full integration of Northern Ireland into the UK, however unrealistic, whereas the Trimble supporters were split on the merits of integration. Both wings appeared divided among themselves over whether British political parties should contest elections in Northern Ireland. On the vexed question of the Orange Order's right to march through nationalist areas, Smyth supporters were adamant in defence of such liberties, whereas Trimble supporters were almost neutral, offering only the slenderest weighting in favour of the assertion of such rights. Finally, Smyth supporters declared themselves almost twice as likely to consider offering vote transfers to the DUP, an ominous portent of what was to come for the UUP.

Beyond the Trimble–Smyth friction, there was no doubt, however, that Orange Order membership was a significant influence upon attitudes within the UUC. Importantly, Orangeism was more influential than the other characteristics which might have been expected to influence political attitudes. Membership of the Orange Order within the UUC was associated closely with a range of positions in opposition to the Belfast Agreement, yielding a *significant independent effect* when controlling for the range of other variables: gender, age, occupation and denomination, on each of the following issues: power-sharing with cross-border bodies (anti); a united Ireland if a majority in Northern Ireland was in favour (anti); the early release of paramilitary prisoners (anti); the Patten reforms of policing (anti); the right to march through nationalist areas (pro); voting rights within the UUC (pro) and vote transfers to the DUP (pro). Only one other variable – that of age – reached significance on more than one issue, youth being significant in terms of two positions: support for power-sharing without cross-border bodies and strong propensity towards DUP vote transfers. Influential across seven key policy positions, however, Orange Order membership was a key determinant of the attitudes towards key issues within the UUC. Most of these positions held by the Orange Order membership were in direct repudiation of the Trimble view.[53]

The Orange Order's link with the UUP came under growing pressure not from Orange delegates within the UUP, who appeared to respect their privileges, but from elsewhere within the Order. In 1999, Antrim became the first County Lodge to vote in favour of disaffiliation. Previously, such calls had been confined to District Lodges and ignored at county level. Yet, as late as the end of the twentieth century, other County Lodges were not similarly inclined to disaffiliate. Grand Lodge and the UUC had both set up committees to look at the issue in 1995, but little of substance arose prior to a change of personnel in the Grand Lodge's committee in 1999, when a grouping more hostile to the UUP emerged. The UUC was split on the affiliation issue and fudged the matter in 2002 by proposing that, rather than have their voting rights removed, Orange delegates should each pay a levy to the UUP and that UUC places would be reserved strictly for Orangemen who were also local party members (a stipulation that had become lax). Grand Lodge wished to retain some control over Orange delegations to the UUC and in any case the Orange elite were already looking to the UUP's rival as their preferred unionist vehicle. The grand master, Robert Saulters, quit the UUP in 2002, although he did not join the DUP, unlike the grand secretary, Dennis Watson, who joined Paisley's party. The DUP was no longer seen by traditional Orange elites as a pariah organisation, whose leader was associated with a Free Presbyterianism eschewed until this point by the Order.

Strikingly, the serious discussions over the link with the Orange Order which had developed within the UUP owed less to a perceived need to de-sectarianise the party than to a perception that, first, some Orange delegates caused trouble and, second, that structures needed altering to allow the leader greater control of his party. Had the UUP severed the link, it would not, therefore, have been a move designed to chase Catholic votes. The view of Martin Smyth, expressed at the 1995 UUP conference, held sway. To risk 160,000 Orange votes to chase a maximum of 50,000 Catholic votes (probably in any case an exaggeration) was 'bad mathematics'.[54] In an ethnically divided polity, vote maximisation within the bloc was what mattered and Smyth's sectarian sums had carried much clout. They nonetheless grossly exaggerated the size of the Orange vote, if measured in terms of the Order's actual membership. They also assumed, not unreasonably at the time, that this sectional interest within the party had the capacity to deliver votes. In other western European parties, reliance upon sectional interests has been diminished, mainly due to the lack of electoral value.[55] Three years after Smyth's calculations, the UUP president, Josias Cunningham, confirmed that any Orange–UUP divorce would not arise due to the onset of civic unionism, but would instead be a consequence of party modernisation:

> The adoption of a 'Party' structure, with no formal representation from the Loyal Orders and other groups ... may make it easier for some of the Roman Catholic faith to identify and join with us. But this is not the reason why the matter has been under consideration for the last nine years. The thinking has been driven by an earnest desire to streamline and modernise our structure, so that

we may have effective discipline and cohesion, which is difficult in the present federal structure.[56]

Liberal unionists had long criticised what they saw as the unacceptably sectarian tag attached to the UUP.[57] By the time of Orange separation, however, the UUP would have gladly called in any unionist voters, Orange or otherwise. While the exit of the Orange Order may have helped modernise a hitherto ethno-religious party, it did not improve the UUP's electoral fortunes.

Following disaffiliation, the new messages were those of Orange political non-alignment (rather than re-alignment with the DUP), the need for unionist unity and the offer of and brokerage between the UUP and DUP. Had the severance decision been put off for two more years, it might have been interesting to see the result. By then, the DUP, as the dominant unionist force, had supported a rather slight re-negotiation of the Belfast Agreement, albeit with a crucial change on Sinn Féin's attitude to policing, via the St Andrews Agreement and re-entered the Executive, heading a coalition with Sinn Féin. Those elements within the Orange Order still opposed to mandatory power-sharing, Sinn Féin in government and an all-Ireland dimension could find comfort within neither the UUP nor the DUP. Anti-Agreement Orange stalwarts now had to look to a new vehicle, Jim Allister's Traditional Unionist Voice party. Departure from the UUP appeared to deepen the isolation of the Orange Order. It had removed itself from a political party which, despite its post-1998 electoral catastrophes, would at least enjoy a modicum of influence given the restoration of devolution to Northern Ireland. However, the presence of solid Orange contingents within the DUP and UUP Assembly representatives would perhaps ensure that the Orange voice could still be heard.

The Orange–UUP link was finally severed in 2005 in low-key fashion, following a resolution proposed by a UUP supporter, the county master of Tyrone (and later grand master), Edward Stevenson. His resolution was originally put forward in 2004 and received majorities at its first and second readings. The third and final reading took place in March 2005, when the resolution proposing the 'severing of all links' between Grand Lodge and the UUC was carried by eighty-two votes to sixteen, with eleven abstentions.[58] Thus a century-old alliance was ended with little fuss or fury. Many UUP branches continued to meet in Orange Halls without acrimony (the DUP claimed responsibility for reducing the rates paid for such halls, ensuring their viability). It was the institution which had once feared being pushed from the UUP that in the end jumped. Ironically, the focus of much Orange hostility, David Trimble, was soon to disappear from Northern Ireland politics. Two months after the severance of the Orange Order–UUP link, Trimble's marginal support within his own party failed to extend to the broader unionist electorate, the Nobel Peace Prize winner being beaten by the DUP in his Upper Bann constituency at the general election, a defeat followed by his elevation to the House of Lords. Trimble's electoral humiliation was merely the headline scalp in a bigger story; his party lost five of its six Westminster seats and its vote fell by 9 per cent.

Two years after severance of the link, a majority (60.3 per cent) of Orange Order members believed it was right that the Order no longer held voting rights in the UUC, with only 23.6 per cent dissenting. Support for the ending of the formal link did not extend to a desire for the cessation of all connections. A majority (61.4 per cent) supported the continuation of the holding of UUP meetings in Orange Halls, with only 15 per cent in disagreement. Divorce had not been without pain, but, as is common in such cases, the bitterness at the time of the split rapidly subsided.

CONTEMPORARY VOTING AMONG ORANGE ORDER MEMBERS: STRUCTURAL AND ATTITUDINAL INFLUENCES

By the time of the 2001 general election, there was greater support among Orange Order members for the DUP than the UUP, a preference which, by the 2003 Assembly contest, was to be extended to the wider Protestant population. In the 2001 Westminster election, 48.9 per cent of Orange Order members claimed to vote DUP, compared to 45.3 per cent voting UUP.[59] Unionist voters as a whole split 53.6 per cent UUP to 45 per cent DUP at the election, but by the 2003 Assembly election, DUP support had reached 51.2 per cent among unionists. The under-55s, working class, middle class, low-and high-income categories, plus all the Protestant denominations displayed majority support for the DUP.[60]

Among Orange Order members, party choice was, unsurprisingly, linked to support or opposition to the Belfast Agreement, confidence in which had collapsed to only one-third of Protestants by 2002 and to only 12 per cent of Orangemen by 2004.[61] By this point, among those who had voted 'Yes' to the Belfast Agreement in 1998, majority preference (56.1 per cent) remained for the UUP but among opponents of the Agreement, there was very strong (80.2 per cent) backing for the DUP.[62] 'Thermometer' ratings of the unionist party leaders highlighted the unpopularity of the UUP leader, David Trimble. On a 0 (maximum dislike) to 10 (maximum like) scale, Ian Paisley scored 7.32 among Orange Order members, more than double Trimble's score of 3.47.[63] Trimble's rating lay closer to the utter antipathy (a 0.19 score) displayed towards the Sinn Féin president, Gerry Adams, than it did to the DUP leader. It was not that Orange Order members rejected the idea of devolved government at the heart of the Belfast Agreement. When the Assembly was suspended from 2002–7, 78 per cent of Orange Order members wanted its restoration and only 15 per cent believed that direct rule from Westminster was the best political option. It was the particular terms of the Belfast Agreement which caused consternation.

For the decade following the Belfast Agreement, the switch of the Orange Order and the broader Protestant population from the UUP to the DUP continued apace. The UUP still enjoyed more support (37 per cent to 35 per cent) among the over-55s in the Order, suggesting that those politically socialised in an era of UUP dominance were affected by that upbringing, but the UUP was out-supported by the DUP by two-to-one among 35–54-year-olds and by nearly four-to-one among those under 35.[64] Given that the overwhelming majority of Orange Order members claim to vote, the high figure of one-third who claim not to support a particular political party (the official position of the Orange Order) does at least offer the UUP a modicum of hope if it can re-connect to Orange interests. Table 5.5 reports Orange Order preferences and voting patterns.

TABLE 5.5 REPORTED PARTY SUPPORT AND VOTES AMONG ORANGE ORDER MEMBERS (2005 GENERAL AND LOCAL ELECTIONS)

	Support Generally	Vote in 2005 General Election	Vote in 2005 Local Election
DUP	39.9	60.2	58.4
UUP	24.7	30.7	32.4
Don't Support a Party	31.2	n/a	n/a
Did Not Vote	n/a	4.7	4.9
Other	4.2	4.4	4.3

Since the survey, some evidence has emerged of disillusionment among a section of the Orange brethren over the eventual willingness of the DUP to do a deal with Sinn Féin in the 2006 St Andrews Agreement and re-enter devolved power-sharing government in 2007. Among the broad Protestant population, the DUP performed strongly at that year's Assembly election, effectively cementing the new arrangements. Paramilitary prisoner early releases, opposed by 90 per cent of Orangemen, had long been completed, the Provisional IRA had gone, its weapons had been removed and, crucially, Sinn Féin now supported the Police Service of Northern Ireland. Nonetheless, a hardline core in the Orange Order still questioned the morality of sharing power with those who they regarded as unapologetic terrorists. Moreover, the changes to policing included 50:50 Catholic to non-Catholic recruitment until 2012, a measure backed by only 11 per cent of Orange Order members. The Traditional Unionist Voice (TUV) party, led by the DUP defector and former MEP Jim Allister, attempted to tap this resentment by opposing mandatory coalition government with Sinn Féin. The TUV performed well in the 2009 European election, where Allister lost his seat but achieved a respectable 14 per cent of first preference votes, but weakened in the 2010 Westminster contest, obtaining less than 4 per cent of the vote.

How important are demographic and structural factors relative to attitudes, notably original attitudes to the Belfast Agreement, in determining Orange support for the DUP or UUP? This is tested using a three-stage binary logit model constructed via the authors' 2007 survey of members and deploying the obvious party support question, 'how would you vote if an election were held tomorrow?' as the dependent variable, coding 0 for the UUP and 1 for the DUP. Age is categorised three-fold: under-35, 35–54 and 55 and over. However, in order to test the influence of the political socialisation model more fully, we also include the year of joining the Orange Order. Almost one-quarter (23.2 per cent) of members joined in the 1920–66 era; the bulk (58.3 per cent) joined at the onset of, or during, the Troubles, between 1967 and 1997 and 18.5 per cent joined 'post-Agreement' between 1998 and 2007. A six-fold occupational class structure, based upon Goldthorpe classifications, is used, to see if the more proletarian elements of the Order are more inclined to support the DUP, as working-class loyalist support has been a strong feature of that party's electoral base.[65] Manual workers account for 29 per cent of the Orange Order (split fairly evenly between unskilled/semi-skilled and skilled) and the salariat forms only 10 per cent. The economically inactive form a large chunk of members, just over one-third. Educational qualifications are included in the model. O-Level/GCSE qualifications are the most common highest qualification, held by 32.9 per cent of members, with a further 12.9 attaining at least one A-Level as their highest qualification and 29.7 per cent holding no qualifications. Just over 15 per cent hold undergraduate or postgraduate degrees. The significance of Protestant denomination is tested. Free Presbyterians, likely to back the DUP, are used as the reference category, to be contrasted with the mainstream denominations, while religiosity is tested using frequency of church attendance.

Beyond demographics, social structure and religion, the second test in the model factors is attitudinal. Two tests are deployed. One is the 'hardline loyalist' test, using the proposition 'all Roman Catholics are IRA sympathisers', a view with which 63.3 per cent of Order members agree and from which 26 per cent dissent. Left–Right divisions are tested using the proposition that 'private enterprise is best', a view with which 47.9 per cent of members concur and 25.1 per cent dissent. Most Orange Order members view themselves as right-wing. On a 0 (Left) to 10 (Right) continuum, only 11.9 per cent placed themselves at 5 or lower, but this form of Left–Right placement is often conflated with constitutional/loyalist views rather than economics, so is not used. Finally, in the third test and full model we include the question on how Orange Order members voted on the Belfast Agreement to see whether this washes out all the structural and attitudinal items. The findings are reported in Table 5.6.

As can be seen in the first test, age has some significance, with younger Orange Order members more favourably disposed to the DUP, but the effect is not as huge as might have been suspected and is washed out by the inclusion of the attitudinal and Belfast Agreement vote items. What does retain significance throughout, however, is the period in which a member joined the Orange Order. Those who joined prior to the Belfast Agreement are more likely to support the UUP relative to those who have joined since 1998, emphasising the anger felt by many members towards UUP support for that deal. The contrast is particularly great between those who joined in the 1920–66 era and the 1998-onwards joiners. Those who joined between the 1920s and 1960s were politically socialised in an era where the Orange Order was a natural extension of the UUP, a party seen as the natural organ of government. The DUP, emergent from 1971, were often seen as unwelcome upstarts, a challenge to the 'rightful' UUP–Orange mode of governance. As might be expected, denomination is

TABLE 5.6 LOGIT MODEL PREDICTING DUP SUPPORT AMONG ORANGE ORDER MEMBERS[66]

	Model 1: Demographics		Model 2: Attitudes		Model 3: Belfast Agreement vote	
	B	SE	B	SE	B	SE
Constant	4.06	1.12	4.50	1.15	1.19	1.21
Age						
Up to 34	0.55*	0.33	0.46	0.34	0.32	0.37
35–54	0.42*	0.24	0.36	0.24	0.21	0.27
55+	-	-	-	-	-	-
Joining Year						
1920–66	-1.17***	0.42	-1.03***	0.42	-1.43***	0.45
1967–97	-0.76**	0.36	-0.81**	0.36	-0.81**	0.38
1998–2007	-	-	-	-	-	-
Class						
Salariat	0.16	0.30	0.18	0.31	0.19	0.33
Self-employed	-0.26	0.24	-0.24	0.24	-0.29	0.30
Routine non-manual	-0.42	0.38	-0.35	0.39	-0.56	0.42
Skilled manual	0.29	0.28	0.25	0.28	0.12	0.31
Unskilled manual	0.42	0.30	0.34	0.31	0.20	0.33
Inactive	-	-	-	-	-	-
Education						
None/GCSE	0.06	0.28	-0.00	0.28	0.04	0.30
Secondary leaving	0.16	0.35	0.16	0.35	0.53	0.38
Tertiary	0.01	0.35	0.03	0.35	0.40	0.38
Other	-	-	-	-	-	-
Church attendance (less than weekly)	0.21	0.17	0.25	0.17	0.29	0.19
Denomination						
Presbyterian	-3.12***	1.03	-3.05***	1.03	-2.59***	1.03
Church of Ireland	-3.15***	1.03	-3.11***	1.03	-2.49**	1.04
Other	-2.93***	1.05	-2.87***	1.05	-2.25**	1.06
Free Presbyterian	-	-	-	-	-	-
Private enterprise best (disagree)			0.16	0.10	0.10	0.11
Most RCs IRA sympathisers (disagree)			-0.26***	0.07	-0.19***	0.07
Vote in 1998 GFA referendum (No)					1.75***	0.18

*p<0.10, **p<0.05, ***p<0.01

significant in that members of the Church of Ireland, Presbyterian and other Protestant churches within the Order are less likely to support the DUP than the Free Presbyterians led by Paisley from the 1950s until 2008. The negative attitudinal item of perceiving Catholics as IRA sympathisers is significant, those disagreeing with that idea being more likely to be pro-UUP. A 'No' vote in the 1998 Belfast Agreement referendum is strongly significant as a likely marker of DUP support.

Also striking are the items that are *not* significant in determining party support. Religiosity, measured by frequency of church attendance, is unimportant. No occupational class reaches significance and 'Left–Right', as defined by attitudes towards private enterprise, is unimportant. Educational attainment does not reach significance. The normal perception of unionist electoral politics as being shaped by structural factors, namely middle-class UUP support and DUP working-class support, does not particularly hold sway within the Orange Order. Here, political socialisation, influenced by the era of UUP–Orange dominance, is much more important, alongside negative perceptions of Catholic political leanings and hostility towards the Belfast Agreement. As anger over the contents of the Belfast Agreement fades, amid the successful implementation of its successor, the St Andrews Agreement, attitudes may change. As power-sharing becomes the norm, ethnic valence may dominate, in that the unionist party of choice may depend upon the perception of which appears most competent in the delivery of agreed goals.[67] However, a decade after the 1998 deal, it was clear that its requirements for power-sharing with 'terrorists', prisoner releases and policing changes still struck a raw nerve among many Orangemen.

Beyond the intra-unionist electoral contest, it might be expected that there are few Orange takers for other parties. Of course this is true in respect of Sinn Féin, with only 1.5 per cent of Orangemen (this might be considered a high figure) saying they would consider giving a lower preference vote to that party, under Northern Ireland's single transferable vote system. However, 35.2 per cent of members say they would consider giving a lower preference vote to the SDLP. Of course, such a transfer may be undertaken for tactical reasons (most obviously to assist the SDLP against Sinn Féin) and an avowed willingness to vote outside one's ethnic bloc may not translate into an actual transfer. Nonetheless the figure is broadly in line with unionist–SDLP lower preference traffic in Assembly elections and indicates that Orange electoral thinking may not be more rigid than that of their non-Orange unionist counterparts. Nearly half (47 per cent) of Orange Order members would consider giving a lower preference vote to the centrist, non-bloc aligned Alliance Party, a party which is mainly populated by Protestants, but not of the Orange variety.[68] Age is significant in respect of propensity to transfer votes to the SDLP and Alliance. Younger members of the Order are most willing to countenance such a prospect. Orange Order members are divided on whether Northern Ireland should be fully integrated into the UK party system, with elections in the region contested by the Conservative, Labour and Liberal Democrat parties. Nearly half (46.5 per cent) favour this, but 28.2 per cent oppose.

DEMANDS FOR UNIONIST UNITY: THE ORDER'S BROKERAGE ROLE

Notwithstanding the apparent mass desertion of many Orangemen from their one-time natural UUP allies to the DUP and amid often fractious intra-unionist rivalry, the ultimate aim of the Orange Order is to unite the unionist parties. As Morrow notes, the Orange Order 'represents the most historically important attempt to produce a pan-unionist front', constructed upon unstinting defence of the Protestant religion, support for the monarchy and defence of the constitutional status of Northern Ireland within the United Kingdom.[69] Although the UUP's backing for the Belfast Agreement angered many within the Order and the switch to the DUP may be permanent, the desire for the two main unionist parties to unite runs strong among the Orange brethren. Some 74 per cent of members support the idea that the DUP and UUP should unite (with 44 per cent 'strongly agreeing' with this proposition) and only 15 per cent disagree.

The severing of the Order's relationship with the UUP was accompanied by renewed calls from the Order's leadership for a united unionist political approach, preferably offered by a single unionist party. Such calls reflected the Order's continuing belief that its fusion of the Protestant religion, Ulster culture and robust politics of the constitution reflected a universal unionism, one which transcended the particular interests of intra-bloc competitive unionist parties. The Order's role had changed from being an institution embedded within the UUP's political elite. Now, it sought continued relevance within unionism in acting as an 'honest broker', attempting to unite different political factions. Calls within the 'unionist family' for unity were not new. A majority of the UUC aspired to unionist electoral pacts in the immediate post-Belfast Agreement aftermath, when the UUP could still negotiate with its main unionist rival from a position of strength.[70] In more recent times, a UUP desire for unity has appeared to be more a bid for survival.

Not everyone is as sanguine about the Order's ability to unite unionism. The Order's attempt to conflate Protestantism and British-ness places its unionism within an ethno-religious category unappealing to liberal and civic unionists. Grounding their unionism on more secular terms, liberal unionists reject the automatic conflation of particular church with constitutional position, arguing instead for the maintenance of the union on the basis of a rational contract between the governed and the governors. Civic unionists acknowledge the need to empathise with the other community and de-sectarianise unionism in favour of a more pluralist political project. Civic unionism goes be-yond the Order's ready acknowledgement of the rights of Roman Catholics to worship and extends into forms of political, cultural and religious ecumenism rejected by the Order.

In attempting to fulfil its ambitions as a harbinger of unionist unity, the Order has undertaken several roles, including representations to parties, brokerage of talks and speeches urging unionists to put aside differences. Strident calls for unity have become commonplace, a feature of speeches at Orange demonstrations. The appeal of Robert Saulters, in his final 12th of July speech as grand master, in 2010, provided a typical example:

> I have said that one big strong unionist party was the ideal situation although I recognised that would be very difficult. People have to forget past differences and work for the maintenance of the Union ... there has been one strong message coming through to me – and that is that unionism needs to think smarter and act as a coherent force against our republican enemies ... Our politi-cians should pay heed to the people who elect them and at the very least work as a co-ordinated unionist bloc ... Sinn Féin have been very clever about leaking out the view that they want to see unionist unity because it would suit their purposes. The truth – as usual – is very different from what Sinn Féin say. Republicans are extremely frightened of a strong united unionist voice.[71]

Saulters' call for unity was echoed elsewhere that year, although the difficulties of creating a single unionist political organisation were acknowledged. The deputy grand master of County Londonderry, George Duddy, claimed at his Twelfth demonstration that:

> ... the results of the recent general election, where all unionist party leaders failed to win a seat, should provide an impetus for the parties to work and cooperate more closely together. No-one should be naive enough to think unionist unity means any party will be subsumed to form a single party. There is no doubt it will be a huge challenge, considering the history between the two parties. An approach which should be considered would be for the parties to reach a consensus or form a coalition in a bid to work for the betterment of the whole unionist community ... Apathy among the unionist electorate has come about because people are fed up with the constant fighting among our politicians.[72]

Unionist unity talks followed two strands. In December 2009, inclusive discussions were brokered by the Orange Order, embracing a broad spectrum of unionist opinion, with Jim Allister of the TUV present. Allister had insisted that his party would 'occupy the traditional unionist ground so wantonly abandoned by others for the sake of office'.[73] It was clear, from focus groups conducted by the authors, that the TUV commanded sympathy from a section – albeit clearly only a minority – of the Orange Order, uneasy at the DUP's willingness to head a government with Sinn Féin, notwithstanding the dramatic change in the republicans' modus operandi.[74] The Order's sympathy with some of Allister's arguments ensured he was invited, but a rapprochement between him and former DUP colleagues, whom he regularly accused of betrayal, appeared unlikely. The concern of the UUP was that 'unity' was a codeword for a DUP takeover of their party, now operating in hugely reduced circumstances. Tom Elliott, elected UUP leader in September 2010, went public on his suspicions of Grand Lodge's support for unionist unity, arguing that the (outgoing) grand master, Robert Saulters, 'always takes the DUP side on things'.[75] Elliott, an Orangeman, urged the Order to remove itself from party politics.

The second strand of unionist unity talks was brokered early in 2010 by the then shadow secretary of state for Northern Ireland, Owen Patterson, a curiosity given that the Conservatives had at that time nailed their colours to the Ulster Unionist Party mast. The Conservatives might have found it more difficult to restore their old alliance with the UUP, defunct since the 1970s, had the Orange Order still been a presence within the UUP. Now the issue was not the sectarian connotations of any Conservative–UUP alliance, but its point-lessness. Given the plight of the UUP at the time, the decision to create the Ulster Conservative and Unionist New Force (UCUNF) was extraordinary and the election dividends reaped were predictably zero at the 2010 general election. The UUP lost its solitary remaining Westminster seat, North Down, with its MP, Lady Sylvia Hermon, resigning and successfully standing against her former party, effectively ensuring that the new–old alliance would again be buried. While the unionist unity talks covered salient issues of the period, notably the devolution of policing and justice, the issue of a single unionist party was raised, even though the Conservative–UUP alliance was an obvious barrier at the time.[76]

The term 'unionist unity' is broadly defined within the Orange Order. For several decades it was a thinly-veiled appeal to support the Ulster Unionist Party. During the crisis years of direct rule, the plea for unity in opposition to the Anglo-Irish Agreement had some resonance, but the Order's pleas were undermined by its position as part of the UUP. After the Belfast Agreement, the Order's demands for unity appeared hollow given its role in undermining Trimble's leadership of the UUP and strident opposition to the Agreement. Since the 2006 St Andrews Agreement and the return of devolved government, a more positive role for the Order has been possible, in promoting unionist unity on issues as an honest broker with no party axe to grind. This role has the support of those members who retain a suspicion of parties and politicians. A longstanding, 1955 joiner of the institution insisted:

> I think the Orange Order has nothing to do with party politics …
> it's a big enough body, there's enough men in it and it's well
> enough financed and all the rest of it to form its own opinions of
> what's happening in this province of ours without tying itself to
> any political party. I remember my father advising me as a young
> Orangeman, always watch an aspiring politician who seeks
> membership to the Orange Institution.[77]

Not all take such anti-party or anti-politician views and the Order usu-ally highlights fondly, via the *Orange Standard*, those members of the Northern Ireland Assembly who belong in its ranks. However, most members now take the view that the only possible alignment of the Orange Order is with unionism, not a particular unionist party, and that the Order can help those parties unite on the key issues facing unionism. These key issues may be less along the traditional constitutional and sectarian faultlines and more around securing maximum resources for the unionist community in Northern Ireland. As the 1955 joiner put it, 'now we're going to have to work together, and our biggest competition isn't going to necessarily be Roman Catholic versus Protestant, Irish versus UK.'[78]

CONCLUSIONS

The Belfast Agreement prompted a dramatic rapid electoral re-alignment of the unionist population, which gravitated en masse towards the DUP. There does not exist previous data on voting patterns within the Orange Order so we cannot measure the extent of possible shifts even before the Belfast Agreement. What is clear is that Orangemen deserted the UUP in droves after the Agreement, as indeed did the wider unionist population. While some of the DUP's electoral success and UUP's decline was exacerbated by middle-class Protestants abstaining, Orangemen did vote – and increasingly for the DUP.

The evidence in this chapter shows that older members of the Orange Order who joined in the distant era of UUP hegemony are those most likely to have retained affection for the party to which the Order was affiliated for a century, amid that party's electoral and political disarray. However, this grouping was overwhelmed by the tide of Orangemen prepared to desert the supposed 'natural' party of Orangeism. Year of joining the Order, age and attitudes to the Belfast Agreement, allied to continued suspicion of the political leanings of the nationalist minority, were the key determinants of political choice. Structural factors of class, occupation and education, or religious aspects, such as choice of Protestant church (overwhelming DUP support from Free Presbyterians aside) or frequency of church attendance, were not of sizeable import in respect of Orange party allegiance.

Given that the DUP's ascendancy was based upon the opprobrium displayed towards the Belfast Agreement, the question begged is what happens as that Agreement and its modifications in the St Andrews Agreement continue to consolidate? The painful medicine on prisoners and policing was swallowed by unionists, the DUP did a deal with Sinn Féin and the constitutional question, although unlikely to entirely disappear, may have diminished salience. These developments may embed ethnic valence as the determinant of the unionist vote, with Orange voters, along with other Protestants, choosing their unionist party on the basis of superior perceived competence in delivering services for the unionist community. Despite the elite-level consociation governing Northern Ireland, unionist versus nationalist zero-sum game electoral polarisation is unlikely to dissipate in the near future. The original basis of DUP electoral success was opposition to the Belfast Agreement and the belief among unionists that they would deliver a better deal for that community. The latter aspect of this appeal will continue to be important and among Orange Order members the ability of the DUP to deliver 'for Protestants' will be closely monitored. However, the party will now also be judged on its achievements in office, having been obliged to move from oppositional, sectarian stances into a party of governance. The reduced size of the Orange Order means that its capacity to deliver votes for any party is severely reduced. A more credible role is its continued brokerage position in attempting to unite unionist parties, not in terms of merger, but in respect of tactical electoral pacts or shared political strategy.

NOTES

1. D. Morrow, 'Suffering for Righteousness' Sake? Fundamentalist Protestantism and Ulster-Politics', in P. Shirlow and M. McGovern (eds), *Who are 'The People'? Unionism, Protestantism and Loyalism in Northern Ireland* (London: Pluto, 1997), p.67.
2. G. Walker, *A History of the Ulster Unionist Party: Protest, Pragmatism and Pessimism* (Manchester: Manchester University Press, 2004), pp.22–3.
3. E. Kaufmann, *The Orange Order: A Contemporary Northern Irish History* (Oxford: Oxford University Press, 2007), p.21.
4. Cited in E. Moloney, *Paisley: From Demagogue to Democrat?* (Dublin: Poolbeg, 2008), p.93.
5. Walker, *A History of the Ulster Unionist Party*, p.73.
6. P. Bew, P. Gibbon and H. Patterson, *Northern Ireland, 1921–2001: Political Forces and Social Classes* (London: Serif, 2001).
7. Walker, *A History of the Ulster Unionist Party*, p.121.
8. For essentially sectarian justifications of how the different curricula supposedly positively affected the economic fortunes of Protestants and counted against Catholics, see T. Wilson (ed.), *Ulster Under Home Rule* (Oxford: Oxford University Press, 1955); *Ulster: Conflict and Consent* (Oxford: Blackwell, 1989).
9. P. Bew, P. Gibbon and H. Patterson, *Northern Ireland, 1921–2001: Political Power and Social Classes* (London: Serif, 2001).
10. H. Patterson and E. Kaufmann, *Unionism and Orangeism in Northern Ireland Since 1945* (Manchester: Manchester University Press, 2007).
11. D. Bryan, *Orange Parades: The Politics of Ritual, Tradition and Control* (London: Pluto, 2002).
12. Kaufmann, *The Orange Order: A Contemporary Northern Irish History*, p.38; *Belfast Telegraph*, 13 June 1968.
13. 'Orange Order numbers in decline', *News Letter*, 18 January 2010.
14. Ibid.
15. Patterson and Kaufmann, *Unionism and Orangeism in Northern Ireland Since 1945*, p.123.
16. Walker, *A History of the Ulster Unionist Party*, p.180.

17. Minutes of Grand Lodge Central Committee, 5 December 1975, cited in Patterson and Kaufmann, *Unionism and Orangeism in Northern Ireland Since 1945*, p.204.
18. J. Tonge, *The New Northern Irish Politics?* (Houndmills: Palgrave Macmillan, 2005).
19. Bryan, *Orange Parades*, p.104.
20. 'David Trimble: worthy champion of unionism', *Orange Standard*, October 1995, p.11.
21. D. Hume, *The Ulster Unionist Party, 1972–92* (Lurgan: Ulster Society, 1996).
22. J. Harbinson, *The Ulster Unionist Party, 1882–1973* (Belfast: Blackstaff, 1973), p.95.
23. B. Kennaway, *The Orange Order: A Tradition Betrayed* (London: Methuen, 2006), p.39.
24. For details see Kaufmann, *The Orange Order: A Contemporary Northern Irish History*, pp.165–7.
25. Grand Lodge internal survey report 1997; Kaufmann, *The Orange Order: A Contemporary Northern Irish History*, p.194.
26. Speech at the Waterfront, Belfast, 3 September 1998. Available at: http://www.davidtrimble.org/speeches_toraiseup5.htm; accessed 6 May 2011.
27. 'NO', *Orange Standard*, May 1998, p.1.
28. Kennaway, *The Orange Order: A Tradition Betrayed*, pp.241–5.
29. 'NO', *Orange Standard*, May 1998, p.1.
30. Independent Commission on Policing (the Patten Commission), *A New Beginning: Policing in Northern Ireland* (Belfast: HMSO, 1999).
31. *Orange Standard*, July 1998, p.1.
32. Patterson and Kaufmann, *Unionism and Orangeism in Northern Ireland Since 1945*, p.231.
33. B. Hayes and I. McAllister, 'Who Voted for Peace? Public Support for the 1998 Northern Ireland Agreement', *Irish Political Studies*, 16, 1 (2001), pp.73–94.
34. J. Tonge, J. Evans, R. Jeffery and J. McAuley, 'New Order: Political Change and the Protestant Tradition in Northern Ireland', *British Journal of Politics and International Relations*, 13, 2 (2011), forthcoming.
35. BBC Northern Ireland, 'Hearts and Minds', 17 October 2002.
36. Hume, *The Ulster Unionist Party, 1972–92*, p.197.
37. A. Downs, *An Economic Theory of Democracy* (London: Harper & Row, 1957).
38. J. Evans and J. Tonge, 'Problems of Modernising an Ethno-Religious Party: The Case of the Ulster Unionist Party in Northern Ireland', *Party Politics*, 11, 3 (2005), pp.319–38.
39. Stephen King, Lecture at Manchester Metropolitan University, 23 April 2002.
40. Kennaway, *The Orange Order: A Tradition Betrayed*, p.167.
41. Conversation (Tonge) with David Trimble, UUP HQ, Glengall Street, Belfast, 15 March 2001.
42. Kennaway, *The Orange Order: A Tradition Betrayed*, p.29.
43. Kaufmann, *The Orange Order: A Contemporary Northern Irish History*, p.218.
44. Kennaway, *The Orange Order: A Tradition Betrayed*, p.29
45. E Kaufmann and H. Patterson, 'Intra-Party Support for the Good Friday Agreement in the Ulster Unionist Party', *Political Studies*, 54, (2006), pp.509–32.
46. E. Kaufmann and H. Patterson, 'Intra-Party Support for the Good Friday Agreement in the Ulster Unionist Party', *Political Studies*, 54, 3 (2006), pp.509–32.
47. *The Times*, 24 March 2000.
48. *Belfast Telegraph*, 24 March 2000.
49. *Belfast Telegraph*, 27 March 2000.
50. J. Tonge and J. Evans, 'Faultlines in Unionism: Division and Dissent within the Ulster Unionist Council', *Irish Political Studies*, 16, 1 (2001), pp.111–32.
51. Ibid., p.121.
52. A postal questionnaire survey of the UUC was conducted by Tonge in 2001. There were 292 respondents, more than one-third of the entire UUC membership.
53. For the full model, see Evans and Tonge, 'Problems of Modernising an Ethno-Religious Party'.
54. Walker, *A History of the Ulster Unionist Party*, p.253.
55. J. Blondel, *Political Parties: A Genuine Case for Discontent?* (London: Wilwood, 1978); S. Scarrow, *Parties and their Members* (Oxford: Oxford University Press, 1996).
56. *Orange Standard*, July 1998, p.6.
57. See, for example, A. Aughey, *Under Siege: Ulster Unionism and the Anglo-Irish Agreement* (Belfast: Blackstaff, 1989).
58. Kaufmann, *The Orange Order: A Contemporary Northern Irish History*, p.234.
59. J. Evans and J. Tonge, 'Unionist Party Competition and the Orange Order vote in Northern

Ireland', *Electoral Studies*, 26, 1 (2007), pp.156–67. The findings in these two paragraphs are based upon the pilot survey of the Orange Order conducted by the authors in 2004. Subsequent findings are based upon the full 2006–7 survey.

60. Ibid., p.161.
61. The 2002 figure is from the BBC Northern Ireland 'Hearts and Minds' programme, 7 October. The 2004 figure is taken from the authors' pilot survey, reported in J. McAuley and J. Tonge, '"For God and for the Crown": Contemporary Political and Social Attitudes Among Orange Order Members in Northern Ireland', *Political Psychology*, 28, 1 (2007), pp.33–52.
62. Evans and Tonge, 'Unionist Party Competition and the Orange Order Vote in Northern Ireland', p.160.
63. Ibid.
64. Tonge, Evans, Jeffery and McAuley, 'New Order: Political Change and the Protestant Tradition in Northern Ireland', p.11.
65. G. Evans and M. Duffy, 'Beyond the Sectarian Divide: The Social Bases and Political Consequences of Nationalist and Unionist Party Competition in Northern Ireland', *British Journal of Political Science*, 21, 1 (1997), pp.47–81; J. Evans and J. Tonge, 'Social Class and Party Choice in Northern Ireland's Ethnic Blocs', *West European Politics*, 32, 5 (2009), pp.1012–30.
66. Tonge, Evans, Jeffery and McAuley, 'New Order: Political Change and the Protestant Tradition in Northern Ireland', p.15.
67. See P. Mitchell, G. Evans and B. O'Leary, 'Extremist Outbidding in Ethnic Party Systems is Not Inevitable: Tribune Parties in Northern Ireland', *Political Studies*, 57, 2 (2009), pp.397–421.
68. J. Evans and J. Tonge, 'The Future of the "Radical Centre" in Northern Ireland after the Good Friday Agreement', *Political Studies*, 51, 1 (2003), pp.26–50.
69. Morrow, 'Suffering for Righteousness' Sake?', p.66.
70. The majority in the UUC in favour of electoral pacts was slight: 53.6 per cent to 46.4 per cent. The DUP was the most favoured partner (52.6 per cent) followed by the now defunct UK Unionist Party (14.9 per cent). Some 25.3 per cent of UUC members wanted pacts with 'all unionist parties'. See Tonge and Evans, 'Faultlines in Unionism', p.126.
71. 'Saulters calls for unity', *News Letter*, 13 July 2010, p.2.
72. 'The Twelfth', *News Letter*, 13 July 2010.
73. A. Rankin and G. Ganiel, 'DUP Discourses on Violence and their Impact on the Northern Ireland Peace Process', *Peace and Conflict Studies*, 15, 1 (2008), pp.115–35.
74. Unfortunately, the survey of attitudes of DUP members was completed before the TUV was launched and we are mostly reliant upon qualitative evidence here.
75. http://www.orange-order.co.uk/chronicle/?item=orange-order-urged-to-stay-out-of-politics-by-uup-orangeman; accessed 24 May 2010.
76. http://www.timesonline.co.uk/tol/news/politics/article7011727.ece; accessed 2 February 2010.
77. Interview with the authors, 3 June 2008.
78. Ibid.

CHAPTER SIX

Religion, Politics and Change

Adherence to the principles of Protestantism has provided a discourse of continuity for the Orange Order, amid considerable social and political upheaval.[1] Support for the Protestant faith and the (Protestant) crown remain cornerstones of the Orange Order's outlook. The Order describes itself as 'unashamedly Protestant, for the protection of Protestant people and property' and 'rooted in the scriptures of truth'.[2] Its ability to unite Protestants on an egalitarian basis around a common religious and cultural heritage, with a strong political derivative, has been sustained for over two centuries. Holding political power from the 1920s until the early 1970s via its presence in the UUP, the Orange Order also contained the capacity to unite Protestants across social class and denominational divides. These features ensured that the institution's prominence always exceeded that of its Catholic counterpart, the Ancient Order of Hibernians.[3] Religion is second only to family tradition as the basis of Orange Order membership according to the membership of the Order, two-thirds of whom assert that religion is more important than politics. In traditional Orange Halls, talk of party politics can still meet with disapproval, with the brethren anxious to stress religious credentials and highlight the cultural roles of the Order.

This final chapter assesses how the Order's promotion of Protestantism remains central to its mission, but has been obliged to evolve under pressure from differing forces. These include political change in which even the supposedly ethno-religious DUP has largely divested itself of religious trappings in decision-making; the onset of secularism which has displaced religious identification from its previous prominence in shaping the conduct of everyday life in Northern Ireland and the continued association of the Order with sectarian attitudes by those critical of the institution. These developments have caused considerable disquiet within the Order, prompting debates over whether adaptation is necessary, inevitable or desirable. Historically, the Orange Order offered a religious dimension to a mainly territorial argument. If that quarrel diminishes in salience and society increasingly rejects religion, this raises questions over the future significance of the Orange Order.

PROTESTANTISM AND THE ORDER

The promotion of Protestantism (often seen negatively and pessimistically as a 'defence' of Protestantism) is the raison d'être of the Order. The institution offers itself as a bulwark against secularism and atheism and fishes in a gradually shrinking pool in terms of potential religious recruits. Some 11 per cent of Northern Ireland's population responded that they had 'no religion' or did not state their religion in the 1991 census. By 2001, this figure had increased to 13.9 per cent, while the number of Protestants fell slightly from 798,136 to 767,924 and the Roman Catholic population rose from 605,639 to 678,462.[4]

Although the Orange Order is an ethnic association of Ulster Protestants, it does not highlight its cultural roles in its rules. Instead, the institution's credentials are presented in religious terms, stressing the importance of being a good and worthy Protestant.[5] Lodges begin meetings with prayers or readings from the Bible, charitable works are frequent and church parades are common. Bands participating in church parades are normally required to also attend the accompanying church service.[6] Collarettes worn on parade contain emblems designed to 'reflect a belief in religion and a way of life based on Bible Truth and obedience to the Crown as a symbol of lawful authority'.[7] Adherence to faith and religious practice are supposed to be the dominant features of an Orangeman's life. As a former chief executive of the Order put it, 'Orangeism is not about the Twelfth of July or numbers on the books, it is about living out the faith and principles every day of the year.'[8]

Although the Order's politics and parades may have dominated attention towards the institution in recent times, both are derivatives of the Protestantism which conditions outlook. Support for the union has been synonymous with the defence of Protestantism. Orange influence in legislative programmes during the 1920–72 era, such as the requirement for Bible instruction in non-Catholic schools, stems from the Order's religious outlook. Parades are intended to be visible testimonies of loyalty to faith and crown. There has been considerable debate within the Orange Order in the last few decades over whether the controversies in which it has been involved have been at the expense of its religious mission. One Orange chaplain complained that 'Politics (bordering on sectarianism) has become the master rather than the servant of the Institution ... The institution must declare itself to be either a political organisation within an interest in Christianity; or a Christian organisation with an interest in politics.'[9]

Amid much internal political change within the Order, the institution's religious rules are basic and unchanging. To join, a person must obviously be a Protestant believer in God, who must display 'a sincere love and veneration for his Heavenly Father'.[10] Although formal religious tests are not set, an individual wanting to join a local Lodge is supposed to satisfy the standards required of faith in Christ, adherence to the authority of scripture and respect for the Sabbath.[11] In some cases a letter may be requested by the Lodge from a local clergyman, but such cases appear to be rare nowadays. The standards required are set informally by local Lodges and may be nominal. Being 'Protestant in outlook', to quote one urban Orange interviewee, is normally all that is required, although some Lodges are stricter. A Ballymena District Lodge official, for example, insisted that 'we are very, very particular and we emphasise we would expect members to be at church services in connection with the Battle of the Somme, the Twelfth anniversary service and your affirmation service'.[12] The religious within the Orange Order tend to take umbrage at Protestants whose religion appears to be purely of the tribal variety. A school headmaster within the Order highlighted a particular case:

> There was a rash of 'Proud to be a Prod' t-shirts that came out when things were very bad, and I sent a number of youngsters home, told them to remove these t-shirts that were not to be worn at school, and I knew that there would be no comeback from parents, because they were aware in the village that I was deeply involved with the Orange Institution. So I was sending these youngsters home to take off 'Proud to be a Prod' t-shirts. It was not because I myself did not have a strong Protestant conviction ... there was one lad in particular, I actually told him he wasn't a Protestant, because I was aware of the fact that he had a Sunday School connection, and I knew that neither he nor his parents nor his brothers ever entered the door of a church. So I said you're not a Protestant, so you shouldn't be wearing the t-shirt. But anyway, I didn't ever have any comeback.[13]

In keeping holy the Lord's Day, it is 'deemed an offence for any member to take part in organised games, sports, entertainments and dances on a Sunday', but it is questionable whether many Orange Order members adhere to these strict regulations.[14] Despite urgings from Orange leaders to respect the traditional Sabbath, nearly two-thirds of members admit to shopping on Sunday, although only 9 per cent do so often and one-third claim to 'never' shop on this day. Among the over-55s, frequent Sunday shoppers amount to only 5 per cent, with nearly half (45 per cent) insisting that they 'never' shop on the Sabbath.

The level of religious practice among the Orange brethren appears high. Some 90 per cent claim to be practising Protestants and 60 per cent claim to attend church weekly, with a further 28 per cent attending on a monthly basis. Within the Orange Order, those aged fifty-five and over are significantly more likely to be weekly church attendees than younger members (whose local Lodge activity may exceed church duty), as Table 6.1 demonstrates.

TABLE 6.1 RELIGIOUS PRACTICE BY AGE AMONG ORANGE ORDER MEMBERS[15]

| | Age Church Attendance (%) | | | |
	Weekly	Monthly	Yearly	Never
Up to 34	47.3	34.9	14.3	3.5
35–54	54.1	10.6	10.6	1.7
55 and over	74.7	6.5	6.5	1.0

N=1,354
X2 = 75.16 (6df, p<0.001)

Although the Orange Order initially only recruited Church of Ireland members, the admission of Presbyterians from 1834 onwards broadened the movement and fitted better with Protestant contentions that the Bible is more important than a particular church. The widening was also a response to the growth of Presbyterianism, whose adherents had moved on from support for the United Irishmen at the end of the eighteenth century and overcome their initial disapproval of Orangeism as too extreme, to unite with other Protestants in opposition to home rule.[16] The fusion of Anglican descendants of English settlers and Presbyterian descendants of Scottish settlers meant that Orangeism became the definitive representative of Protestant sentiment. Indeed the Order expanded quickly beyond its Episcopalian origins, appealing to the growing Presbyterian working class in industrialised Belfast and its

surrounds in Antrim and Down. The Order also overcame the initial
scepticism of radical Presbyterians towards the Order's links to the
Conservatives and the 'High' Church of Ireland. The Order's appeal
to a radical egalitarian tradition has been based upon the claim that the
republican ideals of 'liberty, equality and fraternity stand at the heart of
ethical Orangeism', but are fused with obedience to the Protestant
monarchy.[17] Today, Presbyterians form almost half of the Orange
Order's current membership, as indicated in Table 6.2, although the
number of Presbyterian clerics remained low until shortly before the
Second World War and has tailed off in recent years.[18] The proportions
for each denomination are close to those among the wider Protestant
population, with Presbyterians slightly overrepresented and Free
Presbyterians more substantially present than might be expected, given
past rivalries. Orangeism has been described as the 'glue' which bonds
different Protestant groupings.[19]

TABLE 6.2 PROTESTANT DENOMINATIONS IN NORTHERN IRELAND
AND IN THE ORANGE ORDER MEMBERS, 2007[20]

Denomination	As % of the Protestant population	As % of the Orange Order
Presbyterian	45.4	49.3
Church of Ireland	33.6	34.2
Methodist	7.7	6.5
Free Presbyterian	1.5	4.4
Other	11.8	5.6

Clergy within the Orange Order are required to 'discourage contro-
versy among Orangemen on any point of difference among or within
the denominations'.[21] There are no significant differences in the level
of religious observation across the Protestant denominations, but there
are sharp theological differences between liberals and fundamentalists
and between ecumenics and strong opponents of 'Romeward drift'.
Many within the Orange Order are unaware or uninterested in these
divisions. Indeed, it has been claimed that 'many within the institution
today do not have any credible Church connection [and] many do
not have any, even a nominal, membership of any Church'.[22] Equally,
however, it is clear that many Orange Order members are regular
churchgoers. While time series data does not exist to track changes, it
is possible that the reduced numbers in the Order, with membership

only at just over one-third of the figure of the late 1960s, contain within their ranks a higher proportion of committed members. After all, there are no pecuniary or political benefits to modern membership.

A majority of these members (58 per cent) see the relationship between their church and the Orange Order as good, with only a small minority viewing it as unsatisfactory. A survey in the late 1980s found that 12 per cent of clergy in Northern Ireland belonged to the Orange Order.[23] However, the accounts of Kennaway and Kaufmann both suggest a haemorrhaging of clerical membership in recent decades.[24] Elsewhere, in the Orange pockets found in Britain, there have been some tensions between the main Protestant church and the Order. In Liverpool, the Order found itself barred for a time from holding an annual service in the city's Anglican Cathedral.[25] Such friction has been less evident in Northern Ireland, but has existed since the unease expressed by some Church of Ireland clergy over the use of their churches for Orange services at the height of the Drumcree church parade dispute during the 1990s.[26] During that period, the head of the Church of Ireland, Dr Robin Eames, demanded that the Orange Order adhere to three principles of good behaviour, encompassing the sanctity of worship, obedience to the law and respect for church property.[27]

The declining popularity of the Orange Order in recent decades has led to some Church of Ireland clergy engaging in a process of 'progressive disengagement' from Orange associations, amid a desire for a new relationship due to 'profound difficulties with the Orange Order that must not be disguised or ignored'.[28] To the anger of the Order in Northern Ireland, the Church of Ireland archbishop of Dublin, the Reverend John O'Neill, claimed that his church had been 'compromised very seriously' by association with the Order.[29] Difficulties with the Orange Order among Protestant clergy were not doctrinal. As even a key Church of Ireland advocate of a more distant relationship with the Order conceded, 'the doctrinal basis for the Orange Order is orthodox Reformed Christian teaching. In the essentials of doctrine there seems to be no case to make for a relationship to be inappropriate.'[30] The main problem concerned the association of the Orange Order with sectarianism made by critics, with the Church of Ireland increasingly concerned to examine this issue at parish (where the flying of Orange flags was discouraged) and diocesan levels. There have also been political difficulties. Of the denominations to which most Orange Order members belong, only the Free Presbyterian Church clearly opposed the Belfast Agreement and Orangeism has thus assumed a greater distinctiveness as a religious-political entity.

While members of all denominations and of various unionist political hues are welcome within the Order, there have been tensions among Protestants. Although the Independent Orange Order was formed in 1903 partly due to working-class suspicions of upper-class unionism, that organisation was also created because the unionist and Orange Order leadership was viewed as 'insufficiently anti-Catholic' by the leader of the independents, Thomas Sloan, who was dismissed from the main Order.[31] Kaufmann has highlighted the tensions between rebel unionists, drawn particularly from the evangelical or Presbyterian traditions and whose Protestantism is a form of dissent, but also including less religious working-class elements and loyal or traditional unionism, more associated with the established Church of Ireland.[32] The former type of Orange unionist tends to be more militant and was less deferential to the Grand Lodge Orange leadership, before effectively assuming those leadership roles in modern times, whereas the Church of Ireland traditionalist Orangeman, a diminishing breed, tended to be more supportive of the 'Big House' patrician UUP and Orange leaderships when the two were smoothly integrated. 'High' versus 'Low' Church orientation contributed to the existence of two distinct traditions within the Orange Order.[33] Kaufmann's analysis is indeed persuasive in explaining intra-Orange friction, and the existence of a 'rebel unionist' tradition cannot be disputed. However, since the Belfast Agreement, the key faultlines within the Orange Order have been based around political socialisation, age and period in which the Order was joined (see Chapter 5). The old Establishment/High Church/Anglican versus radical Presbyterian are not politically significant markers among Orange Order members.

Hardcore fundamentalists and born-again Christians have at times also been viewed with suspicion by the Orange Order, a wariness reciprocated by those who see the Order as too culturally oriented and insufficiently religious. The Free Presbyterian Church was not officially recognised as a Protestant denomination by Grand Lodge until 1998, meaning it was barred from holding events in Orange Halls. Its founder (in 1951) and leader until 2008, Ian Paisley, remained outside the Orange Order for much of this period, fusing his brand of Protestantism with his militant political vehicle, the DUP, which he led from 1971 until 2008. Paisley had risen to become a district chaplain within the Order by the end of the 1940s, a position which normally led to later election to one of the County Grand Lodges. However, the refusal of the Orange Order to accept Free Presbyterians as chaplains to Lodges (a member of clergy would normally become chaplain of his local Lodge) until the 1990s led to some Free Presbyterians preferring membership of the Apprentice Boys of Derry.[34]

Marginalised, Paisley left the Orange Order in 1962 citing the Order's softening of its approach to the Church of Rome, a trend undetectable to other observers, and criticising the attendance of one of its members, the lord mayor of Belfast, at a Catholic Mass.[35] His virulent anti-Catholicism, expressed via the *Protestant Telegraph* from the mid-1960s onwards, remained too extreme for Establishment figures within the Orange Order and the criticisms by Free Presbyterian clergy of other Protestants offended many in the Order. Grand Lodge regarded his religious organisation as a sect rather than a bona fide church and were offended by comments attributed to Paisley at an Independent Orange Order rally that membership of the (Loyal) Orange Order was not compatible with being a Christian.[36]

The Protestantism commonly associated with the Orange Order is imbued with less political significance than that attributed to the fundamentalist Protestant interpretations espoused by the Free Presbyterian Church and for many years associated with Paisleyism. That fundamentalism offers a mythical interpretation of the Bible which likens the suffering of the innocent Jesus on the cross to the suffering of Ulster Protestants, but with the outcome that 'Ulster Protestants, although currently the persecuted victims, will ultimately be justified by divine retribution.'[37] Offering a political agenda trading on Protestant insecurities, Paisleyism attracted some Orange adherents from the outset, drawn by the idea of Ulster Protestants being a chosen people aided by God to resist the Babylon of the Roman Catholic Church. Paisley was effectively removed as Free Presbyterian leader by his own followers after the DUP deals with Sinn Féin in 2006–7.

ANTI-CATHOLIC OR ANTI-CATHOLIC CHURCH?

In supporting the Protestant reformation, the Order's members are required to oppose the 'false doctrines' of the Roman Catholic Church, on the basis that God 'is the only Mediator between a sinful creature and an offended Creator'.[38] Salvation is via grace alone and the roles of the Roman Catholic Church hierarchy are entirely rejected. The universal claims of the Catholic Church and doctrines such as papal infallibility, the immaculate conception and the assumption of the Virgin Mary into Heaven are seen as having no basis in scripture.

Orange Order members are required to respect scripture as the literal word of God and all that is required for the maintenance of religious faith. The Order insists that its members should 'make the Holy scriptures the rule of their faith and practice'.[39] Subscription to the Order requires an 'unambiguous rejection of the themes of the Roman Catholic Church'.[40] This requires resistance to what is seen as the growth by stealth of Roman Catholicism, conducted principally via the 'capturing' of witless moderate Protestants. Thus the *Orange Standard* insisted in June 2003 that 'the naivety of ecumenical-minded Protestants never ceases to amaze'.[41]

The Roman Catholic Church is viewed as idolatrous, with its religious images and prayers to saints, the Sacred Heart and Virgin Mary taken from wrongful traditions, while the 'false acceptance of the authority of tradition leads to departure from God'.[42] An Orangeman is required to 'strenuously oppose the fatal errors and doctrines of the Church of Rome' and 'should, by all lawful means, resist the ascendancy of that church, its encroachments and the extension of its power'.[43] Whereas the Roman Catholic Church places emphasis upon baptism as a means of salvation, Protestant belief stresses the roles of repentance and personal faith. The use of the Mass as the main mode of Roman Catholic worship, incorporating a belief in transubstantiation (that the body and blood of Christ are literally present) is seen as particularly incorrect, a total departure from the teachings of the Bible. The authority of the Vatican and pope are also challenged as a departure from such teachings and the Orange Order opposed the papal visits to Britain in 1982 and 2010. The Order argued in respect of the latter visit:

> … we are not denying him his right to visit his flock, but we are denouncing his unscriptural claims and those of the Church of Rome … we deny to the Pope of Rome the title 'the vicar of Christ', which means the 'replacement for Christ'. Such a claim is totally at variance with the Biblical message that salvation is by grace alone, through faith alone, in Christ alone.[44]

Despite the Orange Order's uncompromising rejection of the mechanics of the Catholic Church, it insists upon respect for Roman Catholics. Indeed an Orangeman is required to be 'gentle and courteous to, not acting with hostility towards, his Roman Catholic neighbours, but seeking by his example and conversation to spread the Protestant faith'.[45] Members are required to respect the religious rights of others; they must be 'incapable of injuring, persecuting or upbraiding anyone on account of his religious opinion'.[46] Orange members tend to deny anti-Catholicism. Some 57 per cent agree with the proposition that the Order is 'anti-Roman Catholic Church' but 35 per cent reject this contention, despite the strident opposition to its 'false doctrines'. However, only 20 per cent of Orangemen accept the proposition that the Order is 'anti-Roman Catholic' (the individual rather than institutional charge) with 71 per cent disagreeing. Many practising Protestants within the Order dispute charges of sectarianism and stress how the institution takes seriously tolerance as one of its religious responsibilities.

The Orange Order has demonstrated its support for the religious rights of Roman Catholics. The grand master from 1996 until 2010, Robert Saulters, was abused by some loyalists for visiting Harryville Roman Catholic Church in Ballymena in 1997 to show solidarity with Mass-goers running the gauntlet of a sustained militant loyalist picket. The picket was in defence of loyalist marching 'rights' and contained some grassroots Orange Order members. The Order has also always been steadfast in its condemnation of attacks upon Roman Catholic churches and property. Respect for the rights of individual Roman Catholics is thus distinguished from rejection of the trappings of their dangerous, expansionary church and the evils of 'popery'. Only 21 per cent of Orange Order members believe that 'there is no harm in ecumenical projects', with over 60 per cent opposed, although given the stridency of the Order's rejection of Rome there may be surprise that one in five members do not mind such projects.

That the Order is associated with anti-Catholicism derives from several historical and contemporary aspects of its activities. Its main commemoration celebrates the victory in 1690 of the Protestant Prince William of Orange at the Battle of the Boyne over the Catholic King James, and the Order was founded after Protestants won the Battle of the Diamond in 1795. While Order members commonly celebrate this event as a triumph 'for civil and religious liberties ... it wasn't a battle about Protestant versus Catholic ... it was the securing and the preserving of a way of life, the constitutional democracy that we all enjoy today', the nuances of this messages are often lost.[47] Critics see the commemorations in sectarian terms, as historical triumphalism.

Sensitivities over overt displays of religious sectarianism have grown. Orange parades through predominantly Catholic areas, although small in number and defended on grounds of tradition and liberty, are criticised as sectarian coat-trailing exercises. A critical account of the Order, strongly repudiated by many brethren, concluded that sectarianism was a dominant image and that:

> Its [the Orange Order's] basic problem lay, perhaps, in the glaring contradiction between what it purported to stand for and what it was actually seen to be. It claims to be based on Christian principles and on a premise of tolerance towards Catholics, although opposed to Catholic doctrine. Yet is has a well-attested reputation for bigotry, tolerance and inciting sectarian passions[48]

Applicants to the Orange Order are required to confirm that they were born to Protestant parents (although this is rarely, if ever, checked), that they were educated in the Protestant faith, that they have 'never been in any way connected with the Church of Rome' and that their wife is a Protestant or that they are unmarried.[49] As Kennaway has pointed out, this ban on marriage to a Catholic was introduced in 1863, nearly seven decades after the Order was established.[50] The sanction is taken seriously, in that approximately 200 of the 600 expulsions of Orange Order members from 1964 to 2005 were because of marriage to, or co-habitation with, a Roman Catholic, with a further 11 per cent of ejections due to attendance at Catholic religious services, making 'Catholic' offences the biggest single category of expulsion.[51] The Catholic Church's Ne Temere decree provides one Orange justification for the ban on intermarriage, the decree being offered as evidence of Catholic expansionism. Introduced in 1908 (after the Orange Order's mixed marriage prohibition), Ne Temere required a Catholic bringing up children in a Catholic–Protestant marriage to educate their children in the Roman faith. Such a requirement diminished prospects for the generational transmission of Protestantism. The Orange Order is fond of highlighting the impact of the decree (along with other forms of discrimination against Protestants) in reducing the Protestant population in the Republic of Ireland from 320,000 in 1922 to below 100,000 by 1997.[52] The Catholic Church is still seen as influential in the Irish Republic by the vast majority (over 80 per cent) of Orange brethren.

The prohibition upon mixed marriages is waning within the wider Orange movement. The Order in Canada and the US has abandoned the ban and in Scotland and on Merseyside, where mixed marriages are now common, unlike two generations ago, the rule appears to be ignored. In Northern Ireland, where mixed marriages form only 9 per cent of unions, an Orangeman taking a Catholic wife would be far more visible and vulnerable to sanction.[53] Election to the Orange Order takes place by ballot, 'where one black bean in ten shall exclude', while in the case of an applicant who has been a Roman Catholic, or married to one, permission has to be given by majority vote of 75 per cent of Grand Lodge and of the District and County Lodges respectively following election to a private Lodge.[54] Orange Order members do not relish the idea of their own offspring engaging in 'mixed' marriages. Only 6 per cent would be happy for their child to marry a Roman Catholic (the age of Orange Order members is not significant in terms of attitudes), with 81 per cent admitting that they would be unhappy, most 'strongly' so, if such an eventuality transpired. Although moderates within the institution have long argued against the ban on members attending Roman Catholic Church services, the ban remains. The prohibition has placed the Order in a difficult position, heavily attacked for antediluvian sectarian attitudes when, for example, criticisms were voiced of David Trimble, who, when still in the Order, attended the Catholic funeral of three victims of the Real IRA's Omagh bombing in 1998 in his capacity as UUP leader and met the pope during the following year. Educational segregation also persists in Northern Ireland, with Orange Order members divided on the issue. Some 31 per cent believe that the education system should be integrated, with 51 per cent disagreeing.

The Order's avowed respect for Roman Catholics has been juxtaposed with a past determination to bar them from the Ulster Unionist Party and from ministerial office in Northern Ireland.[55] Orangeism thus infused unionism with an apparent sectarianism which bemused and baffled the main allies of the Ulster Unionist Party, the Conservative Party, even if Conservative Party members rarely ventured onto the ground of open criticism. Opposition to Catholics joining the UUP during the 1921–72 era of devolved government appeared nakedly sectarian. Negative political images of Catholics persist; almost two-thirds of Orange Order members agreed with the contention that 'most Roman Catholics are IRA sympathisers'. The belief of the overwhelming majority (88 per cent) of Orange Order members is that it is Protestants who are discriminated against in Northern Ireland today. The Orange Order complains of the 'disparity in allocation of resources between the Protestant and Roman Catholic communities over the past generation'.[56]

The context in Northern Ireland has also changed, to the disadvantage of the Order's promotion of Protestantism. A religious aspect to unionism has not disappeared, but it has been seen increasingly as anachronistic. Many unionists do not see the need for unionism to be inextricably linked to the Protestant religion and prefer secular civic or liberal forms.[57] In contrast, the Orange Order sees Protestantism as a defining characteristic of Britishness, one linking the people of Northern Ireland with their 'parent state' via a shared faith and Protestant crown, regardless of the religious indifference of many in Britain.[58] Therein lies the difficulty for the Order. Religious zealotry, or fundamentalist Protestantism, is internally generated and makes the Orange Order seem less 'normally' British to many other British citizens, yet is still seen by Orange Protestants as an essential component of Ulster-British identity and an integral part of resistance to incorporation within a Catholic Ireland. The question begged is whether Protestantism will remain as a bond across unionism's divides, given the diminished nature of the current constitutional 'conflict'. The Order can legitimately highlight the importance of Protestantism to unionist identity throughout decades (the 1920s until the late 1960s) when Northern Ireland was relatively peaceful, but Christian religious faith did not face severe challenges during that era.

Moreover, the interchangeability of Protestantism, unionism and Britishness remains a given, with the Protestant monarchy the unifying institution uniting these strands. An Orangeman is required to be 'faithful and bear true allegiance to Her Majesty Queen Elizabeth II, and to her Protestant successors'.[59] Irish nationalism and republicanism are regarded as the 'traditional enemies of Protestantism and unionism', regardless of the claim of republicans to distinguish the two, i.e. desire the end of unionism but accommodate 'Catholic, Protestant and dissenter' within new constitutional structures. The frequent attacks on Orange Halls are seen as evidence of continuing ethno-religious cleansing of Protestant unionists by republicans, while restrictions on Orange parades are viewed as anti-Protestant. Indeed antipathy towards such restrictions unites most of the Order's members, 86 per cent of whom support the abolition of the Parades Commission. Support for the Orange Order's right to march through nationalist areas is extensive, although not overwhelming, backed by 58 per cent of members with 19 per cent opposed and 23 per cent undecided.

THE MORAL MAZE: INCLUSIVE GOVERNMENT WITH SINN FÉIN

As shown in the previous chapter, a substantial majority of Orange Order members were much more comfortable supporting the DUP following the Belfast Agreement rather than maintaining loyalty to the pro-Agreement UUP. After 2007, when the DUP did a deal with Sinn Féin, there were qualms within the Orange Order, but these were less noisy than the 1998–2006 version. The motivations for party re-alignment of ordinary members and many within Grand Lodge were not merely political; the brethren were also being told that the deal was morally unacceptable, one that Protestants could not support in good conscience. The moral aspect of Orangeism had always led to Grand Lodge urging support for the law and rejection of paramilitarism, with Orange Order members required to eschew loyalist armed groups. The Order had offered qualified support for Vanguard during the 1970s, an organisation which could be described as 'quasi-constitutional' given its links to loyalist paramilitaries and whose leader, William Craig, had suggested that the enemy might be liquidated. However, even this tentative (and largely irrelevant) backing from the Orange Order met with disquiet among the more religiously oriented within the institution and for the remainder of the duration of the conflict the Orange leadership distanced itself from armed militant loyalism, urging support for the 'legitimate' security forces. Indeed it is claimed that 'the Orange Order kept a lid on what could have been a much more horrific situation because they offered people an alternative way to deal with matters that wasn't going out and shooting people'.[60]

From 1998 onwards, the Orange Order found unionist political representatives, including the leadership of the party of which it was a part, sat in government with largely unapologetic republican terrorists. Although lax in disciplining members or Lodges displaying support for loyalist paramilitaries, Grand Lodge had supported the rule of law for decades and, in the early years of the Troubles, its members had formed a significant element of the local police force. A total of 297 members of the Orange Order were killed during the 1970–97 phase of conflict, of whom 157 were serving in the security forces.[61] Yet the Order's members were eschewed by the security forces once proudly served. The final chief constable of the RUC, Ronnie Flanagan, indicated he preferred that his officers did not join such an organisation, even though 13 per cent of RUC officers killed had belonged to the Order.[62] The Patten Commission which created the PSNI demanded serving

Orange Order members be 'registered'.[63] The requirement irritated the Order, a Lurgan member arguing that:

> ... you could be a member of Glasgow Rangers Supporters Club and they could be more hardline than the Orange Order, so it's where do you draw the line? I don't think any Orange Order members did anything wrong being members of the RUC, I don't think there was any conflict there.[64]

A political deal which not only rehabilitated the perpetrators of the killings of Orange Order members, security force members and civilians but placed several in government was untenable for Orangemen, who, given the absence of an IRA apology for its armed campaign, were not required to utilise Christian principles of forgiveness (although these were unlikely to be evident regardless of whether an apology materialised). The prime minister, Tony Blair, recognised the Order as still of sufficient standing and significance among ordinary Protestants to be worth meeting in an attempt to sell the Belfast Agreement. He found his audience unreceptive, being informed that the deal was prisoner driven and unacceptable from a 'moral/Christian viewpoint'.[65] The Order emphasised this offence far more than its political objections. The pressure on Orangemen to oppose the Belfast Agreement as a deal at odds with the tenets of their Protestant faith did not come exclusively from Grand Lodge, but was also evident beyond the institution. At an Independent Orange Order Twelfth rally in July 2001, Paisley lambasted moderate Orangemen for the way they had 'cheered after they had defeated their brother-Orangemen and fellow Protestants by joining ranks with the representatives of the IRA murderers thus succeeding in that Iscariot treachery' and insisted that 'a return to the basic principles of Orangeism is imperative'.[66]

When the DUP itself became pro-Agreement – that Agreement being the St Andrews 'successor' to the Belfast deal over eight years earlier – the question begged was whether the new conditions that pertained – a vanished IRA and Sinn Féin support for policing – meant that the revised package was morally acceptable. Not all within the Order backed the new deal, despite the obvious changes that had occurred within mainstream republicanism. The Provisional IRA had vanished but still not repented. The IRA did apologise for the killing of non-combatants but not those of members of the security services and its 'closing statement' in 2005 insisted that the armed campaign had been legitimate.

The Grand Lodge chaplain, the Reverend Steven Dickinson, declared a change in allegiance to the anti-Belfast and anti-St Andrews Agreement Traditional Unionist Voice (TUV). Dickinson insisted that 'many within the Christian community and the Orange family have been disgusted with the delivery of IRA/Sinn Féin into Government'.[67] The TUV appealed to Orangemen now disgruntled with their still-novel DUP bedfellows to switch, arguing that what was morally wrong could not be politically right. Certainly there was considerable disquiet among the Orange brethren over the DUP–Sinn Féin deals in 2006 and 2007. A County Lodge official described his reaction:

> Personally yes, it was surprise, shock and stunned. For the leadership of the DUP to have preached what they did preach for the years they preached, and actually got, there was people probably done time for what that man preached, and then to backtrack, you know, either he [Paisley] was, he was right for forty years and wrong for one year, or maybe not ... At one stage, it was, they would never sit down with terrorists in government, never, never, never. Them's the magic words. And now it's disappeared.[68]

The Orange Order perceived the IRA's campaign as a sectarian onslaught upon Protestants and struggled to adjust to the post-1998 republican modus operandi. In particular, border Protestants, who still saw the Orange Order as an important organisation and where membership held up relative to urban areas, perceived the IRA's actions as a form of ethnic cleansing, a term also applied to the 'exodus of some 15,000 Protestants from the west bank of Londonderry'.[69] Orangemen tended not to identify the remarkable shifts in republicanism that had occurred. Moreover, there was a tendency to make religious connections to republican groupings which had little interest in Catholicism. Grand Master Saulters spoke of 'these fancy names of dissident, real, éirígí, they are all the Roman Catholic IRA and let us not forget that'.[70] The impression conveyed was that there remained a religious dimension to a conflict, even though the Catholicism, if it existed, of dissident republicans was at most tangential. The 262 attacks upon Orange Halls during the Troubles, incidents which have not subsequently abated in volume, add to the sense of siege (and are also expensive in terms of insurance costs).[71]

MODERNISATION AND ORANGEFEST VERSUS ORANGE REFORMATION

While it retains thousands of members and still produces one of the largest demonstrations anywhere in Europe each year on the Twelfth, the Orange Order has struggled for relevance as it operates in reduced circumstances. This has sharpened longstanding debates over the relative weightings of the Order's religious, political, cultural and social missions and its public representation. Modernisers within the Orange Order are content to see some changes to the institution's modus operandi. This grouping believes in the need to broaden Orangeism's appeal, which can most obviously be achieved by capitalising on the Order's biggest day, the 12th of July. Although the bulk of participants are not members, the Order retains the capacity to mobilise tens of thousands of Protestants each Twelfth. Encouraged by the Northern Ireland Tourist Board and some political leaders, the institution has been encouraged to supposedly 'de-sectarianise' the event by transforming it into a less contentious Orangefest, a wide-ranging, unthreatening cultural festival, rather than one grounded predominantly in strident assertions of Protestantism.

The Twelfth and other Orange parades are often dismissed by critics more as forms of tribalism than a religious event, most visibly expressed via the proliferation of 'kick the pope' bands. Although the Order tries to exert some control over such bands in asserting standards of dress and conduct, they are beyond the full remit of the Order. These bands 'offer greater excitement to young people than does the Order itself' in terms of fusing ethnic solidarity, sense of belonging, defence of territory and music, but their religious component may be minimal.[72] The Orange Order is often associated with the activities of 'Orange bands', but senior Order officials tend not to like the term, as a Down County Lodge official explained:

> Band parades are different, but sometimes get mixed up with the Orange Order. You know we were at a meeting one day and the police said the Orange Bands, well excuse me, there's very few Orange Bands, they're all bands on their own. So a lot of the trouble maybe comes from what some of the Nationalist community were seeing as paramilitary displays by bands ... there's been more control in that now and these paramilitary emblems have started to disappear and the Orange Order has, to me, clamped down on hiring these bands.[73]

While there is a tendency to associate 'rough' parading with modern times, Bryan's account of Orange marches makes clear that trouble, excessive drink and concern over parading from more spiritual members of the institution were common in the nineteenth century, but with one difference being the considerable impact of rabble-rousing Orange clerics.[74] Older Order members tend to recall a 'golden age' when Catholics watched Orange parades during the 1950s and 1960s, although the evidence of that period suggests considerable variation in Catholic attitudes according to locality.

The difficulty in reform is that consensus over what the Twelfth constitutes is not always evident. It is part-religious, part-constitutional (a victory for civil liberties), part-festival/holiday, part-traditional gathering of the clans and part-political (an opportunity for commentary on contemporary events). Those desirous of alterations to the Twelfth may overestimate the writ of Grand Lodge to impose change. The Orange Order's structure is egalitarian, with private, District and County Lodges all enjoying considerable autonomy. Changes to the day have been evolutionary and developed at grass-roots level, rather than via central decree.

Assertions of Protestantism remain an aspect of the modern Twelfth, evidenced by vigorous, sometimes uncompromising, religious resolutions affirming the faith, passed by clerics within the Order.[75] The faith resolutions do not differ greatly annually, urging the leading of 'Christ-centred and Bible-based' lives and reminding the brethren that salvation is 'by Grace alone, through faith alone, in Christ alone'.[76] Removal of such affirmations might alienate the Orange core. Moreover, in the pursuit of 'inclusivity', there is a risk that the religious aspect of the event is conflated with religious sectarianism. The concept of 'de-sectarianising' is highly problematic, a difficulty applicable more broadly to Northern Ireland, where the term 'sectarian' is too readily and glibly used to label parties, political identities or communities. Professions of religious faith and constitutional preferences are not intrinsically sectarian; the divide between the two communities in terms of religious identification and political outlook may be strong, but that amounts to communal difference, not sectarianism.

It is unlikely that nationalists, who have used the term 'bigotfest', will accept the concept of Orangefest as a shared event. Changes which occur may not represent inter-communal thawing. Effigies of the pope may be much less commonly burned at the top of 'Eleventh Night' bonfires these days, but the pope has often been replaced by an Irish tricolour, a move hardly designed to endear the occasion to the nationalist community. However, a determined re-branding of the main Orange event was undertaken in the late 2000s, juxtaposed with serious rioting in north Belfast. The Northern Ireland Tourist Board, which has highlighted a sharp increase in the number of visitors to the province for the Twelfth, described the Orange parade as 'one of Europe's largest cultural festivals with music, marching and street pageantry', undertaken in a 'carnival atmosphere', without explaining the religious significance of the event which is the ultimate supposed reason for Orange parades.[77] A substantial proportion, one-third, according to Jarman, of banners carried at Orange parades, are exclusively religious, with a large number of others dedicated to aspects of Protestant history.[78] The Order views parades as testimonies to the importance of the Bible, scripture and Protestant faith, with banners the visible manifestation of this witness. The faith, loyalty and state resolutions are what infuses the Twelfth with meaning for the committed within the Orange Institution.

The Orange Order argues that it cannot ultimately be responsible for the large numbers of 'hangers-on' who view the main Orange marching day as an excuse for drunkenness and sectarianism and whose Protestantism is of the purely notional, tribal variety. Drunkenness is not newly associated with Orange parades; rougher elements, the worse for drink, were in evidence in the 1800s and the Order banned drinking in the field at Twelfth demonstrations, a prohibition which remains in force, with drinking banned among members when they are on parade.[79] According to the rules of the Orange Institution, Lodges should not meet in premises licensed for the sale of alcohol. More commonly, Lodges (but not temperance Lodges) have social clubs attached to their premises or bars within their halls, but meet in a room where alcohol is not sold, with the taking of drink forbidden during a Lodge meeting (but permitted afterwards). Excessive drinking associated with some Lodges has been the subject of internal disquiet.[80] Financially, it would be disadvantageous for many Lodges to not facilitate other gatherings involving alcohol, jeopardising the Orange Hall's role as a broader community social centre.

The Orange Reformation group has provided the most strident demands that the Orange Order 'return' to more robust Protestant positions. It has offered numerous criticisms of the supposed dilution of Protestant principles by the Orange leadership and condemned Orange 'reach-out' events, such as a joint procession with the Ancient

Order of Hibernians in the Irish Republic in 2010. Orange Reformation aims to 'restore the centrality of the Protestant faith, form a circle of like-minded brethren within the Orange Institution, offer a positive alternative to the weakening of the Protestant basis and image of Orangeism, retain the traditional "Twelfth" demonstration and nurture a strong, biblical, Protestant basis to face the challenges of the day in the Institution and society'.[81]

While some of these demands lack precision, the Orange Reformation group has formed a significant part of the ongoing debate over the nature of the Twelfth processions. The Reformationists fervently oppose the religious dilution of the event, insisting:

> The 12th July as a demonstration of our Protestant Faith and Heritage is under attack from within as well as without. Orangefest will destroy the traditional 12th demonstrations as it seeks to turn them into tourist attractions or an economic driver!
>
> The Twelfth July celebrations ought to be the preserve of the Orange Institution alone and ought to be outside, separate and independent of any festival that may be organised before or after the 12th itself.
>
> It's time for the Orange Order to take back full responsibility and control of the 12th July!
>
> It's time for the Orange Order to get back to the traditional 12th! [82]

Opinion among the Orange brethren appears divided on whether the religious proceedings on the Twelfth of July platforms are appropriate. While 21 per cent claimed that the platforms attracted considerable numbers, 28 per cent agreed that they 'attract older people only' and 40 per cent declared that the passing of religious resolutions, along with those of loyalty and state, on platforms 'don't attract many people in proportion to the numbers parading'. Only 10 per cent offered the view that proceedings were 'very appropriate and religious'. Just over one-quarter claimed to always participate in the platform proceedings, a similar figure to those admitting they never attended such events, while 47 per cent claimed occasional participation. In terms of extra activities on the Twelfth, 43 per cent of Orange Order members desired a greater variety of stalls in the field and 20 per cent wanted 'more children's entertainment'. Only 15 per cent of members felt that 'things are fine as they are', suggesting a substantial majority in favour of a broadening of the occasion. One Orange official in Lurgan commented:

I think we're in a different era now. I think you can still have that aspect of it but I think increasingly if it's going to get back to a family day, it has to be attractive to families and I think it should be more about a carnival that everybody, Protestant and Catholic alike, can come and enjoy and watch ... there could be other things that can be dispersed within the parade that can be enjoyed by everybody.[83]

A Grand Lodge official felt that the promotion of Orangefest would help the Order end misconceptions of the organisation and highlighted the possibilities of outreach missions hitherto difficult for the Order to undertake:

Through the Orangefest, I went to a Roman Catholic School, and along with David Scott, the Education Officer, I addressed sixth-formers. It was Corpus Christi on the Falls Road and we answered questions that were put to us. Orangefest is not just about celebrating the Twelfth, it's about promoting the Orange culture throughout the whole year, 365 days.[84]

Yet not all want change and a small number of Lodges have refused to participate in aspects of Orangefest – 'we refused to have a float,' said one proud official.[85] There remains a fear that 'while there is a place for Orangefest ... you need to be careful that you don't compromise your principles or lose the ethos, what you're there to do.'[86] Another member, while supportive of change and supporting the 'sensible aim' of Orangefest, said:

We have to remember we have a certain basic understanding of what the Orange Institution is and what it's about. We can't lose that, simply to be cavorting about, trying to entertain the public. We're not here to entertain the public, at least I'm not.[87]

A District Lodge member from Antrim insisted:

There is a place for all this Orangefest and all that, but you need to be careful that you don't compromise your principles or lose the, the ethos, what you're there to do. You still need to have your platform proceedings if you want to celebrate your culture.[88]

What does unite many within the Order is hostility to the television coverage of the Twelfth. Despite mildly favourable coverage of the event in a dedicated hour-long live programme and a half-hour highlights programme, the BBC's coverage is viewed as unsatisfactory by almost three-quarters of Orangemen, with only 10 per cent describing it as good or excellent. This negative rating may accrue from the tendency of news bulletins to focus on contentious parades, rather than the dedicated programmes, which tend to show the day in a positive fashion.

Orange Reformation has not been the only group to challenge Grand Lodge. The Spirit of Drumcree group formed in the mid-1990s and prominent until its leaders were expelled a few years later demanded an uncompromising approach, based on unfettered rights, to the Drumcree church parade and other Orange marches. Even though many Orange Order members viewed the group as overly divisive, most were also angered by the restrictions on the Drumcree parade. As one member put it, 'No-one should have the right to tell me what way I'll go to church, what I wear when I go to church and what to wear when I come back from church. No-one has that right and that has been forced on us.'[89] Another member, a district secretary from an area close to Portadown, the site of the dispute, lamented:

> That parade may have died a death itself because it was a church parade. Historically the church parades are not very well supported by Orangemen and the one in Portadown was like any other, it was just dwindling away. It was early on a Sunday morning you know, it was quite a long walk, there would have been maybe a couple of hundred going to it and when they first said they would stop it that's where it all mushroomed from.[90]

Despite this anger, the Spirit of Drumcree group was not fully backed by Orange Order members because its activities called into question the commitment to obedience to the law supposedly integral to Orangeism. Rather, the Spirit of Drumcree group contained many who viewed the Orange Order as an 'ethnic self-defence association' for Protestants, rather than an austere and devout religious entity.[91] Even within this rebel group, however, there were different strands, ranging from Spirit of Drumcree's 'leader', Joel Patton, expelled from the Order in 1998 following violence at an Orange religious event, who viewed himself as a Protestant of good standing, to the ultra-rebel David Dowey, who dismissed the idea of the Orange Order being a religious institution and acknowledged that he was a 'sectarian bigot'.[92]

Controversies over parades and Orangefest are the most visible manifestations of the difficulties confronting the Orange Order in developing twin strategies of continuity and adaptation. In walking a tightrope between the traditionalism of some of its brethren and the modernisation demanded by 'outsiders', the Orange Order is required to be cognisant of societal changes. Northern Ireland has not been immune from secularist trends affecting Christian western democracies and the Orange Order has faced an uphill struggle in promoting its traditional, austere version of Protestantism, against a backdrop of social change (ranging from civil partnerships to Sunday opening), indifference or even hostility. The Order's members hold authoritarian stances regardless of their likelihood of realisation, with 71 per cent still supportive of the death penalty and only 13 per cent believing that rehabilitation is preferable to punishment. Some moral issues divide the Orange Order. One-third of members believe that abortion should be legalised in Northern Ireland, but two-fifths oppose the idea. Grand Lodge strongly opposes the extension of the 1967 Abortion Act, liberalising abortion laws elsewhere in the United Kingdom, to Northern Ireland.[93] Amid strong overall support for law and order, 90 per cent of Orange Order members believe that the law should always be obeyed, although one-fifth disagree that loyalist violence was never justifiable.

CONCLUSIONS

There are three particularly important issues concerning the Orange Order and religion. The first challenge is how to recruit more members of substance from a pool where Protestantism is often nominal and to encourage recruits to make a worthwhile contribution to the advancement of religious belief and support for the Reformed tradition. Another, extraordinarily difficult, issue is how to remove the perceptions of critics who perceive the Orange Order as predominantly an anti-Catholic organisation, rather than view it as a benign, charitable, Christian and cultural institution which merely opposes doctrinal aspects of the Roman Catholic Church. The third issue is how to modernise the institution and develop its main parades, in particular those on the Twelfth. The old adage was that Lodge meetings traditionally involved 'spending eleven months deciding what you were going to have for your tea on the Twelfth of July'.[94] Now the grassroots has a potentially bigger role in shaping what occurs on the Twelfth as a broader signifier of what the Orange Order is about. Northern Ireland's tourist and commercial concerns and some Orange modernisers favour the development of a popular cultural festival with a more inclusive, unthreatening ethos, but the Order is anxious for the event not to lose the religious significance which some members hold dear.

The Orange Order has gone some way to modernising its traditions in recent years and worked hard to improve its (previously absent) public relations, not without risk. Modernisation risks aggravating traditionalists, while failing to satisfy those nationalists implacably opposed to Orange parades. Catholics may struggle to be convinced that celebrations of ancient Protestant victories are merely expressions of civil and religious liberty. Traditionalists within the Orange Order are not all drawn from the same constituency. Some wish to return the Orange Order to a 'purer' religious role. As one official put it, he would 'rather see a smaller Orange Institution than see it abandon the very high principles upon which it was founded'.[95] Other traditionalists have different concerns, being determined to resist the perceived erosion of Orange parading rights.

The size of the tasks of image 'de-sectarianisation' and attracting Catholic acceptance remains considerable. The issue of inter-communal relationships with Catholics comes to a head during the marching season. A 2010 survey indicated that only 0.2 per cent of Catholics believed that the Orange Order should be permitted to parade without restriction, compared to 49 per cent of Protestants. A further 28 per cent of Catholics believed the Order should be allowed to march only if prior agreement has been reached with local residents (an option supported by 44 per cent of Protestants) but a large majority, 72 per cent of Catholics, believed that Orange parades should simply not be allowed to proceed through nationalist areas, compared to only 8 per cent of Protestants.[96]

Defence of the Protestant faith remains at the core of Orangeism, even if its other political, social and cultural roles are inextricably linked. The chief threat to Protestantism may be indifference rather than hostility, Irish republicanism or Catholicism. While Northern Ireland continues to offer something of a bulwark against the tides of secularism and atheism, this cannot be guaranteed in perpetuity. It is difficult for the Orange Order to 'sell' the idea of a virtuous and holy lifestyle to a population with a wider range of interests and temptations than existed in the heyday of the Orange state. Moreover, the proletarianisation of the Order and growing perception of the institution as mainly a working-class ethnic and cultural loyalist association has perhaps lessened its religious role. Protestantism in Northern Ireland has become increasingly an ethnic badge rather than a genuinely religious aspect of daily life.

The Orange Order has long appropriated a political role, but this is one at the margins of contemporary politics, notwithstanding its significant brokerage role within unionism. Orangeism can survive without party (severance of the UUP link has not been harmful thus far) and just possibly even the union – the Order still has members in the Irish Republic and elsewhere – but it is surely redundant without a significant religious role, one which at least interests ordinary Protestants in aspects of their faith. Within the Order, there has been an ongoing debate over the claimed rise of the 'political Protestant' at the expense of the 'religious Protestant', amid claims that the institution has diminished as a religious organisation.[97] The challenge for the remainder of the twenty-first century for the Orange Order will be to make either type of membership relevant.

NOTES

1. See J. McAuley and J. Tonge, '"Faith, Crown and State": Contemporary Discourses within the Orange Order in Northern Ireland', *Peace and Conflict Studies*, 15, 1 (2008), pp.136–55.
2. M. Smyth, 'Foreword', in B. Kennedy (ed.), *Steadfast for Faith and Freedom: 200 Years of Orangeism* (Belfast: Grand Lodge, 1995), p.2.
3. Graham Walker argues however that 'insufficient attention' has been paid to the Ancient Order of Hibernians as it was briefly a significant force for Irish nationalism at the time of the home rule crisis, with 125,000 members in 1915. G. Walker, *A History of the Ulster Unionist Party: Protest, Pragmatism and Pessimism* (Manchester: Manchester University Press, 2004), p.32.
4. http://www.nisranew.nisra.gov.uk/Census/censusstatistics/1991/pdf/Religionandgen derbyarea.pdf; http://www.nisranew.nisra.gov.uk/census/Censusstatistics/1991/1991popdetails. htmlhttp://www.nisranew.nisra.gov.uk/Census2001Output/KeyStatistics/keystats.html#d sitrict council level; all accessed 10 December 2010.
5. E. Kaufmann, *The Orange Order: A Contemporary Northern Irish History* (Oxford: Oxford University Press, 2007), pp.3–4; http://www.orange-order.co.uk/chronicle/?item=qualifications-of-an-orangeman; accessed 11 January 2011.
6. D. Bryan, T. Fraser and S. Dunn, *Political Rituals: Loyalist Parades in Portadown* (Coleraine: Centre for the Study of Conflict, University of Ulster, 1995).
7. G. Montgomery and J. Whitten, *The Order on Parade* (Belfast: Grand Lodge, 1995), p.8.
8. G. Patton, 'The Orange Institution: The Future', in Kennedy (ed.), *Steadfast for Faith and Freedom*, p.13.
9. Reverend Dennis Bannerman, cited in the *News Letter*, 13 November 1998.
10. Grand Orange Lodge of Ireland, *What is the Orange Order?* (Belfast: Grand Lodge, 1995), p.2.
11. J. McAuley and J. Tonge, '"For God and for the Crown": Contemporary Political and Social Attitudes Among Orange Order Members in Northern Ireland', *Political Psychology*, 28, 1 (2007), pp.33–52.
12. Interview with the authors, 5 June 2008.
13. Ibid., 7 May 2008.

14. B. Kennaway, *The Orange Order: A Tradition Betrayed* (London: Methuen, 2006).
15. J. Tonge, J. Evans, R. Jeffery and J. McAuley, 'New Order: Political Change and the Protestant Orange Tradition in Northern Ireland', *British Journal of Politics and International Relations*, 13, 2 (2011), forthcoming.
16. A. Boyd, 'The Orange Order', *History Today*, 45, 9 (1995), pp.22–33.
17. W. Bingham, *Making Sense of Northern Ireland: An Orange Perspective* (Belfast: Grand Lodge, 1997).
18. W. Porter, 'Orangeism: A Force for Protestant Unity', in Kennedy (ed.), *Steadfast for Faith and Freedom*, pp.101–3.
19. Interview with Orange Order member, 7 June 2008.
20. Authors' survey for Orange Order figures. See: http://cain.ulst.ac.uk/ni/religion.htm#ni-rel-01 for general figures.
21. Grand Lodge, minutes of meeting, December 1999.
22. Kennaway, *The Orange Order: A Tradition Betrayed*, p.253.
23. D. Morrow, *Churches and Inter-Community Relationships* (Belfast: University of Ulster, 1990).
24. Kaufmann, *The Orange Order: A Contemporary Northern Irish History*; Kennaway, *The Orange Order: A Tradition Betrayed*.
25. P. Day, 'Pride Before a Fall? Orangeism in Liverpool Since 1945', in M. Busteed, F. Neal and J. Tonge (eds), *Irish Protestant Identities* (Manchester: Manchester University Press, 2007), pp.273–88.
26. C. Mitchell, *Religion, Identity and Politics in Northern Ireland* (Aldershot: Ashgate, 2006).
27. http://cdnedge.bbc.co.uk/1/hi/uk_politics/378040.stm (25 June 1999).
28. E. Storey, *Traditional Roots: Towards an Appropriate Relationship Between the Church of Ireland and the Orange Order* (Blackrock: Columba Press, 2002), pp.112–26; Mitchell, *Religion, Identity and Politics in Northern Ireland*, p.54.
29. 'Narrow View from a Broad Church?', *Orange Standard*, October 2007, p.2.
30. Storey, *Traditional Roots*, p.109.
31. Walker, *A History of the Ulster Unionist Party*.
32. Kaufmann, *The Orange Order: A Contemporary Northern Irish History*.
33. S. Bruce, *God Save Ulster! The Religion and Politics of Paisleyism* (Oxford: Oxford University Press, 1986).
34. E. Moloney, *Paisley: From Demagogue to Democrat?* (Dublin: Poolbeg, 2008).
35. Ibid., pp.49–51.
36. H. Patterson and E. Kaufmann, *Unionism and Orangeism in Northern Ireland Since 1945: The Decline of the Loyal Family* (Manchester: Manchester University Press, 2007), pp.146–7, 206.
37. D. Morrow, 'Suffering for Righteousness' Sake? Fundamentalist Protestantism and Ulster Politics', in P. Shirlow and M. McGovern (eds), *Who are 'The People'? Unionism, Protestantism and Loyalism in Northern Ireland* (London: Pluto, 1997), p.60.
38. Report for the Parliamentary Select Committee appointed to inquire into the nature, character, extent and tendency of Orange Lodges, cited as Appendix 3 in E. Norman, *Anti–Catholicism in Modern England* (London: Barnes & Noble, 1968), pp.140–3.
39. M. Smyth, 'Reform the Orange Order', in Grand Orange Lodge of Ireland, *The Twelfth, 1795–1995, Bicentenary* (Belfast: Grand Lodge, 1995).
40. C. Smyth, 'Orangeism and Unionism: A Special Relationship?', in R. Hanna (ed.), *The Union: Essays on Ireland and the British Connection* (Newtownards: Colourpoint, 2001), pp.124–37.
41. *Orange Standard*, June 2003.
42. A. Ashdown, 'Why We Resist the Doctrines of the Church of Rome', *The Reformer* (September–October 2008), pp.2–3.
43. Grand Orange Lodge of Ireland, *Constitution, Laws and Ordinances of the Loyal Institution of Ireland* (Belfast: Grand Lodge, 1967), p.2.
44. Alistair Smyth, grand chaplain, 'The Twelfth', *News Letter*, 13 July 2010.
45. R. Harris, *Prejudice and Tolerance in Ulster* (Manchester: Manchester University Press, 1986), p.166.
46. Ibid.
47. Interview with Orange Order member, 3 June 2008.
48. K. Haddick-Flynn, *Orangeism: The Making of a Tradition* (Dublin: Merlin, 1999).

49. Loyal Orange Institution of Ireland, 'Candidate's Proposal Form', in *Constitution, Laws and Ordinances* (Belfast: Grand Lodge, 1967), Appendix 1.
50. Kennaway, *The Orange Order: A Tradition Betrayed*, p.22.
51. Kaufmann, *The Orange Order: A Contemporary Northern Irish History*, pp.139, 288.
52. 'Denial of civil rights of Protestants south of the border', *Orange Standard*, November 1997, p.9.
53. W. Wigfall-Williams and G. Robinson, 'A World Apart: Mixed Marriage in Northern Ireland', Northern Ireland Life and Times Survey Research Update (2001), no. 8, p.1.
54. Loyal Orange Institution, *Constitution, Laws and Ordinances*, Article 3.
55. See Moloney, *Paisley: From Demagogue to Democrat?*; Walker, *A History of the Ulster Unionist Party*.
56. Ibid., p.2.
57. For a discussion of civic, liberal and religious typologies of unionism, see N. Porter, *Rethinking Unionism: An Alternative Vision for Northern Ireland* (Belfast: Blackstaff, 1996). A. Aughey, 'Recent Interpretations of Unionism', *Political Quarterly*, 61, 2 (1990), pp.188–99; A. Aughey, 'The Character of Ulster Unionism', in Shirlow and McGovern (eds), *Who are 'The People'?*, pp.16–33.
58. J. McAuley and J. Tonge (2011) 'The Old Order Changeth – Or Not? Modern Discourses within the Orange Order', in K. Hayward and C. O'Donnell (eds), *Political Discourse and Conflict Resolution: Debating Peace in Northern Ireland* (London: Routledge, 2010), pp.109–25.
59. D. Bryan, *Orange Parades: The Politics of Ritual, Tradition and Control* (London: Pluto, 2002), p.107.
60. Interview with Orange Order member, 8 June 2008.
61. 'Remembering sacrifices with sadness and pride', *News Letter*, 'Orange Victims Tribute', 7 April 2006, p.2; J. Tonge and J. McAuley, 'The Contemporary Orange Order in Northern Ireland', in Busteed, Neal and Tonge (eds), *Irish Protestant Identities*, p.295.
62. Pat Finucane Centre, *For God and Ulster: An Alternative Guide to the Loyal Orders* (Derry: Pat Finucane Centre, 1997); Bryan, *Orange Parades*, p.110.
63. Independent Commission on Policing, *A New Beginning: Policing in Northern Ireland* (London: HMSO, 1999).
64. Interview with the authors, 3 November 2007.
65. Denis Watson, Armagh Grand Lodge, cited in Kaufmann, *The Orange Order: A Contemporary Northern Irish History*, p.209.
66. *News Letter*, 13 July 2001. See A. Rankin and G. Ganiel, 'DUP Discourses on Violence and their Impact on the Northern Ireland Peace Process,' *Peace and Conflict Studies* (2008), pp.115–35.
67. http://www.jimallister.org/default.asp?blogID=829; accessed 7 December 2007.
68. Interview with the authors, 3 November 2007.
69. 'Protestant Drift Continues', *Orange Standard*, 1 August 1997, p.4.
70. 'Orange Order brands dissident terrorists as "Roman Catholic IRA"', *Belfast Telegraph*, 5 October 2010, p.3.
71. By 1997, the annual insurance cost per hall had reached £1,100. Loyal Orange Institution, *Submission to the Rt Hon Peter Hain MP, Secretary of State for Northern Ireland* (Belfast: Grand Lodge, 1997), p.1.
72. A. Bairner, '"Up To Their Knees?" Football, Sectarianism, Masculinity and Protestant Working-Class Identity', in Shirlow and McGovern (eds), *Who are 'The People?'*, p.101.
73. Interview with the authors, 3 November 2007.
74. Bryan, *Orange Parades*.
75. See C. Stevenson, C. Condor and J. Abell, 'The Minority–Majority Conundrum in Northern Ireland: An Orange Order Perspective', *Political Psychology*, 28, 1 (2007), pp.105–25; McAuley and Tonge, 'The Old Order Changeth – Or Not?'
76. Grand Orange Lodge, '"Twelfth" Resolutions', press release (Belfast: Grand Lodge, 2008); 'The Resolutions', *Belfast Telegraph*, 11 July 2008, p.1.
77. BBC News 'New Face of Belfast's Orangemen', http://news.bbc.co.uk/1/hi/northern_ireland/7503169.stm. See McAuley and Tonge, 'The Old Order Changeth – Or Not?'
78. N. Jarman, *Material Conflicts: Parades and Visual Displays in Northern Ireland* (Oxford: Berg, 1997).
79. D. Bryan, *Orange Parades*, pp.48–9, 125.
80. See, for example, 'Support for Temperance Lodges', *Orange Standard*, October 2006, p.7.
81. Orange Reformation, 'Orange reformation', www.orangereformation.co.uk/vision.html; accessed 10 December 2010.

82. Orange Reformation, 'Hands off our 12th', www.orangereformation.co.uk/handsoffour12th. htm; accessed 10 December 2010.
83. Interview with the authors, 15 May 2008.
84. Ibid., 3 November 2007.
85. Ibid., 3 May 2008.
86. Interview with Orange Order member, 7 June 2008.
87. Interview with the authors, 3 November 2007.
88. Ibid.
89. Ibid., 2 November 2007.
90. Ibid., 3 November 2007.
91. Kaufmann, *The Orange Order: A Contemporary Northern Irish History*, pp.168–70.
92. Ibid.
93. http://www.grandorangelodge.co.uk/press/PressReleases-2008/081017-orange_order_ condemn_extension_of_abortion_act.htm; accessed 15 December 2010.
94. Interview with Orange Order member, 7 May 2008.
95. Interview with the authors, 3 June 2008.
96. Economic and Social Research Council Northern Ireland 2010 General Election Survey, SN 6553, available at:http://www.esds.ac.uk/findingData/snDescription.asp?sn=6553&key= /&flag=true; accessed 10 December 2010.
97. Kennaway, *The Orange Order: A Tradition Betrayed*, p.43.

Conclusion

NEW ORDER

The Orange Order has been obliged to operate in reduced circumstances ever since the end of unionist majoritarian devolved government in 1972. At the advent of the Troubles in 1968, the Order's position in the Northern Ireland polity appeared strong. It was enjoying a record level of membership of nearly 100,000, held an influential position within the still-dominant Ulster Unionist Party and had demonstrated an enduring capacity to unite Protestants of almost all denominations and across the social divide. The Order was the neo-religious wing of a unionist party which dominated a unionist state.

Within three decades, however, the comfortable Orange position of 1968 seemed a very distant memory. The political upheavals within unionism arising from the Belfast Agreement engulfed the Orange Order. Already, at the time of the deal, the Order had become a much more militant organisation. The composition of its membership had veered away from middle-class, deferential unionism towards working-class loyalism and the Order's 'quiet' politics of previous decades switched towards anxious, even noisy, confrontation over the four 'ps': parades, power-sharing, prisoner releases and policing.

Even prior to the Belfast Agreement, the Orange Order was in turmoil. Enraged by prohibitions placed upon the route of its Drumcree church parade, the Order's followers, within and beyond the organisation, had created chaos across Northern Ireland. Initial victories in forcing through the march during the mid-1990s appeared Pyrrhic. Disturbances across the province associated with Drumcree undermined the Order's reputation for support for the forces of law and order which had withstood much provocation during the Troubles. Created in the same year as the Belfast Agreement, the Parades Commission became the particular object of Orange opprobrium, its quasi-judicial status seen as illegitimate and its attitudes and stipulations intrinsically anti-Orange.

More broadly, the Order was confronted by a new political dispensation, in which the old dream of a return to unionist majority government was banished in perpetuity and, worse, the 'terrorist' enemies of the state were in government. Political, religious and cultural equality for nationalists was endorsed globally and locally and the peace and political processes lauded as triumphs, but for the Orange Order, in particular, there were bitter pills to swallow, in the form of measures that were seen as 'anti-Protestant'. Having served the security forces for so long, Orange Order members found themselves now discouraged from membership, while Catholics were recruited on a quota basis. Having opposed terrorism (from both sides) during the conflict, the Orange brethren saw the dawn of a new polity in which perpetrators of violence were released from prison, some even taking seats in the Northern Ireland Executive. While most observers beyond the unionist community saw these political and moral compromises as necessary for the greater good, Orange Protestants were less easily assuaged.

The obvious response to such indignities was to protest via the most appropriate constitutional political means and the DUP harnessed the anti-Belfast Agreement sentiment which permeated unionism for most of the first decade after the deal. What is striking about the pro-DUP allegiances of the majority of Orange Order members after the Agreement is that they are not structurally based, but instead derive from different eras of political socialisation. The Order's membership had long proletarianised (although they tend to be drawn from the skilled working class, the labour 'aristocracy') and attracted a 'rougher' form of adherent since the days when some of its leaders were titled gentry and many members were middle class.[1] However, neither social class nor education nor Protestant denomination have been particularly important variables in charting support for the UUP's rival.

Orange Order members who stayed faithful to the UUP were those who joined the Order in the days when that duopoly dominated the polity. Many of the remainder veered towards the DUP as the stouter defender of Protestant interests. Having seen the UUP removed as a major political player, in terms of local decision-making, since 1972 and then watched it use its lingering influence to negotiate an unsatisfactory deal, most Orange Order members took the instrumentalist view that the DUP would better represent them. As Chapter 5 has demonstrated, Orange delegates within the Ulster Unionist Council formed the most visible bastion of resistance to Trimble-ite support for the Belfast Agreement. They frequently challenged Trimble's leadership and his political strategy in a series of showdowns. It was a battle the Order and Trimble lost. The UUP remained pro-Agreement and was eclipsed, the Order left the UUP, with many members supporting the DUP amid rapprochement with Ian Paisley, but the DUP ultimately became pro-Agreement, once that party had got Sinn Féin to fully commit to the institutions of the northern state. It was the UUP that suffered even more grievously than the Orange Order, however, during this period of upheaval. The UUP lost talented individuals such as Jeffrey Donaldson and Peter Weir to its rival party, but such individuals did not defect from the Orange Order. The clashes within unionism and Orangeism of the 1990s and 2000s were a period when 'rebel' Orangeism – less deferential, more militant, non-UUP aligned – finally displaced the cautious, conservative traditional Orangeism which had dominated for much of the twentieth century.[2]

As the teething pains of the Belfast Agreement recede ever-deeper into memory and devolved power-sharing embeds as a permanent feature, this political re-alignment may be permanent, notwithstanding some Orange disgruntlement over the DUP's comfortable sharing of power with Sinn Féin since 2007. For those Orange Order members struggling to come to terms with the new dispensation, the Traditional Unionist Voice party offered an outlet, but its future soon appeared precarious and raging against already irreversible changes did not seem a fruitful road for the Order to travel.

The Orange Order's modern political role is not as an internal Protestant voice within a particular party, but as an honest broker of inter-unionist party differences and as a unifying force of Protestant political and cultural interests. This task is becoming easier as the intra-unionist divisions over the Belfast Agreement fade. During that era, Grand Lodge became seen as increasingly sympathetic to the DUP. Yet these new leanings were not because of anything orchestrated by the DUP; rather the new allegiances towards the DUP were simply an instrumental re-alignment. Most Orangemen, along with the wider Protestant population, believed that the DUP had become better at articulating and defending unionist interests.[3]

Today, the political divisions between the DUP and UUP are far less apparent than in the old pro- versus anti-Agreement days. Of course, in its brokerage role, the modern Orange Order functions with diminished influence, no longer part of the governing team to which it belonged for the first five decades, the era of the 'Orange state'.[4] Instead the Order operates as a prominent and visible pressure group, bartering for influence. In this capacity the Order is not bereft of influence. Its members include half of the unionist elected representatives within the Northern Ireland Assembly, most of whom have considerable affection for the Orange Institution. As such, the Order is likely to at least have the ear of unionist politicians for the foreseeable future.

In performing its pressure group role, the Orange Order resists radical change and stresses the need for Protestant values to infuse decision-making. Orange scepticism over recent political changes remains considerable. For most members, the conflict has not fully subsided, a belief grounded in the caution, scepticism, even suspicion, which permeates its membership. Many believe that nationalists are still intent on removing Britishness from Northern Ireland, by whatever tactics are seen as possessing the greatest utility at a particular time. Few believe that permanent peace and stability have arrived. Of course, the Order has more reason than most organisations to be less enamoured by the celebration of peace and political change. Its halls are still the regular targets for sectarian attacks and its followers still need expensive policing operations to return safely to their homes after parades through certain interface areas.

THE TRANSMISSION OF CULTURAL AND RELIGIOUS VALUES

The Orange Order commands fierce loyalty from its members, partly because for many members it represents an extended family. A majority of joiners do so because of family tradition. This represents strength and weakness for the Order. There is a high degree of fidelity to the institution among its followers and the extent of horizontal integration is striking, in terms of shared values and outlook, regardless of social background. Family reasons for joining the institution help inculcate a shared set of cultural and religious attitudes surrounding faith, loyalty and state, binding members into a 'grand cultural unionist narrative'.[5] Moreover, the level of mutual assistance offered among members is considerable. Amid fashionable talk of 'big societies' and 'strong communities', the Orange Order represents the embodiment of such.

The weakness of the Order lies in the modern inability, in some parts of urban secular Northern Ireland, to penetrate beyond existing family ties. In other words, the intensity of commitment of those inside the organisation is evident, but the extensiveness of loyalty to the Orange Order outside the institution is of greater concern, as joining is no longer a natural rite of passage for a Protestant male. Characterisations of the Orange Order as an ageing, dwindling band, requiring advances in medical science to preserve the membership base, have been overdone; the organisation's age profile is younger than several political parties in Northern Ireland.[6] Nonetheless, even the Order's leadership does not claim that recruitment has been easy in recent times.

Throughout Northern Ireland, the Orange Order plays important roles, ranging from commemorations and celebrations of historical and religious events to social functions. The latter are often held in Orange Halls which remain a key aspect of rural life, one reason why attacks upon them are perceived as attacks upon the entire Protestant community. The social aspect of Orangeism has declined in urban areas and the pessimism of Belfast Lodge members in this study was often at odds with the more upbeat assessments of those belonging to private and District Lodge members outside the main urban conurbation. Commemorations organised by the Orange Order may not be exclusively Orange events; the Somme events, for example, are part of wider historical memory throughout the Protestant community, but the Order has always linked past events to the present and provides occasions which facilitate such linkages.

Collective memory and cultural transmission provide generational continuity for the Order's membership. The Orange Institution offers overt guidance to how personal life should be conducted – religiously and with respect for authority – and, through a strong (non-party) political discourse, conditions outlook on unionism and its attendant aspects, such as support for the British link and the monarchy. This worldview is palpably not simply a top-down construct, based on an edict from Grand Lodge. The invitation to join and so inculcate existing values often comes from family members, while most who respond favourably and sign up do so because they already sympathise with the longstanding Orange worldview.

Orange symbols, traditions and demonstration endured for so long as to be unquestioned internally until fairly recently, which is why the controversies over the Drumcree parade provoked such anger and an uncomprehending response from within Orangeism. From the Order's perspective, this was a church parade which had taken place for almost two centuries, its legitimacy enshrined in history and in the religious associations of the event. Parading has always been an important, visible aspect of Orange activity, an enactment of the civil and religious liberties which the Orange Order claims to defend. Most are indeed uncontroversial church, arch, banner or hall parades, but a small number are designated as contentious. For any parades to be banned or regulated, or even be subject to negotiation, is seen as an affront by many Orange Order members, while an equally uncomprehending view is offered from the 'rival' community. Although opposition to Orange parades may have been fermented by Sinn Féin for tactical and electoral reasons during the 1990s, even much later than that Drumcree period there remains an absence of cross-community consensus. Most Catholics want Orange parades that pass through nationalist areas to be either banned or negotiated and this cultural contest may continue apace.

MODERNISATION AND ADAPTATION

For the Orange Order, discourses of continuity are far more comfortable than those of change, but the challenge of adaptation to societal and political change is being faced. Perhaps the most difficult issue in future generations will be one of relevance in a more secular age. Northern Ireland's citizens still overwhelmingly self-ascribe Christian labels, but the more austere aspects of religious observance have diminished. The Ulster sabbath has largely dissolved as a feature of a Protestant country for a Protestant people; religious observation is in decline and UK-wide legislation on, for example, same-sex partnerships has impinged upon local moral conservatism, a process that will not be reversed by the relative autonomy of devolution. An organisation anxious to stress its religious credentials faces a struggle to remain a cornerstone of a Protestant community if the religious orientation of society dissipates.

Many of the Order's members are resistant to the diminution of principles of faith and, as Chapter 6 demonstrated, religious commitments are taken seriously by many Lodges. Yet moderate internal critics of the Order have lamented the 'gradual shift from fundamental core values' of Christian worship, charity and respect for the authorities and claimed that the 'Grand Orange Lodge of Ireland has become a "cold house" for those who hold to the traditional values of Orangeism'.[7] That the Order's public face sometimes appears to be a stereotypical one of a sub-culture of drunken, ethno-sectarian bigotry, evident on the streets via bonfires and paramilitary-linked bands, is seen as a gross caricature by many members. Orange brethren prefer the traditions of unfussy, quiet religious observance and respect for the religious rights of others, rather than sectarian grandstanding, while maintaining an unyielding opposition to the doctrines of Roman Catholicism. Yet, as Claire Mitchell has observed, 'urban and fairly secular "blood and thunder" flute band parades are now more popular than the rural and more religious Orange Order parades and are better known for the proliferation of Buckfast than Bibles.'[8]

While the issue of drink has been tackled by legislation prohibiting street displays of alcohol, the more fundamental issue for the Order is one of mission. The purpose of most parades is one or more of commemoration of specific historical events, the celebration of civil and religious liberties, or to bear religious witness. Yet this message does not get across to nationalists amid still-fractured local community relations, while the parading issues also created internal disharmony within the Order for several years. The broader debate over the purpose of Orange parades is found in the promotion of Orangefest as an unthreatening cultural celebration by a broad spectrum of the public ranging from Grand Lodge officers to tourist board officials and rejection of the concept as a dilution of religious principles by militants.

In countries more secular than Northern Ireland, the preservation of the Reformed Protestant tradition and emphasis on scripture have been even more difficult to emphasise to often disinterested, even baffled, local populations. Grand Lodge hosted the World Council of the Orange Order in Belfast in 2009 and, amid the solidarity, engaged in genuine attempts to examine how the Order might recast its message to broaden its appeal, without dilution of its non-negotiable fundamental principles. Several of the countries represented were once strongly Protestant and suspicious of 'Romanism', but older fears of the Catholic Church have declined, in some cases replaced by hostility to militant Islam. As Peter Day's study of the decline of the Orange Order on Merseyside notes, 'the views expressed about Catholicism by members of the Order today would not have been considered exceptional in 1950s Liverpool, or in other towns and cities in England.'[9] Yet the Protestant nature of England diminished sharply from the 1960s, while the Orange Order's outlook remained steadfast, its diminishing number of members resolute in adherence to their values.

The Orange Order has made serious efforts to improve its image in recent years. Until the mid-1990s and the intense scrutiny which accompanied Drumcree, the Order had been insular, suspicious of outsiders and incapable of projecting coherent arguments to the media. Even the sympathetic commentator, Ruth Dudley Edwards, whose book on the Order afforded insights into its importance and fulfilment of mainly benign social and cultural roles in rural areas, was criticised for minor censure of the manner in which the Order conducted itself and, in particular, its lack of cognisance of the image it can convey.[10] For her trouble, Dudley Edwards, a Roman Catholic, was labelled a 'Fenian bitch' by some antediluvian elements, according to Kennaway.[11] Since that particular nadir, much has changed, and while the religious, moral and political certainties of the Order's outlook mean that it will never be a liberal, pluralist institution, it has become an organisation much more receptive to media and academic scrutiny.

While critics still see the Orange Order as inward looking and motivated by unchanging sectarianism, this overlooks the introspection occurring within the institution over how the Order is seen beyond Schomberg House, its Northern Ireland headquarters. Greater consideration of its image has led the Order to deploy a media adviser, while the invitation of the American academic Robert Putnam to speak to the Order on the problem of diminishing social capital (and how to address this) was something the institution would not have contemplated in previous eras. Beyond the persistent charge of sectarianism, the issues of social capital and secularism are the biggest confronting the Orange Order. Diminishing social capital provides a general explanation of why individuals are reluctant to join organisations such as the Orange Order. Secularism, or at least diminished religious fervour, offers a more specific explanation of why the Order's membership has declined. While the common route of joining through family ensures loyalty and bonding, the movement away from Northern Ireland (or indeed internal movement within the province) of young people, combined with social mobility and the atomisation of society, has meant that joining the Orange Order has become exceptional for most Protestant male adults, rather than the common feature it was until the end of the 1960s.

However, in closing, it must be observed that Orangeism remains bigger than the formal membership of the Orange Order. The Order retains the goodwill of many Protestants. It is difficult to imagine an alternative organisation mobilising 10,000 people on a march in Northern Ireland in the modern era, let alone that the Order manages 100,000 on its showpiece occasion. Beyond its previous UUP sinecure, the Order continues to infuse unionism with a cultural form, resistant to liberal and civic varieties. In a polity in which ethnic identity remains easily the most important determinant of education, political choice, even of sporting activity, the Orange Institution still acts as a rallying point for those most proud of their religious and cultural heritage. The Orange Order will never regain the influence or membership it once held and the evidence from the Orange diaspora of ailing or disappearing Lodges acts as a cautionary tale of an organisation in retreat amid political and religious isolation. Nonetheless, Orangeism in its Northern Ireland heartland is robust and is not about to disappear soon, even beginning to stabilise in recent years. The challenge for the Orange Order prior to celebrating its tercentenary in 2095 is to ensure that it retains its relevance as an important religious and cultural vehicle within the Protestant community, rather than become mainly a historical artefact.

NOTES

1. E. Kaufmann, *The Orange Order: A Contemporary Northern Irish History* (Oxford: Oxford University Press, 2007).
2. Ibid; H. Patterson and E. Kaufmann, *Unionism and Orangeism in Northern Ireland Since 1945* (Manchester: Manchester University Press, 2007).
3. For a broader discussion of how the DUP was seen as the stouter defender of unionist interests while not becoming more extreme, see P. Mitchell, G. Evans and B. O'Leary, 'Extremist Outbidding in Ethnic Party Systems is Not Inevitable: Tribune Parties in Northern Ireland', *Political Studies*, 57, 2 (2009), pp.397–421; J. Evans and J. Tonge, 'Social Class and Party Choice in Northern Ireland's Ethnic Blocs', *West European Politics*, 32, 5 (2009), pp.1012–30.
4. The term coined by Michael Farrell in *Northern Ireland: The Orange State* (London: Pluto, 1980).
5. N. Porter, *Rethinking Unionism* (Belfast: Blackstaff, 1996), p.87. See also J. McAuley and J. Tonge, 'The Old Order Changeth or Not? Modern Discourses within the Orange Order', in K. Hayward and C. O'Donnell (eds), *Political Discourse and Conflict Resolution: Debating Peace in Northern Ireland* (London: Routledge, 2010), pp.109–25.
6. At a median age of 45–54, the age profile is younger than that of the UUP, SDLP and Alliance memberships, all surveyed by Tonge. See J. Tonge, *The New Northern Irish Politics?* (Houndmills: Palgrave Macmillan, 2005).
7. B. Kennaway, *The Orange Order: A Tradition Betrayed* (London: Methuen, 2006), pp.252–64.
8. C. Mitchell, 'Religious Change and Persistence', in C. Coulter and M. Murray (eds), *Northern Ireland after the Troubles: A Society in Transition* (Manchester: Manchester University Press, 2008), p.145.

9. P. Day, 'Pride Before a Fall? Orangeism in Liverpool Since 1945', in M. Busteed, F. Neal and J. Tonge (eds), *Irish Protestant Identities* (Manchester: Manchester University Press, 2007), p.287.

10. R Dudley Edwards, *The Faithful Tribe: An Intimate Portrait of the Loyal Institutions* (London: HarperCollins, 2000).

11. Kennaway, *The Orange Order: A Tradition Betrayed*, p.258.

Bibliography

Abdelal, R., Herrera, Y.M., Johnston, A.I. and McDermott, R. (eds), *Measuring Identity: A Guide for Social Scientists* (Cambridge: Cambridge University Press, 2009)

Almond, G.A. and Verba, S. *The Civic Culture* (Princeton, NJ: Princeton University Press, 1963)

Ashdown, A. 'Why We Resist the Doctrines of the Church of Rome', *The Reformer* (September–October 2008), pp.2–3

Aughey, A. *Under Siege: Ulster Unionism and the Anglo-Irish Agreement* (Belfast: Blackstaff Press, 1989)

Aughey, A. 'Recent Interpretations of Unionism', *Political Quarterly*, 61, 2 (1990), pp.188–99

Aughey, A. 'The Character of Ulster Unionism', in P. Shirlow and M. McGovern (eds), *Who are 'The People'? Unionism, Protestantism and Loyalism in Northern Ireland* (London: Pluto, 1997), pp.16–33

Aughey, A. 'From Declinism to Endism: Exploring the Ideology of British Break-Up', *Journal of Political Ideologies*, 15, 1 (2010), pp.11–30

Bairner, A. '"Up To Their Knees?" Football, Sectarianism, Masculinity and Protestant Working-Class Identity', in Shirlow and McGovern, *Who are the 'The People?'*

BBC Northern Ireland, 'Hearts and Minds', 17 October 2002

BBC, 'Alexei Sayle's Liverpool', 2008

Bell, D. *Acts of Union: Youth Culture and Sectarianism in Northern Ireland* (Basingstoke: Macmillan, 1990)

Bell, D. 'Acts of Union: Youth Culture and Ethnic Identity Amongst Protestants in Northern Ireland', *The British Journal of Sociology*, 38, 2 (1987), pp.158–83

Bew, P., Gibbon, P. and Patterson, H. *Northern Ireland 1921–2001: Political Forces and Social Classes* (London: Serif, 2001)

Bingham, W. *Making Sense of Northern Ireland: An Orange Perspective* (Belfast: Grand Lodge, 1997)

Blondel, J. *Political Parties: A Genuine Case for Discontent?* (London: Wilwood, 1978)

Boyd, A. 'The Orange Order, 1795–1995', *History Today*, 45, 9 (1995), pp.16–23

Bradley, J. 'Orangeism in Scotland: Unionism, Politics, Identity, and Football', *Éire–Ireland* 39, 1/2 (2004), pp.237–61

Bridge, C. and Fedorowich, K. 'Mapping the British World', *Journal of Imperial and Commonwealth History*, vol. 31 (2003), pp.1–15

Brockmeier, J. 'Remembering and Forgetting: Narrative as Cultural Memory', *Culture in Psychology*, 8, 1 (2002), pp.15–43

Brown, K. '"Our Father Organization": The Cult of the Somme and the Unionist "Golden Age" in Modern Ulster Loyalist Commemoration', *The Round Table – The Commonwealth Journal of International Affairs*, 96, 393 (2007), pp.707–23

Bruce, S. *God Save Ulster! The Religion and Politics of Paisleyism* (Oxford: Oxford University Press, 1986)

Bruce, S., Glendinning, T., Paterson, I. and Rosie, M. *Sectarianism in Scotland* (Edinburgh: Edinburgh University Press, 2004)

Bruce, S., Glendinning, T., Paterson, I. and Rosie, M. 'Religious Discrimination in Scotland: Fact or Myth?' *Ethnic and Racial Studies*, 28, 1 (2005), pp.151–68

Bruner, J. *Acts of Meaning* (Cambridge, MA: Harvard University Press, 1990)

Bryan, D. *Orange Parades: The Politics of Ritual, Tradition and Control* (London: Pluto, 2002)

Bryan, D. 'Rituals of Irish Protestantism and Orangeism: The Transnational Grand Orange Lodge of Ireland', *European Studies*, vol. 19 (2003), pp.105–23

Bryan, D., Fraser, T. and Dunn, S. *Political Rituals: Loyalist Parades in Portadown* (Coleraine: Centre for the Study of Conflict, 1995)

Cairns, D. and Smyth, J. 'Up Off Our Bellies and Unto Our Knees: Symbolic Effacement and the Orange Order in Northern Ireland', *Social Identities*, 8, 1, (2002), pp.143–60

Cairns, E. and Roe, M.D. (eds), *The Role of Memory in Ethnic Conflict* (Basingstoke: Palgrave, 2003)

Channel 4, 'Billy Boys', Tribes series, 1990

Coakley, J. 'National Identity in Northern Ireland: Stability or Change?' *Nations and Nationalism*, 13, 4 (2007), pp.573–97

Coakley, J. and O'Dowd, L. 'The Transformation of the Irish Border', *Political Geography*, vol. 26 (2007), pp.877–85

Cohen, A. *Two-Dimensional Man* (London: Routledge, 1974)

Cohen, S. 'Winning While Losing: The Apprentice Boys of Derry Walk their Beat', *Political Geography*, 26, 8 (2007), pp.951–67

Colley, L. *Britons: Forging the Nation 1707–1737* (New Haven, CT: Yale University Press, 1992)

Connerton, P. *How Societies Remember* (Cambridge: Cambridge University Press, 1989)

Connolly P. and Maginn, P. *Sectarianism, Children and Community Relations in Northern Ireland* (Coleraine: Centre for the Study of Conflict, University of Ulster, 1999)

Connor, W. 'Nation-Building or Nation-Destroying?' *World Politics*, 24, 3 (1972), pp.319–55

Cooper, D. 'On the Twelfth of July in the Morning ... (or the man who mistook his sash for a hat)', *Folk Music Journal*, 8, 1 (2001), pp.67–89

Cosgrove, D.E. *Social Formation and Symbolic Landscape* (Madison, WI: University of Wisconsin Press, 1998)

Craith, M.N. 'Politicised Linguistic Consciousness: The Case of Ulster-Scots', *Nations and Nationalism*, 7, 1 (2001), pp.21–37

Craith, M.N. *Plural Identities, Singular Narrative: The Case of Northern Ireland* (Oxford: Berghahn Books, 2002)

Day, P. 'Pride Before a Fall? Orangeism in Liverpool since 1945', in M. Busteed, F. Neal and J. Tonge (eds), *Irish Protestant Identities* (Manchester: Manchester University Press, 2007), pp.273–88

Department for Education and Skills, *Curriculum Review: Diversity and Citizenship* (London: The Stationery Office, 2007)

Devine, T. (ed.), *Scotland's Shame? Bigotry and Sectarianism in Modern Scotland* (Edinburgh: Mainstream, 2000)

Devine-Wright, P. 'A Theoretical Overview of Memory and Conflict', in E. Cairns and M.D. Roe (eds), *The Role of Memory in Ethnic Conflict* (Basingstoke: Palgrave, 2003)

Doane, A. 'What is Racism? Racial Discourse and Racial Politics', *Critical Sociology*, 32, 2–3 (2006), pp.255–74

Downs, A. *An Economic Theory of Democracy* (London: Harper & Row, 1957)

Dudley Edwards, R. *The Faithful Tribe: An Intimate Portrait of the Loyal Institutions* (London: HarperCollins, 2000)

Eagleton, T. 'Afterword', in T. McDonough (ed.), *Was Ireland a Colony? Economics, Politics and Culture in Nineteenth-Century Ireland* (Dublin: Irish Academic Press, 2005)

Evans, G. and Duffy, M. 'Beyond the Sectarian Divide: The Social Bases and Political Consequences of Nationalist and Unionist Party Competition in Northern Ireland', *British Journal of Political Science*, 21, 1 (1997), pp.47–81

Evans, J. and Tonge, J. 'The Future of the "Radical Centre" in Northern Ireland after the Good Friday Agreement', *Political Studies*, 51, 1 (2003), pp.26–50

Evans, J. and Tonge, J. 'Problems of Modernising an Ethno-Religious Party: The Case of the Ulster Unionist Party in Northern Ireland', *Party Politics*, vol. 11 (2005), pp.319–38

Evans, J. and Tonge, J. 'Unionist Party Competition and the Orange Order Vote in Northern Ireland', *Electoral Studies*, 26, 1 (2007), pp.156–67

Evans, J. and Tonge, J. 'Social Class and Party Choice in Northern Ireland's Ethnic Blocs', *West European Politics*, 32, 5 (2009), pp.1012–30

Farrell, M. *Northern Ireland: The Orange State* (London: Pluto, 1980)

Farrington, C. and Walker, G. 'Ideological Content and Institutional Frameworks: Unionist Identities in Northern Ireland and Scotland', *Irish Studies Review*, 17, 2 (2009), pp.135–52

Fealty, M., Ringland, T. and Steven, D. *A Long Peace? The Future of Unionism in Northern Ireland* (Wimborne: Slugger O'Toole, 2003)

Finlay, A. 'Defeatism and Northern Protestant "Identity"', *The Global Review of Ethnopolitics*, 1, 2 (2001), pp.3–20

Fish, S. *Is There A Text in This Class?* (Boston: Harvard University Press, 1980)

Fitzpatrick, D. 'Ireland and Empire', in W.R. Louis (ed.), *The Oxford History of the British Empire, Volume III: The Nineteenth Century* (Oxford: Oxford University Press, 1999)

Fraser, T.G. (ed.), *The Irish Parading Tradition: Following the Drum* (Basingstoke: Macmillan, 2000)

Geary, L.M. and McCarthy, A.J. (eds), *Ireland, Australia and New Zealand: History, Politics and Culture* (Dublin: Irish Academic Press, 2008)

Gellner, E. *Nations and Nationalism* (Ithaca, NY: Cornell University Press, 1983)

Geoghegan, P. 'Multiculturalism and Sectarianism in Post-Agreement Northern Ireland', *Scottish Geographical Journal*, 124, 2 (2008), pp.185–91

Gillis, J.R. (ed.), *Commemorations: The Politics of National Identity* (Princeton, NJ: Princeton University Press, 1996)

Graham, B. and Shirlow, P. 'The Battle of the Somme in Ulster Memory and Identity', *Political Geography*, vol. 21 (2002), pp.881–904

Grand Orange Lodge of Ireland, *Constitution, Laws and Ordinances of the Loyal Institution of Ireland* (Belfast: Grand Lodge, 1967)

Grand Orange Lodge of Ireland, *What is the Orange Order?* (Belfast: Grand Lodge, 1995)

Grand Orange Lodge of Ireland, *Submission to the Secretary of State for Northern Ireland* (Belfast: GOLI, 9 February 2007)

Grand Orange Lodge of Ireland, *'Twelfth' Resolutions* (Belfast: Grand Lodge, 2008)

Grand Orange Lodge of Ireland, *The Millennium Book: A History of Orangeism in County Armagh* (Belfast: GOLI Publications, no date)

Haddick-Flynn, K. *Orangeism: The Making of a Tradition* (Dublin: Merlin, 1999)

Halbwacks, M. *On Collective Memory*, edited and translated, with an Introduction by Lewis A. Coser (Chicago: Chicago University Press, 1992)

Hall, M. (ed.), *Orangeism and the Twelfth: What it Means to Me* (Newtownabbey: Island Publications, 1999)

Hall, S. 'Introduction', in S. Hall (ed.) *Representation: Cultural Representations and Signifying Practices* (London: Sage, 1997)

Hammack, P.L. 'Identity as Burden or Benefit? Youth, Historical Narrative, and the Legacy of Political Conflict', *Human Development*, vol. 53 (2010), pp.173–201

Hanna, R. (ed.), *The Union: Essays on Ireland and the British Connection* (Newtownards: Colourpoint, 2001)

Harbinson, J. *The Ulster Unionist Party 1882–1973* (Belfast: Blackstaff Press, 1973)

Harris, R. *Prejudice and Tolerance in Ulster* (Manchester: Manchester University Press, 1986)

Hassner, R.E. *War on Sacred Grounds* (Ithaca and London: Cornell University Press, 2009)

Hayes, B. and McAllister, I. 'Who Voted for Peace? Public Support for the 1998 Northern Ireland Agreement', *Irish Political Studies*, vol. 16 (2001), pp.73–94

Hechter, M. *Internal Colonialism: The Celtic Fringe in British National Development* (Berkeley, CA: University of California Press, 1975)

Hobsbawm, E. and Ranger, T. (eds), *The Invention of Tradition* (Cambridge: Cambridge University Press, 1983)

HMSO, *The Agreement: Agreement Reached in Multi-Party Negotiations* (Belfast: HMSO, 1998)

Howe, S. *Ireland and Empire* (Oxford: Oxford University Press, 2000)

Howe, S. 'Questioning the (Bad) Question: "Was Ireland a Colony?"', *Irish History Studies*, 37, 142 (2008), pp.1–15

Hume, D. *The Ulster Unionist Party 1972–1992* (Lurgan: Ulster Society, 1996)

Hume, D. (ed.), *'When Brethern are Met in their Order So Grand': A Brief History of Orangeism and Orange Lodges in Larne District* (Larne: Vermont Press, n.d.).

Hume, D, Mattison, J. and Scott, D. *Beyond the Banners: The Story of the Orange Order* (Holywood: Booklink, 2009)

Independent Commission on Policing (the Patten Commission), *A New Beginning: Policing in Northern Ireland* (Belfast: HMSO, 1999)

Jarman, N. *Material Conflicts: Parades and Visual Displays in Northern Ireland* (Oxford: Berg, 1997)

Jarman, N. *On The Edge: Community Perspectives on the Civil Disturbances in North Belfast, June–September 1996* (Belfast: CDC, 1997)

Jarman, N. *Drawing Back from the Edge: Community-Based Responses to Violence in North Belfast* (Belfast: CDC, 1999)

Jarman, N. *No Longer A Problem? Sectarian Violence in Northern Ireland* (Belfast: Institute for Conflict Research, 2005)

Jarman, N. and Bryan, D. *Parade and Protest: A Discussion of Parading Disputes in Northern Ireland* (Coleraine: Centre for the Study of Conflict, University of Ulster, 1996)

Jess, M. *The Orange Order* (Dublin: The O'Brien Press, 2007)

Johnson, R., McLennan, G., Schwarz, B. and Sutton, D. (eds), *Making History: Studies in History-Writing and Politics* (London: Hutchinson, 1982)

Jones, A. *Memory and Material Culture* (Cambridge: Cambridge University Press, 2007)

Jordan, G. and Weedon, C. *Cultural Politics: Class, Gender, Race and the Postmodern World* (Oxford: Blackwell, 1995)

Kaufmann, E. *The Orange Order: A Contemporary Northern Irish History* (Oxford: Oxford University Press, 2007)

Kaufmann, E. 'The Dynamics of Orangeism in Scotland: Social Sources of Political Influence in a Mass-Member Organization, 1860–2001', *Social Science History*, 30, 2 (2006), pp.263–92

Kaufmann, E. *The Orange Order: A Contemporary Northern Irish History* (Oxford: Oxford University Press, 2007)

Kaufmann, E. and Patterson, H. 'Intra-Party Support for the Good Friday Agreement in the Ulster Unionist Party', *Political Studies*, vol. 54 (2006), pp.509–32

Kaufman, S.J. *Modern Hatreds: The Symbolic Politics of Ethnic War* (London: Cornell University Press, 2001)

Kelly, R. and Byrne, L. *A Common Place* (London: Fabian Society, 2007)

Kennaway, B. 'All Change But No Change: Can We Learn Lessons from the Past?', IBIS Working Paper no. 101 (University College Dublin: Institute for British–Irish Studies, 2010)

Kennaway, B. *The Orange Order: A Tradition Betrayed* (London: Methuen, 2006)

Kennedy, L. *Colonialism, Religion and Nationalism in Ireland* (Belfast: Queen's University Belfast, Institute of Irish Studies, 1996)

Kinealy, C. 'The Orange Order and Representations of Britishness', in S. Caunce, E. Mazierska, S. Sydney-Smith and J.K. Walton (eds), *Relocating Britishness* (Manchester: Manchester University Press, 2004)

Kinealy, C. 'At Home with the Empire: The Example of Ireland', in C. Hall and S.O. Rose (eds), *At Home with the Empire* (Cambridge: Cambridge University Press, 2006)

King, Stephen, Lecture at Manchester Metropolitan University, 23 April 2002

Kumar, K. *The Making of English National Identity* (Cambridge: Cambridge University Press, 2003)

Kuzmanić, M. 'Collective Memory and Social Identity: A Social Psychological Exploration of the Memories of the Disintegration of Former Yugoslavia', *Psihološka Obzrja / Horizons of Psychology*, 17, 2 (2008)

Kymlicka, W. 'Nation-Building and Minority Rights: Comparing West and East', *Journal of Ethnic and Migration Studies*, 26, 2 (2000), pp.183–212

Lanclos, D. *At Play in Belfast: Children's Folklore and Identities in Northern Ireland* (London: Rutgers University Press, 2003)

Loyal Orange Institution, *Submission to the Rt Hon Peter Hain MP, Secretary of State for Northern Ireland* (Belfast: Grand Lodge, 1997)

MacDonald, D. *Blood and Thunder: Inside an Ulster Protestant Band* (Cork: Mercier Press, 2010)

MacRaild, D.M. 'Wherever Orange Is Worn: Orangeism and Irish Migration in the 19th and Early 20th Centuries', *Canadian Journal of Irish Studies*, 28, 2 (2002), pp.98–117

MacRaild, D.M. *Faith, Fraternity and Fighting: The Orange Order and Irish Migrants in Northern England, c. 1850–1920* (Liverpool: Liverpool University Press, 2005)

McAuley, J.W. 'Peace and Progress? Political and Social Change Among Young Loyalists in Northern Ireland', *Journal of Social Issues*, 60, 3 (2004), pp.541–62

McAuley, J.W. *Ulster's Last Stand? Reconstructing Unionism After the Peace Process* (Dublin: Irish Academic Press, 2010)

McAuley, J. and Tonge, J. '"For God and for the Crown": Contemporary Political and Social Attitudes among Orange Order Members in Northern Ireland', *Political Psychology*, 28, 1 (2007), pp.33–52

McAuley, J. and Tonge, J. '"Faith, Crown and State": Contemporary Discourses within the Orange Order in Northern Ireland', *Peace and Conflict Studies*, 15, 1 (2008), pp.136–55

McAuley, J. and Tonge, J. 'The Old Order Changeth – or Not? Modern Discourses within the Orange Order', in K. Hayward and C. O'Donnell (eds), *Political Discourse and Conflict Resolution: Debating Peace in Northern Ireland* (London: Routledge, 2010), pp.109–25

McCrone, D. and Kiely, R. 'Nationalism and Citizenship', *Sociology*, 34, 1 (2000), pp.19–34

McGlynn, C. and Mycock, A. 'Introduction: A Special Edition on Britishness', *Parliamentary Affairs*, 63, 2 (2010), pp.223–8

McLaughlin, R. 'Irish Nationalism and Orange Unionism in Canada: A Reappraisal', *Éire-Ireland*, 41, 3 (2007), pp.80–109

McLeod, J. and Thomson, R. *Researching Social Change: Qualitative Approaches* (London: Sage, 2009)

Merelman, R.M. 'The Family and Political Socialization: Toward a Theory of Exchange', *The Journal of Politics*, vol. 42 (1980), pp.461–86

Middleton, D. and Edwards, D. (eds), *Collective Remembering* (London: Sage, 1990)

Miller, D. (ed.), *Material Cultures: Why Some Things Matter* (London: UCL Press, 1998)

Ministry of Justice, *Citizenship: Our Common Bond* (London: The Stationery Office, 2008)

Mitchell, C. *Religion, Identity and Politics in Northern Ireland* (Aldershot: Ashgate, 2006)

Mitchell, C. 'Religious Change and Persistence', in C. Coulter and M. Murray (eds), *Northern Ireland after the Troubles* (Manchester: Manchester University Press, 2008)

Mitchell, P. Evans, G. and O'Leary, B. 'Extremist Outbidding in Ethnic Party Systems is Not Inevitable. Tribune Parties in Northern Ireland', *Political Studies*, 57, 2 (2009), pp.397–421

Modood, T. *Multiculturalism* (London: Polity, 2007)

Moloney, E. *Paisley: From Demagogue to Democrat?* (Dublin: Poolbeg, 2008)

Montgomery, G. and Whitten, J. *The Order on Parade* (Belfast: Grand Lodge, 1995)

Morag, N. 'The Emerald Isle: Ireland and the Clash of Irish and Ulster-British Nationalisms', *National Identities*, 10, 3 (2008), pp.263–80

Morrow, D. *Churches and Inter-Community Relationships* (Belfast: University of Ulster, 1990)

Morrow, D. 'Suffering for Righteousness' Sake? Fundamentalist Protestantism and Ulster Politics', in Shirlow and McGovern (eds), *Who are 'The People'? Unionism, Protestantism and Loyalism in Northern Ireland* (London: Pluto, 1997)

Moxon-Browne, E. 'National Identity in Northern Ireland', in P. Stringer and G. Robinson (eds), *Social Attitudes in Northern Ireland: The First Report* (Belfast: Blackstaff Press, 1991)

Muldoon, O., Trew, K., Todd, J., Rougier, N. and McLaughlin, K. 'Religious and National Identity after the Belfast Good Friday Agreement', *Political Psychology*, 28, 1 (2007), pp.89–103

Murtagh, B. 'Social Activity and Interaction in Northern Ireland', *Northern Ireland Life and Times Survey Research Update*, no. 10, February 2002

Mycock, A. and Tonge, J. 'The Future of Citizenship', in Political Studies Association, *Failing Politics? A Response to 'The Governance of Britain' Green Paper* (Newcastle: Political Studies Association, 2008)

Nairn, T. *Pariah: Misfortunes of the British Kingdom* (London: Verso Books, 2002)

Neal, F. *Sectarian Violence: The Liverpool Experience, 1819–1914* (Manchester: Manchester University Press, 1987)

Nelson, D. 'The Message of the Orange Banners', in *Grand Orange Lodge of Ireland: A Celebration, 1690–1990* (Belfast: GOLI, 1990), pp.56–7

Neuheiser, J. and Schaich, M. (eds), *Political Rituals in Great Britain: 1700–2000* (Augsburg: Wisner-Verlag, 2006)

Nic Craith, M. *Plural Identities, Singular Narratives: The Case of Northern Ireland* (Oxford: Berghahn, 2002)

Nora, P. 'Between Memory and History: Les Lieux de Mémoire', *Representations*, vol. 26 (1989), pp.7–24

Norman, E. *Anti-Catholicism in Modern England* (London: Barnes & Noble, 1968)

Novick, P. *The Holocaust and Collective Memory* (London: Bloomsbury Publishing, 2001)

Ó Dochartaigh, N. 'Building New Transnational Networks Online: The Case of Ulster Unionists', unpublished paper, 2003; and 'Reframing Online: Ulster Loyalists Imagine an American Audience', *Identities: Global Studies in Culture and Power*, 16, 1 (2009), pp.102–27

Officer, D. and Walker, G. 'Protestant Ulster: Ethno-History, Memory and Contemporary Prospects', *National Identities*, 2, 3 (2000), pp.293–307

Olick, J.K., 'Collective Memory: Two Cultures', *Sociological Theory*, vol. 17 (1999), pp.333–48

Olick, J.K., '"Collective Memory": A Memoir and Prospect', *Memory Studies*, 1 (2008), pp.23–9

Olick, J.K. and Robbins, J. 'Social Memory Studies: From "Collective Memory" to the Historical Sociology of Mnemonic Practices', *Annual Review of Sociology*, vol. 24 (1998)

Parekh, B. *Report of the Commission on the Future of Multi-Ethnic Britain* (London: Profile Books, 2000)

Parekh, B. *Rethinking Multiculturalism: Cultural Diversity and Political Theory* (London: Palgrave Macmillan, 2000)

Pat Finucane Centre, *For God and Ulster: An Alternative Guide to the Loyal Orders* (Derry: Pat Finucane Centre, 1997)

Paterson, L. 'Sources of Support for the SNP', in C. Bromley, J. Curtice, D. McCrone and A. Park (eds), *Has Devolution Delivered? The New Scotland Four Years On* (Edinburgh: Edinburgh University Press, 2006)

Patterson, B. (ed.), *Ulster–New Zealand Migration and Cultural Transfers* (Dublin: Four Courts Press, 2006)

Patterson, H. and Kaufmann, E. *Unionism and Orangeism in Northern Ireland Since 1945* (Manchester: Manchester University Press, 2007)

Patton, G. 'The Orange Institution: The Future', in B. Kennedy (ed.), *Steadfast for Faith and Freedom* (Belfast: Grand Lodge, 1995)

Peating, G.K. 'Unionist Identity, External Perceptions of Northern Ireland, and the Problem of Unionist Legitimacy', *Éire-Ireland*, 39, 1/2 (2004), pp.215–36

Porter, N. *Rethinking Unionism: An Alternative Vision for Northern Ireland* (Belfast: Blackstaff Press, 1996)

Porter, W. 'Orangeism: A Force for Protestant Unity', in Kennedy (ed.), *Steadfast for Faith and Freedom*

Powell, L. and Cowart, J. *Political Campaign Communication: Inside and Out* (Birmingham: University of Alabama, 2003)

Quigley, G. *Review of the Parades Commission* (Belfast: Northern Ireland Office, 2002)

Radford, K. 'Drum Rolls and Gender Roles in Protestant Marching Bands in Belfast', *British Journal of Ethnomusicology*, 10, 2 (2001), pp.37–59

Rankin, A. and Ganiel, G. 'DUP Discourses on Violence and their Impact on the Northern Ireland Peace Process', *Peace and Conflict Studies*, 15, 1 (2008), pp.115–35

Robbins, K. *Nineteenth-Century Britain: Integration and Diversity* (Oxford: Clarendon Press, 1988)

Ross, M.H. 'Psychocultural Interpretations and Dramas: Identity Dynamics in Ethnic Conflict', *Political Psychology*, 22, 1 (2001), p.158

Ryder, C. and Kearney, V. *Drumcree: The Orange Order's Last Stand* (London: Methuen, 2001)

Scarrow, S. *Parties and their Members* (Oxford: Oxford University Press, 1996)

Simpson, K. *Unionist Voices and the Politics of Remembering the Past in Northern Ireland* (Basingstoke: Palgrave Macmillan, 2009)

Simpson, K. *Truth Recovery in Northern Ireland: Critically Interpreting the Past* (Manchester: Manchester University Press, 2009)

Smith, A.D. *National Identities* (Harmondsworth: Penguin, 1991)

Smith, A.D. *Myths and Memories of the Nation* (Oxford: Oxford University Press, 1999)

Smyth, C. 'Orangeism and Unionism: A Special Relationship?' in R. Hanna (ed.), *The Union: Essays on Ireland and the British Connection* (Newtownards: Colourpoint, 2001), pp.124–37

Smyth, M. 'Foreword', in Kennedy (ed.), *Steadfast for Faith and Freedom: 200 Years of Orangeism* (Belfast: Grand Lodge, 1995)

Smyth, M. 'Reform and the Orange Order', in Grand Orange Lodge of Ireland, *The Twelfth, 1795–1995: Bicentenary* (Belfast: Grand Lodge, 1995)

Southern, N. 'Britishness, "Ulsterness" and Unionist Identity in Northern Ireland', *Nationalism and Ethnic Politics*, 13, 1 (2007), pp.71–102

Southern, N. 'Post-Agreement Societies and Inter-Ethnic Competition: A Comparative Study of the Protestant Community of Londonderry and the White Population of Pretoria', *National Identities*, 11, 4 (2009), pp.397–415

Stapleton, K. and Wilson, J. 'A Discursive Approach to Cultural Identity: The Case of Ulster Scots', Belfast Working Papers in Language and Linguistics no. 16 (Belfast: University of Ulster, 2003), pp.57–71.

Stapleton, K. and Wilson, J. 'Ulster Scots Identity and Culture: The Missing Voices', *Identities: Global Studies in Culture and Power*, vol. 11 (2004), pp.563–91

Stevenson, C., Condor, C. and Abell, J. 'The Minority–Majority Conundrum in Northern Ireland: An Orange Order Perspective', *Political Psychology*, 28, 1 (2007), pp.105–25

Stone, L. and Muir, R. *Who Are We? Identities in Britain* (London: Institute of Public Policy Research, 2007)

Storey, E. *Traditional Roots: Towards an Appropriate Relationship between the Church of Ireland and the Orange Order* (Blackrock: Columba Press, 2002)

Storey, J. (ed.), *Cultural Theory and Popular Culture: A Reader* (London: Pearson Education, 2006), p101

Sutherland, C. 'Nation-Building through Discourse Theory', *Nations and Nationalism*, 11, 2 (2005), pp.185–202

Tajfel, H. *Human Groups and Social Categories* (Cambridge: Cambridge University Press, 1981)

Thompson, S. 'The Politics of Culture in Northern Ireland', *Constellations*, 10, 1 (2003), pp.53–74

Todd, J. 'Two Traditions in Unionist Political Culture', *Irish Political Studies*, vol. 2 (1987), pp.1–26

Todd, J., Rougier, N., O'Keefe, T. and Canas Bottos, L. 'Does Being Protestant Matter? Protestants, Minorities and the Re-Making of Ethno-Religious Identity after the Good Friday Agreement', *National Identities*, 11, 1 (2009), pp.87–99

Tonge, J. *The New Northern Irish Politics?* (Basingstoke: Palgrave, 2005)

Tonge, J. and Evans, J. 'Faultlines in Unionism: Division and Dissent within the Ulster Unionist Council', *Irish Political Studies*, vol. 16 (2001), pp.111–32

Tonge, J., Evans, J., Jeffery, R. and McAuley, J. 'New Order: Political Change and the Protestant Tradition in Northern Ireland', *British Journal of Politics and International Relations*, 13, 3 (2011)

Tonge, J. and McAuley, J. 'The Contemporary Orange Order in Northern Ireland', in M. Busteed, F. Neal and J. Tonge (eds), *Irish Protestant Identities* (Manchester: Manchester University Press, 2008)

van Dijk, T.A. 'Discourse, Ideology and Context', *Folia Linguistica*, nos 1–2, (2001), pp.11–40

Walker, G. *A History of the Ulster Unionist Party: Protest, Pragmatism and Pessimism* (Manchester: Manchester University Press, 2004)

Waller, R. *Democracy and Sectarianism: A Political and Social History of Liverpool, 1868–1939* (Liverpool: Liverpool University Press, 1981)

Ward, S. (ed.), *British Culture and the End of Empire* (Manchester: Manchester University Press, 2001)

Wertsch, J. *Voices of Collective Remembering* (Cambridge: Cambridge University Press, 2002)

Wigfall-Williams, W. and Robinson, G. 'A World Apart: Mixed Marriage in Northern Ireland', Northern Ireland Life and Times Survey Research Update, no. 8 (2001)

Wilson, D.A. (ed.), *The Orange Order in Canada* (Dublin: Four Courts Press, 2007)

Wilson, T. (ed.), *Ulster Under Home Rule* (Oxford: Oxford University Press, 1955)

Wilson, T. *Ulster: Conflict and Consent* (Oxford: Blackwell, 1989)

Wodak, R. and Richardson, J.E. 'On the Politics of Remembering (or not)', *Critical Discourse Studies*, 6, 4 (2009), pp.231–5

Woodward, K. *Social Sciences: The Big Issues* (London: Routledge, 2003)

Zizek, S. *Interrogating the Real* (New York: Continuum International Publishing Group, 2005)

WEBSITES

Jim Allister: http://www.jimallister.org/

British Broadcasting Corporation: www.bbc.co.uk

Conflict and Politics in Northern Ireland: http://cain.ulst.ac.uk/

Conservative Party: www.conservatives.com

Democratic Unionist Party: www.dup.org.uk

Economic and Social Data Service: http://www.esds.ac.uk/

Fabian Society: www.fabians.org.uk

GfK NOP: www.gfknop.com

Grand Orange Lodge of Ireland: http://www.grandorangelodge.co.uk

Grand Lodge of Scotland: http://www.orangeorderscotland.com

Northern Ireland Life and Times: http://www.ark.ac.uk/nilt/

Northern Ireland Statistics and Research Agency: http://www.nisra.gov.uk/

Northern Ireland Tourist Board: http://www.discovernorthernireland.com/

UK Prime Minister: www.number10.gov.uk

Orange Chronicle: www.orange-order.co.uk/chronicle

Orange Reformation: www.orangereformation.co.uk
David Trimble: http://www.davidtrimble.org/
Ulster Unionist Party: www.uup.org.uk
YouGov: www.yougov.co.uk

NEWSPAPERS

Belfast Telegraph
Daily Telegraph
Catholic Herald
Irish Post
Glasgow Herald
The Guardian
Londonderry Sentinel
News Letter
Orange Standard
Sunday Herald
The Scotsman
The Times

Index